HARRY PRICE

HARRY PRICE

THE PSYCHIC DETECTIVE

RICHARD MORRIS

SUTTON PUBLISHING

First published in the United Kingdom in 2006 by
Sutton Publishing Limited · Phoenix Mill
Thrupp · Stroud · Gloucestershire · GL5 2BU

British Library Cataloguing in Publication Data
A catalogue record for this book is available from the British Library.

ISBN 0-7509-4271-1

For my parents and late grandparents,
with love and gratitude

Typeset in 15/10.5pt Photina.
Typesetting and origination by
Sutton Publishing Limited.
Printed and bound in England by
J.H. Haynes & Co. Ltd, Sparkford.

CONTENTS

LIST OF ILLUSTRATIONS

Harry and Connie Price pose on their honeymoon in Scarborough, *c.* 1908
Stella Cranshaw aboard a Channel steamer, 1923
Harry Price in his workshop in Pulborough, 1930
A stylish Lucy Kay outside 16 Queensberry Place, London, *c.* 1926
Price, Lucy Kay and *Daily Mail* reporter Charles Sutton
An athletic Price on holiday in 1929, at about the time of his 'heart attack'
Price and Lucy in Vienna, *c.* 1930
Price and the Austrian medium Rudi Schneider, 1930
Price's investigating council, including Kathleen 'Mollie' Goldney
The 'Poltergeist Girl', Eleanore Zugun
Lees Farm, Walcot, Shropshire
The grave of Harry and Connie Price at St Mary's, Pulborough

David Meeker photographs courtesy of The Harry Price Library of Magical Literature, Senate House Library, University of London. (HPC/DM)

ACKNOWLEDGEMENTS

Many people have helped with the compiling and production of this book, some with advice and material, others with proofreading. The acknowledgements I should like to make would take up many pages, but as I only have a limited number I must first thank Andrew Clarke, author of the excellent *Bones of Borley*, a forensic account of the haunting of Borley Rectory, to whom I owe a huge debt of thanks. He provided me with clear thoughts, ideas and at times stopped me from appearing a fool.

John L. Randall helped me at the very beginning of this project; Logan Lewis Proudlock at the College of Psychic Science rooted through scores of letters, discovering valuable material. Professor Dr Frank-Rutger Hausmann at the University of Freiburg helped me to establish the character of Dr Hans Bender; Coleen Phelan at the American Society for Psychical Research (ASPR) in New York helped to clarify Price's early journalism. Thanks are also due to David Meeker, Alan Roper, Uwe Schellinger and Eberhard Bauer at the Institut für Grenzgebiete der Psychologie und Psychohygiene (IGPP).

Work on this project has also taken me to various institutions, and I am indebted to staff of the University of London Special Collections Unit, especially Alun Ford, Stephan Dickers and Chris Smith. My thanks also to the staff of the National Archives, the LSE, James Turner at the Imperial War Museum, Adrian James at the Society of Antiquaries, Thomas Becker at the University of Bonn, Ottilia King for translating German into easily understood English, and to Peter Meadows and his staff at University of Cambridge Library, as well as the Society for Psychical Research for allowing me access to their archives.

My thanks also extend to Paul Adams and to Eddie Brazil for the excellent Harry Price archive at www.harryprice.co.uk, and to the International Survivalist Society for their valuable website.

A special word of thanks must go to my brother Peter, Carol and my two nephews Jake and Kit Morris-Hall, to Alison Healy at Shropshire Archives, to Sebastian Morgan David Hyde, Marion Jamieson and to Jeff Sorrell, without whose help this book would have been written in twice the time that it was.

Particular thanks go to my commissioning editor Christopher Feeney, Elizabeth Stone, Jane Hutchings and the board of directors at Sutton Publishing. Finally, I express enormous gratitude to Kate, for her help in a strange year and for bearing all my 'off' moments with love and understanding.

LIST OF ABBREVIATIONS

ASPR	American Society for Psychical Research, New York
BCPS	British College of Psychic Science (formerly the LSA)
HPC	Harry Price Collection, Senate House, University of London
HPC/DM	David Meeker photographs, courtesy of The Harry Price Library of Magical Literature, Senate House Library, University of London
JSPR	*Journal of the Society for Psychical Research*
LPL	London Psychical Laboratory
LSA	London Spiritualist Alliance
NLPR	National Laboratory of Psychical Research
SFT	Harry Price, *Search for Truth* (an autobiography)
SFHP	Trevor Hall, *Search for Harry Price*
SOA	Society of Antiquaries
SPR	Society for Psychical Research
TNA	The National Archives
WSRO	West Sussex Record Office

INTRODUCTION

There was a time, just within living memory, when countless people were gripped by spiritualism. It was comforting to think, especially after the millions of deaths of the First World War, that the dead walked in a new place and could come back to earth to see loved ones for a quick chat and a hug. In the early 1920s, mediums who claimed they were able to photograph auras, apparitions, seances, levitations and the spirits of the dead were in great demand, helped in part by the fanatical advocacy of Sir Arthur Conan Doyle, who had turned towards spiritualism several years earlier after having lost his son Kingsley, his brother, his two brothers-in-law and his two nephews in the bloody trenches and fields of the Great War.

Although many of the public believed the photographs mediums were producing to be fakes, it was hard getting evidence to prove it since they were understandably reluctant to sit for psychical scientists. Then one man exposed the movement for what it was. Harry Price was a 41-year-old amateur photographer, paper bag salesman, freelance journalist, former spiritualist and conjuror, who had successfully won membership of the Magic Circle, that exclusive body of magicians.

In early 1922, together with the Society for Psychical Research (SPR), Price used his spiritualist contacts (who were blithely unaware of what he was up to) to lure the spirit photographer William 'Billy' Hope into a carefully crafted sting. Through this he was able to show the world that Hope's 'celestial' photographs were nothing more than pictures ripped from long-forgotten periodicals or family albums, which had been pasted on to photographic plates before a photograph was taken in the normal way. It was enough to give Price the status of a minor celebrity; a position he had enjoyed some years earlier after a short journey into archaeology ended when experts, amazed at his luck in discovering rare artefacts, found he had forged a Roman silver ingot which on closer inspection turned out to be a crude slab of lead.

Following his success at unmasking Hope, he was invited to accompany the SPR foreign research officer Eric 'Dirty Ding' Dingwall to witness the astonishing feats of an Austrian medium named Willi Schneider, who claimed to have the gift of communicating with the spirit world via his guide Lola, the former mistress of Ludwig I, the blind king of Bavaria. When Willi produced such remarkable phenomena as invisible hands playing an accordion, discarnate lungs puffing chilly breath through witnesses' hair and a crawling disembodied hand, Price set himself the task of establishing a laboratory in Britain that would test mediums and supply the world with unknown facts about the paranormal.

He got off to a remarkable start by being told about a 21-year-old untried medium called Stella Cranshaw, a tractable young nurse who claimed to possess supernatural powers. In a series of exhaustive experiments with Price, she was reported to be able to summon a violent force that broke tables. Chairs levitated and mysterious objects were seen to crawl along the floor of seance rooms: and through her the dead prophesied the future. The seances with Stella were reported as a world first, but other psychical investigators, notably those from the Society for Psychical Research, distrusted Price's experiments and as a result he found himself marginalised, a situation he responded to with calculated insults, attributing the society's attacks on his character to sectarian jealousy.

After falling foul of the SPR, Harry made several attempts to prise money from leading spiritualist organisations with a view to establishing his own psychical organisation. In 1925 he managed to form the National Laboratory of Psychical Research (NLPR), a project backed by the London Spiritualist Alliance.

With his celebrity rising, he made friendships with well-known magicians, scientists and show people including Harry Houdini, a relationship that petered out a few years later after he accused the great escapologist of fraud. But that did not matter. At the NLPR, Price had the ear of eminent men of letters and, since he now regarded life after death as proven, had become a friend of Conan Doyle. He was given the necessary money by wealthy supporters to investigate areas of the occult others had only dreamt of.

He attempted to contact the planet Mars, a fascination that had begun with the late Victorians after the Italian astronomer Giovanni Schiaparelli had claimed to see canals on the planet through his telescope, a claim supported by his colleague Camille Flammarion. At first Price used clairvoyants who claimed a familiarity with the solar system and stars, then he used an odd invention made by a City of London solicitor to try to contact Martian savages. When this proved inconclusive he travelled to the Jungfraujoch in Switzerland, where he considered making an attempt to contact the Red Planet using a huge beam of light, but the project was abandoned on account of the cost.

Each experiment at the NLPR was too preposterous, too remarkable for any sensible person to ignore. Every strange incident or miserable plaything of the dead was publicised to keep pace with the public's appetite, which Price had whetted. He was rapidly becoming the natural leader for a nation in thrall to what happened to the soul after death. No newspaper report or broadcast on a haunted house was complete without Harry's thoughts about the matter. He had a status and reputation that no ghost hunter of today can hope to share.

He claimed that his findings were bolstered through his training as a scientist and engineer but in reality the man who had left school at 15 was an academic failure. His scientific methods were nothing more than an act, using scientific apparatus and the trappings of a chemical laboratory merely to convince people that he was a scientist. He thought instinctively and impulsively and, instead of trying to disprove his theories, he sought only to prove them. At one stage in his career, he believed he had discovered the very substance that ghosts were made of and thought it might be possible to re-create them from what turned out to be a piece of regurgitated cheesecloth, iron filings and albumen.

He sought out a talking mongoose called Gef on the Isle of Man, who it was said spoke several languages, could recite poetry, travelled around the island on a bus to bring back gossip and was partial to cream buns. Price also set out to prove the uselessness of transcendental magic by showing how attempting to turn a goat into a handsome man on top of the Harz mountains in Germany was bound to fail. It did, but he got to smear the chest of an attractive girl with a sticky black substance which he claimed was an alchemical ointment, though *The Times* described it as 'looking and smelling exactly like boot polish'. The event, though, did bring him an appreciative audience, largely made up of prominent Nazis.

Impatient for academic and financial success, which had eluded him in Britain, Price was wooed by the Third Reich to establish an institute for psychical research, a project Hitler took great personal interest in. It was an idea the Führer had promised Erik Jan Hanussen, his personal seer, he would carry out – before he had him murdered. When war looked inevitable, and warned off by MI5, Price dropped the idea, but not before writing a letter asking Hitler if he could witness the 1939 Nuremberg Rally planned for that August 'in some comfort'. Following the failed airlift of his laboratory to Bonn, Price's offices in London were closed, the contents crated up and transferred to the University of London after his friend, the philosopher Cyril Joad, had successfully negotiated their safe berth.

Now on his own, Price, still selling paper bags for a living and without money to fund experiments, began to invent phenomena to supplement his earnings. Perhaps the best example of this is the haunting of Borley Rectory in Essex. It was a time when he would do anything for money.

Since his death in 1948, two biographies have been published. Paul Tabori, his literary executor, paved the way with his *Biography of a Ghost Hunter*, a book written under strict terms of engagement with Harry's widow, so that anything that deviated from her husband's carefully crafted autobiography was snuffed out and replaced with tall 'facts'. In 1978, Trevor H. Hall, a successful businessman and author on the esoteric, published a revised version of Harry's life, *Search for Harry Price*. Though he discovered that a lot of what Price had written was invented, Hall just skimmed the surface of who the real Harry Price was – partly due to the sheer quantity of documents his subject had bequeathed to the University of London. Only in 2005, fifty-seven years after Price's death, was his vast archive at last catalogued, a project undertaken by Lesley Price (no relation) and Stephan Dickers at the university's Special Collections Unit; and this has helped considerably in writing this biography.

This is not a book about psychical research as such. I have aimed to understand Harry Price and his complex personality. I have tried to give him a voice by searching through thousands of documents in his archive and elsewhere, many of which are published here for the first time. There are also questions that have not been asked before. For example, could Price have been forging artefacts alongside Charles Dawson, the Piltdown Man hoaxer? Did he make one of his secretaries pregnant? How did Price, a lowly paper bag salesman, manage to afford Rolls-Royce cars and rare books and keep a string of mistresses on a small wage? Was it he who suggested police should raid a prominent spiritualist organisation after he had fallen out with their president, Sir Arthur Conan Doyle? What was the truth behind his friendship with Houdini? Did he forge every piece of evidence at Borley Rectory, 'the most haunted house in England', so people would buy his books? Have his previous literary executors deliberately hidden the truth from the public? Did Price meet Adolf Hitler? This book answers each of these searching questions. I believe that the Harry Price I have written about is the closest the reader can come to knowing who he really was.

Richard Morris
September 2006

1

THE RED LION AND THE SANCTUARY OF NEW CROSS GATE

owards the end of his busy life, Harry Price increasingly resembled Max Schreck playing Count Orlock in *Nosferatu*, the 1922 film version of Bram Stoker's *Dracula*, so it is perhaps appropriate that he became famous that year for dabbling with the souls of the dead, which would later make him a celebrity the world over.

Price chose to tell his readers, in his ironically titled autobiography, *Search for Truth*, that he had been born in the tidy moral climate of a family from leafy Shropshire,[1] when in fact his first home had been a cramped tenement at 37 Red Lion Square, Holborn, in London, a former factory belonging to the celebrated pen and ink maker James Perry & Co. (though in a peculiar twist of fate, the building is now home to the Ethical Society).

Harry was born on the bitterly cold morning of Tuesday 17 January 1881, in the filthy no man's land between the City and the affluent West End. During the day there was the stink and general clattering of assorted Victorian industry; at night it was an area synonymous with prostitution, so much so that a band of moralists, the Midnight Meeting Movement, set up their offices at 55 Red Lion Square to be near the women who needed to make money quickly and without fuss. The area figured on Charles Booth's famous poverty map a little later as one of the poorest parts of the district: people living there were described as very poor and in chronic want.

It had not always been like this. Harry's 44-year-old father, Edward Ditcher Price, once a successful grocer from an affluent Shropshire family, had been born in the small village of Rodington, where his father, John, had managed to climb the twin ladders of respectability and wealth. A district magistrate, landowner, postmaster, innkeeper of the Bull's Head and friend of the rich and powerful, John Price was a valued member of the Victorian middle class.

In 1853 Edward, the youngest of five brothers and three sisters, decided to leave the burgeoning coal mines, steelworks and agriculture of Shropshire and settle in London, where he hoped to find prosperity, and settled in trade as a grocer.

After consulting his copy of Frederick Copestick's *Prophetic Almanac* of 1852,[2] which assured him his life was 'set faire', he travelled among an odd walking caravan of gypsies, hucksters and the hopeful. Edward was bound to William Witt, a master grocer in Skinner Street, Bishopsgate, in the City, and then graduated as a journeyman in the Worshipful Company of Grocers a few years later.

In a little more than two decades, he took part in a flurry of activity by opening five businesses in twenty years. That was until 1875 when it seems he was faced with a crisis. Now a man in his 40s and still single, he had met a young girl of 14 named Emma Randall-Meech and made her pregnant. It is pure supposition, but once his customers heard of this scandal, gossip spread and they deserted him.

To try to head off disaster Edward married Emma, now aged 15, on 11 January 1876 at St Andrew's, Holborn. The only family member to witness the wedding was the bride's mother, Emma Dunnett; her husband, Henry, who had worked as a solicitor's clerk and latterly as a newspaper reporter, was dead, and the Price family were snowed up in Shropshire.

If Edward and Emma had arranged the marriage to try to save the family business, then the strategy failed dismally. With his customers gone, he sold his business at 70 Theobald's Road in Holborn's impressive thoroughfare to the future Queen's grocer, Henry Harrod, and began work as a commercial traveller for Edward Saunders & Son Limited. Based at Cannon Street, a few hundred yards from St Paul's Cathedral, it was one of the largest paper suppliers in London, and looked after the grocery and bakery trade by selling paper bags, tea wraps and twine.

Within three months of Harry's birth the family had made the move west. The 1881 national census shows them living at 34 Walpole Street in Chelsea, a respectable early Victorian white stucco four-storey terraced house near Chelsea Women's Hospital, owned by the Worshipful Company of Grocers. It perhaps signifies that a member of the family, possibly Emma, was seeking treatment nearby.

A short while later the family moved east, into a smart, nearly new, six-bedroomed house at 6 Amersham Road, New Cross, rented out at £10 a year and fitted out from scratch. The surrounding streets may have been monotonous and near the smoke and noise of the railway, but they were decent, solid, substantially built traders' homes that spilled out across the former medieval thoroughfare of New Cross Gate. This was a world of comfort, and although geographically and socially indeterminate, it offered privacy, seclusion and a chance for life to begin again. The Price family would live here for three years before Edward had earned or inherited money to buy a house nearby called Cloverley, at 36 St Donatt's Road. Such a purchase would have set him apart from his neighbours, since only 15 per cent of people then owned their own homes.

When Harry was 6 he started at the London Board School in Waller Road, New Cross, a street named after the poet Edmund Waller and where his sister Annie would later settle down to married life.[3] It was not a happy time for Harry. He was bullied by other boys, who jeered and taunted him for his diminutive size, and he developed a nervous stammer, which stayed with him for the rest of his life.

Strangely, his own accounts of his early life give the impression that he was a virtual orphan.[4] Not only are his parents largely missing from any autobiographical work (he mentions his mother in passing and his father twice) but he ignores his sister and his schoolfriends, as if they made no great or favourable impression: it seems that his childhood was dominated by a vague sense of solitude.

School holidays sometimes get a look-in, but innocent friendships, happiness and bliss are all dismissed, as if inviting readers to think he was someone permanently deprived of affection. He hints that he was a boy who enjoyed being alone, who delighted in inventing games for himself, with the lonely child's habit of making up stories and holding conversations with imaginary people.

From these thin-on-the-ground reminiscences we can sense that from the start of his boyhood his strongest feelings were of being self-contained. It was a formative time for him, and he claimed that one incident he witnessed around the age of 8 transformed his world, the encounter ranking above all his earlier childhood memories.

One cold January morning the 'Great Sequah' with his brass bands, gilded chariots, and troop of 'boosters' in the garb of Mohawk Indians, pitched his tent – so to speak – in Shrewsbury's principal square. And, to the accompaniment of the sounding brass and tinkling cymbals, announced in stentorian tones that he was there to extract every bad tooth in the county and to cure every ailment with which his bucolic listeners were cursed.

During the whole of this eventful morning I stood, cold but happy, open-mouthed at this display of credulity, self-deception, auto-suggestion, faith-healing, beautiful showmanship, super-charlatanism and 'magic'. The miracles of the market-place left me spellbound.[5]

The Sequah was probably William Henry Hartley, an eloquent northerner, a quack, a money-grabbing pretender, or, in Ben Jonson's colourful phrasing 'a lousy-fartical rogue'. A regular at fairgrounds and market squares throughout Britain, Hartley became so successful that Sequah franchises were set up throughout the British Empire, becoming a limited company with more share value than Boots the chemist.[6] Tooth-pulling was the most popular of his acts, at a time when dentistry was still in a painfully primitive state. Once the patient was in Hartley's grip he set to work with his forceps, removing teeth at a steady machine-gun rattle – contemporary newspaper accounts claim he removed as many as 320 teeth in 40 minutes, or eight a minute.

Though hypnotised by the show, Price said he did not believe a word he heard or a thing he saw: 'It was the novelty of it all, rather than genuine amazement, that made such an impression on me,' he wrote, adding that although he rushed home to tell his parents what he had seen and pestered his father to buy him a copy of Professor Hoffman's *Modern Magic*, the fact that 'I demanded how it was done, is proof, I think, of that inherent scepticism coupled with the critical faculty, with which my existence has been cursed.'[7]

Modern Magic was a well-known primer, disclosing the secrets of the latest in Victorian drawing-room conjuring, and became the starting point of a library that one day would become one of the most comprehensive collections of occult and magical books in the world. In later life Price recalled reading the chapters on conjuring, card-sharping and producing doves out of a stovepipe hat in happy competition with an unnamed friend.

He may have become interested in magic to impress his peers, or from the need to learn various tricks because they imparted secrets, hoping that these puzzles might award him a special place among his friends. And he certainly knew that magic was power.

The following Christmas his father gave him another book that was to leave a profound impression on his childish mind. *The Tiny Mite, Describing the Adventures of a Little Girl in Dreamland, Fairyland, and Wonderland and Elsewhere*,[8] is the story of the adventures of a small girl, her cat, a dog and a doll in a magical kingdom. Fifty years on, in *Search for Truth*, he wrote of his fondness for a book that had opened out a mysterious world of night hags, hobgoblins, fairies, giants, dragons, witches and magicians.

'The book still fascinates me, and as I gaze at my father's inscription on the verso of the frontispiece, a lump comes into my throat as I think of those happy childhood days when my love for the miraculous was as boundless as it is now.'[9]

Aged 11, each day Harry would walk the short distance to join more than 500 other pupils attending the Haberdashers' Aske's Hatcham Boys School in Pepys Lane. The school's vision, then, as now, was to inspire all pupils to reach their full potential, no matter what their ability or background, and to continuously raise their aspirations and achievements.

Haberdashers' kicked away the usual terror of Victorian classroom rules, where children were caned regularly if they happened to be left-handed or beaten for ignorance if they put up their hands up pretending to know an answer but did not.

The school had an advanced curriculum, concentrating heavily on new subjects such as elementary physics, practical chemistry and botany, which in turn enhanced the school's reputation for science teaching. Headed by William Spratling, a geologist rather than a vicar, the Victorian norm, it could afford passionate, inspired teaching.

The young Harry enjoyed playing chess, collected old coins, kept small animals and could recite strange and sinister facts of nature or history. His scrapbooks also confirm his interest in performing theatre and music hall acts. His biggest interest, however, was in the arcane. He collected cigarette cards, magazines on magic and spiritualism, in fact anything his pocket money and jobs were able to muster; Harry devoured whole articles on hypnotism and trance mediumship, and lived his youth through magazines such as W.T. Stead's *Borderland*, a publication designed to appeal to 'the great mass of ordinary people' in revealing the 'study of the spook'. He was entering into a new world.

These literally wonderful periodicals spoke of men being turned into horses, larger-than-life phantasmagoria, fairy folk, apocalyptic bogeymen and eyewitness sightings of mad flibbertigibbets seen roaming the hinterlands of the Yorkshire Dales and visits to ruined cloisters and haunted spots such as Fyvie Castle in Scotland, which, according to *Man and Boy* magazine, was cursed by a wizard and had 'a murder room, with ineffable bloodstains and rotting brain matter on the floor'.[10]

The footprint of the so-called 'new revelation' (the rapid growth of spiritualism), and how it affected Harry Price's family and millions of others throughout the world, seems alarmingly innocent. The radical ideas of Charles Darwin's *On the Origin of Species* and *The Descent of Man* had so thoroughly shaken the concept of the divine, years earlier, that evolution and creationism were still hotly debated issues when spiritualism arrived in Britain from America in the 1850s.

It all began on 11 December 1847 at Hydesville, a hamlet some 20 miles from Rochester in New York State, when two sisters, Kate and Margaret Fox, aged 10 and 12 respectively, heard a series of thuds and raps on their bedroom wall.

The small wooden clapboard shack where the family lived had a reputation of being haunted, especially when the wood wheezed and knocked as the temperature outside rose and plummeted. It was around the middle of March 1848, so the children later told their mass audiences, that they were so alarmed at what was happening that they refused to sleep apart and instead slept with their parents.

Then, on 31 March of that year, Kate Fox made history. She challenged the mysterious unseen power to repeat the snaps of her fingers: it did so. The entity, whom the girls later called Mr Splitfoot, had, according to Kate, been murdered in the shack. As newspapers began to report these peculiar events, the girls' brother, David, learned that he could talk on an intelligent level with the spirits by devising an alphabet they could follow.

Now the atmosphere changed: a 'violent, wanton force' began attacking the family until at last they realised that the spirits were trying to tell them something. Sitting down with the spiritual alphabet David had invented the sisters communicated with the noises and worked out what they were saying:

Dear Friends, you must proclaim this truth to the world. This is the dawning of a new era; you must not try to conceal it any longer.

When you do your duty, God will protect you and good spirits will watch over you.

This remarkably convenient message, reported in newspapers throughout America, was soon earning the Fox sisters up to $300 a night, and when they signed to Phineas T. Barnum they popularised the idea of seances, induced trances and manifestations. Table-tipping and tea parties became common, and as religion questioned spiritualism's innocence, the movement became a byword for survival after death.

In the teeming streets of New Cross and dark squares of Hatcham, in meeting houses in Piccadilly, all manner of fanatics gathered believers to their cause. The movement, which prided itself on its classless appeal, emphasised that a talent for communicating with the spirits was well within the grasp of every man and woman. It thus provided a tremendous consolation for the bereaved and a window into the timeless joys of a spiritual afterlife that beckoned from beyond the grave.

In the spiritualism mania, pictures were seen to throw themselves off walls, furniture to move and even levitate without being touched; famous people, who so few people knew in life, appeared in the most humble of drawing rooms; ectoplasm became a buzzword.

The late Victorians, in George Bernard Shaw's view, were addicted 'to table rapping, clairvoyance, palmistry, crystal gazing, and the like',[11] just as their parents had been spellbound by hypnosis, muscle-reading and phrenology.

One of the most distinctive aspects of this mystical revival was the broad embrace of the Orient and the emergence of groups such as the Theosophical Society, headed by Madame Helena Blavatsky, a Germano-Russian aristocrat, thanks to whom the society rapidly became the most famous occult group in late-Victorian Britain.

Also from this time came 'high-magic' societies, such as the secret Hermetic Order of the Golden Dawn, where initiates studied astrology, alchemy, the cabala, tarot definitions and basic magical techniques. Members graduated to access the secrets of ritual magic, through which invisible forces could be influenced and controlled.

Back at Haberdashers', Price, the future psychist, had begun to contribute small articles to the school magazine, *The Askean*, on topics he was fascinated with, such as coin collecting, archaeology and how things in general worked; all the time drawing on his developing interest in language.

If his mind ranged widely, it was not entirely surprising. During his school years his mother was stricken with various severe illnesses, and to ease the strain on his family Harry frequently decamped to Shropshire. In the school holidays he went to stay either with his unmarried uncle Joseph at Lees farmhouse, a three-gabled, whitewashed building that still stands today in the hamlet of Walcot near Withington, or with one of his father's two sisters, Aunt Jane, who lived at Constitution Hill in Wellington with her daughter Caroline, or with Rhoda, who lived at Rodington Heath.

Trevor Hall suggests that Lees Farm was the place Price fictionalised as Parton Magna and that it was here Price had his first supernatural experience, an event that shook the certainties of his sane world and signalled the possibility of things not being as they first appeared, where his endless interest in the occult blossomed and broadened his understanding about the supernatural.

If hard analysis is made of the tale Price called *The Ghost that Stumbled*,[12] then major doubts as to the truth of his story of a rich recluse who 'strangled his niece' come bubbling to the surface, especially when one realises that the Mary Hulse in the story was the name of Harry's long-dead aunt who died not a victim of murder, as he claimed, but after a sustained and painful cancer in 1835, a year after her brother Edward was born.[13]

Price forgets to tell the reader that the Lees was at one time owned by his family and was where his grandfather, a man deeply embedded in Shropshire society and a one-time Tory candidate in Sir Robert Peel's first government, died from heart failure in 1868 at 73 years of age. Unfortunately, the work is not in Price's archive, but we can hazard a guess about its contents since Harry also used the Lees in *A Tragedy of the Night*, a ghoulish unpublished short story set in haunted Shropshire that he wrote on 12 March 1901.[14]

The narrator of the story is a wealthy London doctor whose main interest other than medicine is ghosts; spirits are his 'dearest friends', spectres his 'one and constant study'. The doctor is invited by an old school friend, Dick Corbet, to view a house he has bought called Walcot Lees, near Wellington, the 'finest place in Shropshire'. Price's nameless adventurer sets out to visit Corbet after closing his surgery early. When he arrives at Wellington railway station he realises he is too late for a cab, so he decides to walk the 5 miles to the house. After trudging through fields and along quiet lanes he arrives at Walcot Lees, enjoys a meal and falls asleep; but in the early hours of the morning he is awakened by a young woman 'wearing a flowing gown of the purest whiteness which failed to hide the beautiful symmetry of her body and which contrasted strangely to her glistening, nut brown hair, that fell in profusion over her snowy shoulders'.[15] After being murdered by her lover, her ghost comes back to haunt the house. The killer then drowns himself. The end of the story is limp and uninspired: the hero wakes up and decides the adventure was the result of having eaten too much before going to bed.

As always in his early stories, there are elements of autobiography. In *Confessions of a Ghost Hunter* and *Poltergeist over England: Three Centuries of Mysterious Ghosts* Price tells his readers he spent many happy weeks in the house, his heart beating faster than its accustomed rate because of a certain young woman. The descriptions of the ghost, and of his future wife, Constance Knight, are so exactly alike it seems probable that he was dating Connie when he wrote the story.

Where the essence of the story came from is unknown, but it may well have come from Shropshire local legend and history learned at his father's knee: Edward certainly had a taste for adventure and believed in the supernatural, as most of his generation did.

There was once a flourishing and comforting oral literature in the English countryside, where tales of legendary figures, stories of witchcraft, ghosts, giants and incarnations of fairies were heavily localised, sometimes borrowed from other villages, and mixed in with a villager's own tales, which were then recounted off the cuff. Before the days when most people could read and write, folklore was vital to the rural community, supplying villages with a fund of narrative, humour, satire and social comment everyone could understand and in which everyone could participate.

The way in which Harry gives no sympathy to his aunt or his great-uncle is suggestive of a Restoration comedy or a gory rural tale:

At about half-past eleven my companion thought he heard a noise in the room overhead (the traditional apartment of the murdered niece). I too heard a noise but thought it might have been caused by rats. A few minutes later, there was a thud overhead that left nothing to the imagination. It sounded as if someone had stumbled over a chair. The fact that we were not alone in the house paralysed us with fear.[16]

Then, suddenly, the presence made a dash for the stairs but they found nothing that could account for 'it'. After a short wait, the noise of stamping

returned. Price pressed a remote switch rigged up to a flash made from
gunpowder and magnesium powder: there was a loud bang and, no doubt
shocked and disorientated, he heard the ghost distinctly stumble. But the
photographic plate was bare except for an overexposed picture of a staircase.
If he thought the supposed trip to 'Parton Magna' (a name derived from
Upton Magna, a village close to Rodington) was a failure, he still recognised
the importance of his disappointment and wrote about it after his return to
school in London.

Instead of noting down points about the ghost in the school magazine,
Harry sought to improve on the tale by creating a drama about his
experiences and formed a small amateur dramatic company, the Carlton
Dramatic Society, to perform his play, The Sceptic,[17] but that would be two
years in the making. In the meantime, shortly before he left Haberdashers',
Price's amateur dramatic society put on their first show, in (so he claimed)
the large coach-house at the side of his parents' house:

We used to keep a phaeton and a dear old mare named 'Sallie' (on whose
back I used to ride into the country two or three times a week) and my
father thought that we could convert the coach-house into a first-class
auditorium as there were two doors opening on to the roadway.[18]

The family was now living in the middle of New Cross, which makes it
unlikely that there was in fact a coach-house attached to the property, and
although both 6 Amersham Road and Cloverley, at 36 St Donatt's Road, had
brick-built workshops (as they do today), there is barely room to swing a cat,
let alone turn around a horse or the eighty persons Harry claimed he
managed to cram into the 'theatre.'[19] According to yellowing posters in his
archive, the evening of entertainment was actually performed at the Club
Rooms in Brockley rather than on the rough stage he claimed a carpenter
had erected in Sallie the mare's huge stable.

Price's academic life was less successful than his life outside the school, and
he left at the age of 15 with rather little to show for it. He himself said that
he was not a distinguished scholar, but a clever, quick and knowing young
man, strongly able and competent. He had a flair for English composition,
for which he won a couple of prizes.[20] The rigour of school life had one
beneficial influence, however: it turned a rather shy child into a person of
charm, able to develop a rejoinder equal to every social contingency.

Vituperation was a skill Harry developed early, to cope with the difficult world around him.

To his family's chagrin, he was not destined for a university education, and Harry claimed that straight after school he was to begin an apprenticeship at the railway engineers Merryweathers in Shrewsbury, 'but my father suddenly changed his mind! He decided that I should enter the paper trade, with which he was intimately connected.'[21]

Merryweathers' of Shropshire had closed years earlier and the only two remaining outlets were in London, an administrative address at Long Acre in Covent Garden and an engineering works in Greenwich Road, south-east London, so this account does not ring true.[22]

There are scattered clues in Harry's archive that he did in fact set out to become an engineer, until the fateful day when he failed his exams. Bitterly disappointed, his father recruited him into Edward Saunders, where he worked as a part-time travelling salesman during the daytime and studied electrical engineering at Faraday House in the evenings.

It was during his time here that he gave his first press interview,[23] during which he claimed that on 2 April 1899, soon after his eighteenth birthday, he and some friends carried out a small experiment into radio waves. He had made a portable transmitter and receiver as a course project, and then placed them in the tower of St Peter's Church, in Brockley, and on Telegraph Hill, in New Cross, which were a mile or so apart, with the aim of transmitting a continuous radio signal. The experiment was a success, and Price even managed to record flashes and waves on to a photographic plate. His efforts caused some interest, and accounts appeared in the local press and in the *Westminster Gazette* for 2 May 1899. 'I believe my portable wireless was one of the very earliest to be constructed,' he told his readers.[24]

If this experiment did take place, then it would have been a milestone in the history of radio. At that time the existence of radio waves had been demonstrated by Hertz, and Sir Oliver Lodge had invented the coherer to detect sparks from a transmitter, but very little was known about them, which makes it most unlikely that Price could have photographed a radio wave. If Price had achieved the seemingly impossible one would expect to find the photographic plate somewhere in the huge archive of curios that represent his life; one would also need to explain why he failed the qualifications he needed to progress into the fast-moving world of communication. The truth is that he probably wrote the story himself;

and the newspapers printed it without first checking the integrity of their source.

Around this time Price talks of nursing himself to sleep with a copy of *Burke's Peerage* and *Who's Who*. It is not hard to understand why he would want to be able to recite the names of those considered important, topical, or noteworthy, those that lived great lives.[25] His parents were perhaps a little in awe of his vitality, competence and strength of character. He was a stylist, an instinctive performer and, like all born entertainers, a petitioner for attention and applause.

His local fame gave him a taste for the sort of adulation he most desired; it also gave him the excuse to have his portrait painted by a schoolfriend, the artist John Dumayne.[26] The picture, paid for by his father, now hangs in the Harry Price Magical Library at the University of London, and depicts Price as a romantic rebel, impatient for success – a fledgling novelist, perhaps. If the artist Henry Hoppner Meyer had been wandering around New Cross in the last years of the nineteenth century he might have thought Price was a young Lord Byron.

Meanwhile, having failed as an electrical engineer, Price attended evening classes at Goldsmiths College adjacent to his home. Here he studied photography, photographic optics, chemistry and mechanical engineering, while keeping his day job at Edward Saunders. He claimed that his evenings at the college were some of the most pleasant he had spent in his life, and 'the chemical experiments (the department was then in charge of Charles Loudon Bloxham) especially interested me'.

A good description of a young scientist, one might think, but Bloxham, one of the most distinguished of nineteenth-century minds, had died in 1887 when Price was aged 6, so we can count this as another piece of Harry's retrospective gloss, an afterthought applied after his fame had been established.

But it was in chemistry that, with a burning sense of destiny, Harry and a friend and fellow Goldsmiths College student, Walter Creasy, found an early berth in business, forming, with startling originality, a glue-making company called Price and Creasy. With the intention of building a monolithic business, the pair started out from Cloverley's workshop, baptised 'the Laboratory', with the brand name of Quexol, a version of 'quick solvent', marketing a range of adhesives throughout London and in some of the Home Counties. Unfortunately, there is no indication in any of Price's writings of the outcome of the enterprise, though one can be sure that if it had been successful he would have written about it.

Not the least of their achievements was an idiosyncratic foot-rot cure. Price and Creasy planted hit-and-run newspaper stories, portraying the medicine as a miracle therapy. A news item in the morning edition of the *Kentish Mercury* of 4 May 1902 read:

> This specific, which has been termed the acme of veterinary science as regards this complaint, absolutely cures both the contagious and non-contagious forms of foot-rot. Besides being a preventive of the disease, it has the advantage of being inexpensive, economical, and exceedingly simple to use. It is the outcome of painstaking experiments conducted with a view to permanently curing the sheep, and eliminating all traces of the infection.

After the Quexol enterprise, armed perhaps with a little surplus cash, Price pursued photography, a great love of his early teenage years. Throughout his life he studied up-to-date techniques, and after attending a particularly dubious seance where the medium had produced a photograph of a ghostly figure, he went home and, with help from a gnarled family retainer, 'George the gardener', he duplicated the medium's miracles.

At one time he took pictures of shop frontages for local newspapers (the images were then made into line drawings for advertisement purposes) but, perhaps because it was a less tractable craft than he had hoped for, he was certainly disinclined to turn photography into a full-time career, despite setting up a small studio at his parents' house.[27]

In his leisure time he was writing more light comedies for the stage, including a 30-minute squib called *Half-Hours with the Mediums*, ostentatiously choked with magical effects. Others were *The Poltergeist, Cut in Half* and *The Cuckoo's Nest*, 'a romantic romp of a comedy with magical scenes' performed at the Club Rooms in Brockley.[28]

Another composition was a surreal semi-musical based on the Gallic highwayman Claude Duval, who had come to the nation's attention in *Memoirs of Du Vail: Containing the History of his Life and Death*, by William Pope, again performed in Brockley.

That same year he left England for the first time, now 21 years old, to visit Paris, where he not only wanted to experience more of the world but to 'see how vast and interesting fairs can be. In France, fair life, or the *vie foraine* is a very organised business.'[29] Here he experienced the extraordinary café life and astonishing streetscapes of cosmopolitan France. He visited the exhibitionistic Foire aux Pains d'Epice, an annual Easter fair in central Paris, where he squeezed his way into a tent to witness horrible sideshows, and gawped at fetishistic sights such as 'Fat Fifine', who perched cushion-like in a box, wearing extremely short shorts, anaesthetised, waiting for her body to be pricked by customers who had bought pins for a few francs.

When Harry and his nameless companion had finished stabbing Fifine's flesh with pins they walked away leaving her 'just like a good looking hedgehog' and went on to see Olga, the girl with cast-iron skin, 'nude except for a loin cloth', imprisoned in a glass coffin, who lay reclining on a bed of 'two hundred broken wine bottles'.[30]

Clearly relishing the intensity of the shows, Price moved on to other pleasures, such as two hypnotised subjects making love to one another, and then witnessed the entombed Tavern of the Dead, where for one franc customers could see a dead woman, suitably laid out in a coffin draped in red satin, slowly rot into a skeleton in front of their eyes.[31]

He was living life to the full and had found a trade he was comfortable with; and at the back of his mind he was in no doubt of his own ability to make an impact and become the discoverer of some outlandish or knavish invention. But there were obstacles to his happiness, not least the health of his mother.

Emma had become much weaker during the last two years of her life. Edward hired an 18-year-old domestic, Louisa Highland, to help look after her and to do odd chores such as black-leading the kitchen stove, dusting and scrubbing the front step. Nevertheless, Emma was admitted to St Thomas's Hospital for an operation to remove ovarian cancer: in these days when cancer surgery was at best a quasi-scientific enterprise, the chances of survival were extremely low. Shortly after half past three on 22 August 1902, she died from a massive heart attack while still in theatre. She was 42 years old, and had enjoyed no intensity of life to set against her early death.[32]

The year 1902 marked a new stage in Harry Price's life. Unsure of his future and how to earn his living he joined his father at Edward Saunders & Son as a full-time commercial traveller selling stationery and paper to the grocery and baking trades, a job he retained for the rest of his life. It was a complacent career in business rather than a rapturous one. This is not to say that this phase of Harry's life was a boring one. As a seller he was able to enter into other people's offices, shops and lives, and was paid to travel.

In public he made only elusive statements about his trade, but whenever he did refer to it he speciously assured his listeners that his father was a well-known paper manufacturer, no mere salesman.[33] It was a job Price junior seems to have enjoyed, and one that would see him rise to a clutch of senior positions in the firm, first as sales manager and then sales director, an amiable figure perched above his staff in Little Sutton Street.[34]

Whatever happened around him in his career, writing and magic were still the centre of his universe. Price's literary focus still lay with *The Askean*, the magazine of his old school, and he was able to indulge a growing mania for contributing to its pages, the range of his writing moving on to chemistry, photography, radiotelegraphy, archaeology and a little book reviewing.

The magazine, intended for school circles and erstwhile pupils, found only a limited audience, but at least enabled Price to reach a readership beyond his own family.

Even at this stage he knew that writing would eventually offer him a way of coming to terms with the conflicts of his upbringing, allowing him to create and experience the things that most fascinated him; and getting his work published represented fame of a sort. He began writing breezy short articles for *The Captain*, a magazine edited by Old Fag,[35] the pen name of R.S. Warren Bell, and so his work was read by public schoolboys, or those who wished they were schoolboys still.

Writing and getting paid for writing became one of his long-standing ambitions, an activity he thought would set him apart from his less emotional and clever friends as well as foreshadowing the life which he so desperately wanted, that of a full-time author. And here was proof of the distance he had travelled since leaving school.

In Harry's anecdotal autobiography he makes out that it was his interest in coin collecting that led him to write his first 'serious work'. But behind the authoritative, all-knowing façade was simply someone armed with scissors and a can of homemade glue. Trevor Hall's scathing biography of Price alerts readers to the fact that Price was not the great coin expert he said he was but a rather inexpert journalist, and a dishonest one at that.

Hall suggests that much of the material for the series of articles Price wrote between 1902 and 1904 for the *Kentish Mercury* and the *Wellington Journal* (in Shropshire) were lifted directly from George C. Williamson's revised edition of William Boyne's *Trade Tokens Issued in the Seventeenth Century in England, Wales and Ireland*, a standard, three-volume work on numismatics. Indeed, according to Hall, Price was no more than a duplicitous hack, one who had a self-imposed regime of flicking through dusty, hand-cut, greenfly-blotched volumes, copying out quantities of material – facts, styles, sophisticated tone and opinions – with editors taking him at his word.

In his defence, this is not to say his task was an easy one, since his many raids and pillages meant he was faced with the prickly chore of subediting, sifting and mixing material written with a clear-cut readership in mind. He did it because he had something to prove to his former schoolfriends. Though he had failed to secure the career he wanted, journalism was a sunny calling: it was the lifestyle and image he wanted, and it brought with it character. Price began to look like a hack, with his odd, rumpled, unmistakable fashion sense, and journalism gave him the power to stand outside established authority, with the possibility of propelling him into places where he least expected to go. It was the supreme anti-profession: it brought a craving to snitch and spill secrets. It was a foreshadowing of his future life.

Although his local reputation was established, Harry needed to spread his fame wider and he still yearned for people's approval. Accordingly, in 1902 he nonchalantly began yoking unearned initials to his name. For instance, when he joined the Royal Astrological Society in that year he became Harry Price MRAS, and after joining the Numismatic Society, which after 1903 became the Royal Numismatic Society, he began sporting MRAS FRNS, even announcing his attendance at the society's meetings – and his entrance into the starry world of the Royal Societies Club – in the personal announcements column of his local newspaper.[36]

Price's literary pilfering also brought him a highly ambiguous appointment in Ripon, in Yorkshire. Benjamin Fields of the Ripon Naturalists' Club and Scientific and Literary Association wrote asking Harry to become their honorary curator. It was a strange offer, made queerer by having no official requirement to attend conventions in Yorkshire or to offer advice on coins. Whether he made it to Yorkshire for a meeting is not known, but he was obviously delighted that someone had recognised his talent. He accepted the post and for a good part of his life wore the title as a respectable battle ribbon, only dropping it when his fame, as a ghost hunter and writer, was established.

Scrawled on the letter in red pencil is 'I am elected as honorary curator Ripon Museum'; and no doubt this was a letter he waved in front of his friends' faces as proof of his rising status. Contrary to Harry's later claims, however, the post was an advisory one and had nothing whatever to do with the numismatics department at Ripon Museum. Harry later commissioned John Dumayne to draw a design for his own private token, which he used as a Christmas card for friends and potential business clients.

Harry's writing career had so far proved moderately successful, but he wanted to move it forward and extend himself. In the forefront of his mind, he had only one clear idea for the future: to become rich. His early writings indicate that he fantasised about making thousands of pounds by becoming an inventor.

Certainly by the time Price was 21 he had some fixed goals, or so he told his faithful readers. Writing in 1940 he reflects on having lunch with Frank Whitaker, the then editor of *John O'London's Weekly*, a middlebrow literary magazine, and touching on the thorny subject of ambition.

Here are some of my 'ambitions' that foolishly possessed me when I obtained my majority as confided to Frank Whitaker.

(1) I wanted to be a writer and to write for the *Encyclopaedia Britannica*
(2) I wanted to appear in *Who's Who*
(3) I wanted to collect the largest magical library in existence
(4) I wanted to be offered a doctorate, *honoris causa*, of some university
(5) I wanted to possess a Rolls-Royce car. Later when the radio was in its infancy, I wanted to broadcast.[37]

When he could afford it, he lost no time in buying a Rolls-Royce, which he first hankered after when one 'stopped in front of our house in, I think 1897. The driver had tyre trouble of some sort.' This was at a time when most people walked, travelled by horse or train, and only the wealthy had a car.

After leaning over the Rolls and chatting to its driver, Harry said he became entranced by its beautiful workmanship and coveted not the car but the engine: 'I consider that the Rolls-Royce is the poor man's car. You can get a used one very cheaply (I saw a magnificent specimen, ten years old, at a dealer's in South Kensington: it was marked £89 10s); they never want repairing, and they never wear out. So much for my youthful ambitions!'[38]

If he did compile his ambition list at the age of 21 then it was truly prophetic, since Henry Royce did not meet Charles Rolls until 1904, and the first Rolls-Royce car, a six-cylinder Silver Ghost, did not purr from the production line until 1906. In his leisure time, perhaps encouraged by his father, he continued to tunnel into the esoteric. With an unnamed friend he visited mediums in his area of London, particularly the epicentre of the movement around Manor Road (now Manor Avenue) in Brockley, where he may have seen the medium artiste Straw Dolly, who conjured up a 'cleft-palate negro Papa Issacs' who promised to cure various diseases by spirit magnetism.

Price settled on regularly visiting one woman spiritualist who played hostess to an ever-shifting congregation of people playing psychic pot luck, hoping to witness astounding acts or phenomena from once famous mediums such as Charles Eldred, one of the first materialisation mediums – causing a spirit to appear in bodily form – that Price saw perform.

Eldred, a former fishmonger, had a truly bizarre act. Protected by the half dark, he would appear wearing various disguises: one minute he was ramrod straight, wearing a thin black moustache, stretching out a dead hand to shake before being claimed by a sitter as her departed Uncle Peter; then he was a girlish figure dressed in white lacy top 'just like a lady's chemise', shrieking for Mabel in a masculine but squeaky voice, until a woman rushed forward and embraced 'her' as her long-dead niece.[39]

Harry was not impressed with Eldred's mechanical exaggerations. He saw him through the eyes of a magician as

> most interesting, but not convincing . . . the whole display was very artificial, and there was no control of the medium's person. The search of his clothes was perfunctory, and the various effects – both visual and aural – could have been introduced into the cabinet without the sitters' being aware of the fact.[40]

Eldred was later exposed as a fake. During a particularly emotional seance one observer, Dr Abraham Wallace, a member of the Society for Psychical Research, seized the clairvoyant's Canterbury chair (which he insisted on taking with him from seance to seance because the horsehair stuffing was 'saturated with his magnetism') and up-ended it.

Wallace discovered that the back of the chair was really a locked box stuffed full with theatrical garb, including wigs, beards, costumes, masks and faces, a collapsible dummy, dresses, hats, a musical box for producing spirit music and perfume to 'simulate the sensation of spirit flowers'.[41] The old man was finished.

Others, such as Madeleine G, a singer and dancer, fitted well into London's vaudeville atmosphere: she outrageously tripped and pranced about the stage in a transcendental state, 'softly floating' and singing in a high soprano while 'spirits lurked within her'.

As to the audiences, those souls who waited for their loved ones to be returned to them were ordinary people, and Harry, like so many others, believed in the existence of spirits.

He 'anticipated having a genuine thrill at meeting some denizens of the spirit world' and was very disappointed at the shows he witnessed. 'I concluded that the "spirits" could be explained in terms of normality.'[42]

But that reasoning would come much later. He certainly had good reason to suppose that past lives could be contacted, that table-tipping, the transposition of ornaments, the world of innumerable stilled voices yearning wordlessly for recognition, was real and inexhaustible. His father instilled in him the belief that immortality was a fact, not a pious hope; the dead were all around and had a deep influence on the living.[43]

Towards 1905, however, Edward Ditcher Price, now aged 70, went into a gentle decline, suffering from heart disease and angina. The dread of illness and the deaths of both his wife and mother-in-law in close succession must have left him increasingly withdrawn within the family circle. As the last surviving member of eight siblings Edward was keenly aware of his own mortality.

He and Harry had enjoyed working and living together, and with Annie now married with a young daughter[44] they would have been alone to exchange stories and reminiscences, and for the remaining few years of his life there was a deep and happy friendship between the two of them.

But the times were already moving too fast. Beyond the sanctuary of St Donatt's Road the streets and squares now seemed forbidding and suddenly the inevitable happened. Harry and Edward's relationship came to an end on a scalding hot Saturday in July 1906 when Edward died from a heart attack at home, a matter of days before his seventy-second birthday.

For Harry, his father's death was a shocking event, made worse by his having found his lifeless body, a discovery that would overshadow the rest of his life.[45]

His father's simple death notice, which appeared in the *Wellington Journal* of 14 July, read:

Price 7th Inst. aged 71 at Cloverley, St. Donatt's Road, New Cross S.E., Edward Ditcher, son of the late John Price of Rodington.

Edward had been unprepared for death and had not made a will. Probate was granted to Harry and his sister. The small estate was worth £189 18s 0d, the equivalent of £15,000 when this book was published in 2006.[46]

Soon after his father's death Harry abandoned life in New Cross, sold the house in St Donatt's Road and went to lodge with a work colleague, Alfred Hesson, and his wife, Katharine, at 22 Harefield Road in Brockley so that he could be near his fiancée, Constance Knight.[47]

He was emotionally bereft, but he was also, unwillingly, free. The old pattern of his life was broken in nearly every respect. The new one was to bear little relationship to it and the transition would not be without its difficulties.

2

UNCOVERING LOST WORLDS

When Harry Price left New Cross in the hot summer of 1906 the philanthropist Baroness Angela Coutts became the last person to be interred in Westminster Abbey; James Hyslop, professor of logic and ethics at Columbia University, New York, one of the most distinguished American propagandists on survival, published three books on psychical research; and Harry, recently bereaved, settled on curious figures who dealt in the occult. Among these was Cecil Husk, an eccentric former tenor with the Carl Rosa Opera Company.[1]

During his singing tours Husk had become an earthly instrument for the faithful who felt pressed for evidence of survival after death. From 1870 he conducted sittings on a regular basis, and from around 1875 began to produce ectoplasm, that ethereal energy, the cloud-like mist, solid white mass or milky emission that gave life to spirit forms. The material originated from the medium's nose, mouth and sometimes his sexual organs. It took on semi-solid forms, with features that the compliant sitters could recognise, but on more than one occasion tuned out on closer inspection to be a snarl of coarse cheesecloth or thin netting. Some witnesses claimed it smelt musty like death or an old man's clothes.

Husk specialised in materialising seances, bringing those spirits just out of reach of mere mortals back to earth for a quick chat, hug and squeeze from their relatives. Price was not impressed by these wonders, but certain 'telekinetic phenomena', or moving objects around the room, did impress him.

Towards the end of autumn he was persuaded by a friend to go to a seance held by Husk at Swanley in Kent, 12 miles from his new base in Brockley. He made the journey on an elaborate invention of his, a cycle-yacht – apparently a Heath-Robinson-style bike with 'a largish sail' attached to its front.[2] He constructed the cycle in his workshop and 'with a following wind one could travel very rapidly by means of this sail, which created quite a sensation as we made our way through Catford, Bromley and Orpington'.

At the end of this epic journey by mast, Price found that the seance was held in a large barn loaned to a local spiritualist group by an expert grower of spring cabbages.[3] As the congregation of thirty embarked on singing hymns, ropes holding a tarpaulin, used as a sheet to stop dust and ears of corn falling on the celebrating group below, were gnawed through by a rat, which then fell on top of the penitential hopefuls. The sitting ended with women pulling up their petticoats to try to escape a storm of feathers, straw, spring cabbages and a family of rodents. 'I tremble to think,' he wrote later, 'what would have happened if it had been a dark seance.'

Harry's first important act after his father died was to marry. Though he had earlier girlfriends, his brush with Constance Mary Knight was a serious affair of the heart, her laid-back caution and emotional steadiness providing the much-needed weight for his rocky moods.

In appearance Constance was short, with nut-brown hair – good looking in a quiet-featured way. The impression that survives of her is that of a sweet-natured, unambitious woman. She had been born into a well-to-do family and had had the best of starts. Her father, Robert Hastings Knight, had begun working life as a hairdresser, and her mother, Marianne, as a domestic, though it would be a brief outing into the world of work and earning.[4] By the time Robert had celebrated his twenty-first birthday he had inherited a sizeable amount of money from his late father, a perfumier in the City of London, and from then on he decided to live life as a gentleman, his wealth increasing every so often by shrewd investment in stocks and shares.[5]

His daughter, although younger than Harry, perhaps also less sharp, less assured and less remarkable, was the product of a socially more elevated family. Connie was more sophisticated and more finished than Harry; but her rarest quality was her character, which everyone who knew her intimately agrees was the most selfless and unworldly they ever encountered.

The Knight family were on good terms with the Price family, each household inviting the other for dinner and other social occasions. The friendship continued until 39-year-old Robert was diagnosed with an aggressive lymphoma. Within a few months, the cancer had rapidly spread to his face, which in a short time was literally being eaten away.[6] He died on 2 February 1906, five months before Edward Ditcher Price. In his will, dated 30 June of the previous year, he had appointed his son Robert Henry and his wife Marianne as trustees to his estate. A substantial amount of money, property and government bonds, which produced a fluid income for the family trust fund, was shared between the three surviving members of the family.

In the final hours of his life, just before he died, Robert expressed the wish that Harry, whom he held in high esteem, should, 'when I'm gone, take care of my little girl'.[7] With this blessing, Price married Connie eighteen months later, on 1 August 1908 at the twelfth-century St Mary's Church in Pulborough, West Sussex, the village to which Marianne had moved and where she had relatives. This, in any case, is the story according to family tradition.

But there is a competing narrative, a story that focuses on Harry Price's extraordinary capacity for getting himself into a tight spot, his sheer reckless appetite for life and his ability to bounce from one disastrous entanglement to another. This is the story told by the late Sidney H. Glanville, a man of absolute integrity, an adviser to Price and perhaps the nearest he had to a confidant – his 'best friend', as Connie called him.

Glanville was also Harry's first choice as literary executor and authorised biographer, someone he trusted to build his house of veneration; and so the story is not without plausibility. In the fragmented archive of papers that Mrs Cecil Baines, a one-time friend of Harry and favoured executor of the Borley legend, gathered in the 1960s in preparation for a biography, there is an unpublished interview with Glanville, whom she met to chat about their friend's life.[8]

Glanville told her that one evening over a convivial drink Harry scoffed that he only agreed to marry Connie Knight after her parents discovered that they had slept together as teenagers. Connie's parents believed her adolescent fumbling had robbed her of the chance of marrying anyone else. Her single life was over, and she received a simple one-way ultimatum, a punishment of sorts. Although Harry was far from being a wealthy man, after a decent period he would have to marry her and put up with the consequences. If Robert and Marianne Knight (census returns name her as Mary Anne or Marion) were worried that they were handing over their only daughter to a man with little earning potential, the problem was solved by presenting Connie with an income of £500 a year from a trust fund. This was a generous bequest, but not enough for her to live on independently for the rest of her very long life.[9]

According to this story reported by Glanville, Price never slept with Connie again, but instead embarked on numerous affairs with other women. He was remote even to his nephews and never showed any great interest in his new, extended family. Perhaps this had a lot to do with Harry's belief that he could make himself invisible when he chose to. His skewed thinking extended to the belief that if he chose not to see others, others could not see him. He got his own way through sweetness and charm (though he was also pugnacious and mercurial), and it was these qualities that allowed him to move freely among the social circles of both London and Sussex.

Harry was an opportunist, unlike his wife, who seems to have been uncomplicated, less profane, and later in life so overwhelmed by self-doubt and introspection that she believed if it were not for her unstinting loyalty she would be superfluous. For Harry it must have seemed a perfect arrangement: he looked to Connie to fathom the small domestic details he found too boring to consider, and he turned to her for focus; otherwise he was entirely indifferent to her. With Connie's income, money from his regular job and with chance earnings from journalism, which he began increasingly to seek, they hoped to live well and comfortably.

The new Mr and Mrs Price spent their honeymoon enjoying the traditional, genteel delights of the English seaside at Scarborough, with its bathing machines, tea shops, military bandstands and zoological gardens, and then went to live with the taciturn Marianne Knight at Riverside, her home in Pulborough.

Surrounded by fields and near the church of St Mary, Riverside presented a quiet, unassuming but privileged aspect to passers-by who glimpsed it on their way to matins or vespers. It was a place that had minded its own business and one that might be expected to accommodate a successful businessman or affluent civil servant. Instead, it was occupied by a family who traded in insults, strained to get at each other's throats and engaged in exhausting battles of wit. Here Harry was up against a household dominated by women, where men, for once, did not take precedence.

Strait-laced, truculent and intimidating, Marianne did not get on with her equally fiery son-in-law. Moralising and critical, she projected a great deal of guilt and misery on to Harry's eggshell personality. In this harsh and emotionally stifling atmosphere, relationships quickly deteriorated, and from this time on Harry and his mother-in-law were barely on speaking terms, communicating with each other only when they had to.[10]

According to surviving members of Price's family, there were endless outbursts and loud shouting matches, so much so that it must have become a subversive performance art to have a polite conversation.

It did not help matters that as soon as Harry had settled into the area he managed to drag himself into a bad-tempered dispute over a motor boat he was trying to buy, a dispute that ended, typically, in court.[11] He won the case, which had been plastered over the headlines of the local paper for two weeks, when the owner of the boat finally admitted the craft was too wide to cruise the narrow width of the River Arun.

Connie and Marianne came to the conclusion that the answer to the dreadful consequences of them all living under one roof was to buy an adjacent parcel of land. Consequently, a new home was built for the newly-weds. The house, named Arun Bank, on the corner of Allfrey's Wharf, had the typical layout of an early well-to-do Edwardian home – a scaled-down version of a grand house. The front door opened to a wide hall with a low-pitched ceiling and a long hallway, which ran to Price's study and home library. Upstairs were four bedrooms. There were neatly planted gardens with balsam firs, bryony and a fishpond, and added to this idyll at the bottom of the garden was the bubbling River Arun. Positioned on a ridge overlooking the banks of the river, Arun Bank (which today is divided into flats) has a distinguished view scanning the Downs, while in the distance the Chanctonbury Ring bobs over a crest and hills and fields give way to a wilder headland.

The area has a wild, old-world feeling, full of picturesque nooks and delicious places of solitude where one can quite believe the many stories that the Devil had a hand in forming the ring when he discovered the inhabitants of Sussex were being converted from previous pagan religions to Christianity, and decided to drown them. They say you can raise the Devil at Chanctonbury Ring by running around the clump of trees seven times in an anti-clockwise direction. When he appears he will offer you a bowl of porridge in exchange for your soul.

While their neighbours in this ideal spot dodged malign influences and devoted time to celebrating marriage, the Prices' lives together were filled with an overpowering atmosphere of permanent marital strife. Yet, for all its apparent deficiencies, the marriage seemed to work. Connie slavishly endorsed her husband's needs yet she was ambivalent about Harry's interests: she could not quite bring herself to embrace its more extreme moments, and stayed away from psychical events and get-togethers.

In fact in all his writings and notes of his experiments his wife is seldom mentioned. Even in his autobiography his wedding is only marked by a brief remark in the appendix. At the back of the book is a chronological list of important events in his life, which reads 'Lifelines – 1908 married. (Aug 1)'. Even Paul Tabori, Price's authorised biographer and literary executor, who obviously had close contact with Connie, limited his description of the liaison to the uncommitted 'he married a girl he had known since childhood'.[12]

Just before his marriage Harry made much of helping Jose Weiss, the landscape artist and early glider enthusiast, with his flying experiments at Amberley Mount on the South Downs.[13] There is no mention of Harry in any press reports of the time, so it is likely that any assistance he gave Weiss was along the same lines as the help given by the hundreds who helped in the futile attempt to get him and his plane *Albatross* airborne; it is another of Harry's exuberant claims, a nod of faint interest at the time which three decades later became a spring of athletic action.

His claim to some local prominence in the rarefied world of Sussex archaeology is also a little awry. For a man as canny as Harry Price, the obvious next step to settling in this small village was to insinuate himself into the local culture, and in this he was fortunate to meet Canon Frederick Baggallay, then Rector at St Mary's Pulborough, a keen Romanist who possessed one of the finest collections of Roman antiquities in Sussex. For a time they fished together and obliterated pheasants and rabbits, until they found safer common ground.[14]

Frederick's extended family included the chemist, inventor, magician and psychic researcher William Wortley Baggallay, someone who had tested mediums from the days of the Victorian Daniel Dunglas Home and had patented all kinds of end-of-pier inventions including the first mutoscope or What the Butler Saw machine and the first coin-operated magic lantern machine in 1899. It was William who later recommended Harry to the Society for Psychical Research and the Magic Circle.

Price doubtless told the Baggallay family, as he later told his readers, that he too had an ardent interest in discovering lost worlds, which stemmed from his experiences on archaeological digs, notably that at Greenwich Park in 1902. Here he claimed to have discovered a forgotten hoard of Roman relics, including a denarius of Mark Antony among others. 'I helped excavate the Roman villa Urbana in Greenwich Park. The site (known to have existed for many years) lies midway between the Magnetic Pavilion and the Vanbrugh entrance to the Park. Excavating Roman villas is one of the most exciting jobs imaginable,' he enthused.[15]

That might well be the case, but if his own words are to be believed this excavation was foreign territory to him. Seven years before his marriage he had written a lengthy review of A.D. Webster's *Greenwich Park: Its History and Associations* for *The Askean*.[16] There is no suggestion in this article that he took part in the excavations; in fact, the first time he used the dig as a device to support the story of his vast knowledge and experience about Roman Britain was in the pages of his autobiography some forty years later.

The truth is probably that the Reverend Baggallay introduced Price to his circle of antiquarian friends. Harry was eager for social inclusion and luckily, as so often happened in his life, he was in the right place at the right time and was able to ride on other people's shoulders to get what he wanted from them.

In the Sussex antiquarian circle he found the inspiration to begin talking about a place he knew next to nothing about, culling most of the information from *A Roman History of West Sussex*, privately published by A.D. Dean in 1881.[17] He gave his first lecture on Roman Pulborough in St Mary's church rooms on 28 December 1909, an event fanfared in his local newspaper, the *Sussex Daily News*. The editorial described Price, no doubt following his briefing to the letter, as someone who possessed an 'extensive knowledge of antiquities'. A rather more spicy review appeared in the *West Sussex Gazette*, which described him as 'a good authority on the subject' and explained that part of his lecture included his own hoard of coins, discovered over a period of years.[18] (The coins had in fact been the property of a Yorkshire-born plough-man named Mickelthwaite, who had found them near his home at Arundel and Pulborough at some point during the forty-two years he had spent working on the land before selling them to Price.)

The display of the coins apart, there were also huge sections of Samian ware, Roman lamps, urns and vases, bronze fibulae, jagged misshapes of tessellated pavements and all sorts of Romano-British detritus, belonging mostly to Canon Baggallay. Price characteristically implied that the majority of the exhibits came from his personal collection, and were the result of his own meticulous work.

None of his lecture work could have been either well paid or intellectually stimulating, but it was useful for collecting well-shod friends. Price was not an accomplished speaker. He had a rather gruff voice – a cross-breeding of received pronunciation and Cockney – often stammered, giving sometimes a barely audible address and sometimes a shout. But what he lacked in lucidity he made up for in a resolute desire to share knowledge and open the minds of others. Even when he became better known his oratorical skills were still woefully underdeveloped, as if he neither sought, nor needed, a close relationship with his audience. Later, as a celebrity speaker, his impatience frequently broke over the heads of his audience, and he often snapped back replies to questioners at meetings.

This was certainly his Roman period. Earlier in 1909 Price discovered an ornate and beautiful bronze statuette of Hercules in the bank of the River Arun at the bottom of his garden, glimpsing 'its legs sticking out of the river bank'.[19] According to a family story, which has never been told until now, he found the little statue of the half-god, half-man, measuring 3½in high, one Sunday afternoon in late 1908 after Connie, her brother Robert Knight, his wife and he had returned from their usual post-church boat trip along the banks of the river close to Riverside and Arun Bank where the respective couples lived.[20]

When Connie, Robert and his wife had disembarked, Price, as if stung by a wasp, jumped out of the boat and into the cold river. He began paddling around the landing stage, at the bottom of his garden, and after a few seconds of displacing water, fished out the statuette, much to the amazement of Robert Knight. However, Robert immediately suspected that all was not what it seemed and right up until his death believed Harry had bought the piece either in London or locally, or indeed had cast it himself, then planted the statuette where he had supposedly found it in the river.

Nor was he alone in his suspicions; many others thought Harry was lying, but it was hard to get anyone to notice their protestations since he was taken seriously by several academics.

One of Harry's supporters was Charles Reginald Haines, a slightly shady character who had moved to Pulborough after being ousted as Classics master at Uppingham School, in Leicestershire, for reasons unknown.[21]

Haines was a Fellow of the Society of Antiquaries and a busy member of the Sussex Archaeological Society.[22] He may have found it bewildering that whenever Price went for a walk with his black Labrador or with a friend he would invariably find a lost treasure, but nevertheless he believed his finds to be authentic, since Harry always had a witness to his discovery, a technique that would be repeated years later in his most famous case at Borley Rectory, in Essex.

Harry's innumerable archaeological finds lay in areas where even experienced archaeologists had failed to discover anything worthwhile, and all were conveniently found lying on the surface. If he did indeed find the bronze Hercules by chance then its state of preservation was quite remarkable. The fast current which flows past the garden of Arun Bank contains a great deal of silt and small stones, both highly abrasive substances. Together with the crushing and pounding effect of the river's current, one would have expected the small statuette of the muscle-bound hero to be nothing more than a featureless lump of metal. But there was no sign of wear on the bronze club or Nemean lion skin; there was no patina, pitting or smoothing of the body; and despite his brother-in-law's obvious suspicions, Harry rang the newsdesk of the *West Sussex Gazette* to tell them about his find.

When the story appeared the next day, one of Haines's friends, Richard Garraway-Rice, suggested to Harry that he should exhibit the small statuette, or lar, of Hercules at the Society of Antiquaries in London. Sensing a chance to establish local prominence, Harry jumped at the chance: after all, what was the point of having a rare Roman antiquity if you never got to show it off? The find also had a mention in the internationally respected *Proceedings of the Society of Antiquaries*, an annual catalogue of rare finds; a great achievement for an amateur archaeologist.

As he began putting on archaeological muscle, Price reinforced his local standing by approaching the editors of the *West Sussex Gazette* and the *Southern Weekly News*, suggesting he should write an occasional column on antiquities for Brighton-based newspapers. Their editors, delighted to have such a well-connected freelance expert on their staff, readily agreed to the proposal. It now became possible for Harry to shift the onus of his income-raising efforts on his writing for both a daily and a weekly newspaper, which had the advantages of increased remuneration and an intellectual monopoly that would improve his standing as an expert on Roman Sussex.

Now other archaeological finds followed in quick succession: a perfect bronze hatchet-head of the Early Bronze Age and a crafted bone measuring 6in long by 1½in deep and of great antiquity showed up in a matter of weeks. One side of the bone was inscribed with decorative runic characters and the word 'OLAF', while on the other side were two semicircular lines which, Harry told his readers, 'represented the contour of the South Downs on the one side (near where it was found) and the other, a bend of the River Arun, close by'.[23] 'If this theory is correct,' he postulated, 'we have quite the earliest pictorial representation ever made of Sussex scenery.' Indeed, if it was authentic, it would have been a staggering discovery, an archaeological bridge between two ancient worlds, possibly ranking as one of the oldest works of man in bone.

Its finder supposedly sent the fragment (the sketch of which looks as if a dog had gnawed it), to the British Museum for them to decipher the characters, since Harry firmly believed the bone was a treasure map, which, if the runic characters could be translated, would mark a chieftain's burial place.[24]

By coincidence the museum replied in time for his next column, so he was able to write 'they believe the bone is some form of magical rite and in fact the carved characters are cabalistic. Of course there is a great deal of magic associated with this area so our friends at Russell Square could be right.'[25] With remarkable luck, Harry had the habitual good fortune to find the most interesting part of these associations. But his most sensational find was yet to come.

In the *Southern Weekly News* of New Year's Day 1910, a report details one of Harry's lectures in December the previous year. It was at this talk that he first exhibited an inscribed Roman silver ingot that he claimed he had discovered while walking across a ploughed field some months earlier, in the same area as the bone and his other finds. Again, the find was on the surface of the soil. It was the sort of relic an archaeologist would dream of finding because it established the area as a major historical location.

Only two previous specimens of Roman ingots had been found, one by labourers in 1777, laying the foundations of the Ordnance Office at the Tower of London, the other located a few hundred years later at the Roman Fort at Richborough, in Kent. But both these finds were the familiar double-axe-head ingots; Price's ingot appeared to be a one-off. It was an oblong measuring 3¾in by 2½in and half an inch thick, and is today kept at the University of London in its original black and green velvet-lined box, which Price had made for it. It has some rather curious features, namely its pristine condition, its shape, its weight and its inscription.

For a pure silver ingot, it looks and feels as dense as lead and is excessively heavy for its size. The spidery raised writing stamped on a recessed label and the blocked mark showing a bunch of grapes have survived nearly a thousand years remarkably well.[26]

In fact, the ingot, now covered in a patina of thick black lead oxide, is so regular in shape over its entire length that it appears to have been cast in a recent mould. The texture of the metal has not suffered; it has no feel of history about it.

Price reflected that the inscription 'Ex Offici Hono Reg' meant that it had originated from the workshop of an artisan named Honorius or Honorinus, though he refrained from saying that the legend had anything to do with the Emperor Honorius, which would have made it the only piece of its kind ever found in Britain.

Haines, a self-professed expert on Roman finds, supported his friend's theory by holding lectures of his own based on the find. Price himself, in his regular 'Antiquarian Notes', made the puzzling supposition that the ingot was probably lost in transit 'on its way to Bosham or Chichester harbours en route to Rome to be turned into money'.[27]

He would have known there were mints in France, so there was absolutely no need for the ingot to travel to Rome. And in any case, silver ingots like this were used to pay soldiers and civil servants in the late Roman Empire, so why he wrote this is as mysterious as the find itself.

No one at the time seems to have asked why it had taken him months to report the find, despite its obvious importance; all the more puzzling since Harry was desperate to start his own archaeological exploration with the aid of two prominent Sussex landowners, the 16th Baron Zouche and Sir Walter Bartellet, both of whom pledged their support in his quest for Roman antiquities.[28]

The ingot raises as much suspicion now as it must have done to people who read about it in 1910. But strange things were then happening in the normally sedate world of the Sussex Archaeological Society. Charles Dawson, a solicitor, amateur geologist and antiquarian, dubbed 'the Wizard of Sussex' for his unerring ability to discover rare objects, had unearthed two inscribed bricks from the Roman fort at Pevensey, in East Sussex. The legend 'Hon Aug Andria' stamped on a sunken label referred to the same Emperor Honorius as the inscription on Price's ingot.

The discovery of the brick caused a sensation, since no one before had been able to supply a date for the final phase of reconstruction of Pevensey Fort. A particularly intriguing aspect of the Honorius finds is the fact that while Dawson's inscription made sense, Harry's did not, since it was a strange form of Latin, which one assumes was badly copied from the British

Museum's ingot, a photograph of which lies languishing in his archive of papers at the University of London.

This tenuous link between Price and Dawson is not the only one. There is a letter in the Society for Psychical Research's files at Cambridge University from W.H. Salter, a former barrister, psychical researcher and honorary secretary of the SPR. In a letter to a friend, Salter wrote that Price's discovery of bones at Borley Rectory in Essex (of which we shall read more in a future chapter) bore more than a passing resemblance to the discovery of fossilised bones known as Piltdown Man at a pit in Sussex, estimated to be at least 500,000 years old, which Dawson had excavated in 1913 and sensationally publicised as the missing link in man's evolution.[29] Only when tests were carried out on the remains long after Dawson's death was it confirmed that Piltdown Man was a well-executed hoax, as were the majority of his finds.

It is absolutely conceivable that Dawson and Price worked together. They had plenty of opportunities to meet each other, as both were active in the Sussex Archaeological Society and were members of the Royal Societies Club, that most prestigious social club of scientists and industrialists. Furthermore, Price and Dawson would have shared patrons and supporters.

There are other odd features in Price's archaeological past. After a series of passionate and energetic lectures, in January 1910 he suddenly withdrew from the public glare. His disappearance from the scene coincided with a disagreement with the Society of Antiquaries over an item that appeared in their *Journal*, mention of which would shatter Price's claim to be a distinguished Roman historian. This happened after Charles Praetorious, Secretary of the local FSA, showed the ingot to Professor E.J. Haverfield of Oxford University, the country's foremost expert on Roman history and a Fellow of the British Academy. Haverfield was in no doubt as to its origin.

In his report on the excavation at Borough, Praetorious reported that:

Professor Haverfield said the double axe type of silver ingot was well known and dated from late Imperial times but the one recovered from Sussex was an inferior copy of one found at the Tower of London, with alterations to give it an air of authenticity. Both the shape and lettering betrayed its origin.[30]

It was a forgery, as Charles Dawson's Honorius brick had been. The chance of discovering two sham Honorius finds just 45 miles from each other (the distance from Pevensey to Pulborough) in a small area of Sussex must be millions to one; a remarkable coincidence. Price saw his integrity and expertise crumble, and his conduct was enough to bring the local archaeology society into disrepute. Though members stopped short of telling the press, word still got around and within a month the *West Sussex Gazette* had sacked him, though he regained some sort of equilibrium by continuing to write for the *Southern Weekly News* for a further twelve months. Interestingly, in these later columns, chastened and observed from all quarters, uncertain as to whether his position made him look like a man of honour or the school dunce, he altered his style of contribution. But instead of tales of highly lucrative finds, there came a mish-mash of edited letters from treasure hunters who had been fortunate enough to discover coins of earlier centuries, brooches and bangles from their Saxon predecessors and Roman bricks that may have formed part of a cryptoporticus.

The scandal was not a final farewell for his lectures, though it did halt them for a time. His final lecture, on the Roman occupation of Pulborough, came at the Petworth Men's Mutual Improvement Society in winter 1911.[31] After this valedictory address Harry began a series of lectures on the history of the castles and abbeys of Sussex (a speciality of Charles Dawson), but abandoned his intended publication of a book called *Two Thousand Years of Sussex*. His hand-written notes and rough drawings of coins made in expectation of publication lie forlornly in a file at the University of London.

The fakery did, however, cost Price some of his friends, including Hugh Davies-Colley, which in turn ended his association with the Pulborough Players, who continued to stage drama until the late 1930s.

Despite this, three decades later Price repeated the false history of the ingot and the mysterious runic bone in his autobiography, thinking that after thirty years it would be safe to do so.

The scandal undoubtedly affected the perceived probity of his friend Charles Reginald Haines, too, as he resigned from several local organisations, and moved out of the village to London, only to resurface briefly in Pulborough in 1921. As we shall see, Price's useful friendship with Haines would continue and help propel him to international fame some years later.

Although some time in 1913 Harry ceased to write his column for the *Southern Weekly News*, this was not the end of his curious link with relics of the past. What finally put an end to his years as a collector of artefacts was the peculiar and suspicious telling of the theft of his 'fine and rare collection of ancient gold coins of the Sussex princes – most of them washed up at Selsey',[32] from the nave at St Mary's Church, Pulborough, in September 1923.

Like all old churches, St Mary's was forever in need of care and money, funds were running short and the fabric of the building was suffering. A diocesan report noted that: 'The main roof is in a very bad condition. The buttresses on the north side are only held together by ivy and there are signs that the walls are perishing.'

To raise the urgently needed cash, Price came up with the idea of staging an exhibition of his most important coins, as well as the fake silver ingot and other archaeological discoveries. Placed in a glass display cabinet along with St Mary's own valuable collection of hammered silver coins dating back to the reign of William the Conqueror, they included two Roman coins recently donated by Charles Haines, which he had found in 1907. Other coins in Harry's collection were items he had bought the previous year from three sources: from his friend Edward Heron-Allen, a chiromancer, musician, expert asparagus grower, erotic novelist and fellow magician, who lived along the Sussex coast at Selsey; and from two London dealers, Spink and Co. and A.H. Baldwin, where he paid a total of £29 12s 3d for a set of gold and silver Norman coins.[33]

In his memoirs Harry wrote that he had nearly completed his numismatic history of Sussex and that 'all the plates had been engraved' when, on Wednesday 26 September, a thief walked into the church 'as visitors were allowed to go in and out as they pleased' and stole his gold coins and St Mary's rare hammered pennies. The coins were probably taken by a collector, he assumed.[34]

An interesting sidelight to the raid comes ten days earlier in Price's petulant letter to the Reverend Ernest Frost, the vicar of St Mary's, asking him to make sure that his collection of artefacts had been insured: 'I have spoken to an insurance man and he feels quite certain that the objects can be insured and strongly advised me to protect my property in this way. It is difficult to place an exact value on the artefacts but I estimate the following values – coins £150, ingot £50 and others £50.'[35] In the event, Frost failed to insure the coins, probably because the church was so poor he was unable to do so.

According to Harry's account, written some fifteen years after the event, he received a telegram in London from the churchwardens of St Mary's Parochial Church Council telling him about the theft and expressing their 'sincere regret' at his loss.[36]

The telegram is not in any of Price's correspondence files, so we cannot verify his statements. Unusually though, he decided to take no further action above asking the vicar to contact the Metropolitan Police as he believed the coins would now be out of Sussex and into London's chain of pawnbroker shops.

The theft of these rare artefacts (Harry's coins alone would be worth at least £25,000 in today's market) failed to find space in any of the local newspapers. There is no mention of the robbery in any edition of St Mary's Parish Magazine and as far as can be ascertained scant attention was paid to it by the Parish Church Council. In fact, the only mention of the theft was in *Reynolds's Weekly News*, a mass market Sunday tabloid subsidised by the Co-op. A small paragraph in the 30 September issue tells the reader that police were 'searching for three men who stole silver and gold coins, some of which had been in the church since the days of William the Conqueror. They were considered of priceless value.'[37]

In his autobiography Price added the rider: 'if the loss had occurred anywhere except in my own village, I would have taken drastic action in the matter. It was an unfortunate business . . . I received no compensation.' The fact that Harry showed vague indifference to the theft for a decade and a half should have alerted readers that there was something rather fishy about the whole business. The only evidence that the coins went missing was from his own pen, which was as trustworthy as fiction.

A quick scan through the property he bequeathed the University of London on his death some forty-two years later reveals that some of the coins are locked in one of their strongrooms, along with the little statuette of Hercules, the ingot, other sentimental bric-a-brac and hammered pennies, identical to those stolen from the church.[38]

A string of uncomfortable questions is raised here: did Harry's light-fingered exercises materialise in anything he wanted? How did coins identical to those in St Mary's own priceless collection end up in his archive? Did he steal the coins after believing Ernest Frost had insured them, so that he could claim compensation? Should we ever trust Harry Price's probity? It is a question one has to ask repeatedly.

3

HARRY PRICE AND THE PRIMROSE PATH

Life in Sussex in the golden Edwardian years was a heady mix of socialising and gentle decisions. Harry was dabbling with producing plays for the professional stage. In 1910 he had written an adaptation of John Bunyan's *Pilgrim's Progress*. He could have cast himself as one of the jury in Vanity's trial, perhaps Mr No-good, Mr Malice, Mr Love-lust or Mr Live-loose, but he preferred instead a reverential role as Lord Hate-Good, the judge, casting Connie as Humility. The production, by the Pulborough Drama Society, toured the village halls of Pulborough and Horsham to great acclaim and was charitably compared – by Harry – to the Passion Play at Oberammergau.

In February 1913 he wrote to the editor of *The Stage* saying he was looking for a director to tour the British Isles with the play, but it seems that no one contacted him.[1] So, he contemplated new ventures, including writing magic books, the possibility of astral travel, and articles on bibliomania – the symbol, he thought, of a man with a cultivated and achieving mind.[2] For fun, and to dissipate the accusations of fraud surrounding his ingot, he set up a Liar's Court (convened in pubs) where 'sinners' were presented with a certificate by his 'Infernal Majesty', a piece of blue vellum which allowed them to lie 'and should he (obviously lying was a male preserve) be detected telling the truth he will be subjected to penalties'.[3]

Between the winding down of his writing for his local newspaper and the end of 1913, a period of three years, Price was living a steady, rather mundane existence in the paper industry. When he was not working for Saunders, he organised cricket matches, athletic meetings and nights of fun, where he sang near-the-knuckle humorous songs.[4]

The Russell Cricket Club, which his father had founded in 1900, became a flourishing part of Edward Saunders' social diary and a fashionable feature for those involved in the industry. Harry was an enthusiastic supporter and served a term as vice-chairman; though there is no record that he ever played.

In his spare time he won two first prizes in photographic competitions, one organised by the *Sphere* magazine and the other by *Amateur Photographer*, both for a picture of his Sheltie dog, Laddie. Later that year he became prominent in local and national politics when, like his father and grandfather before him, he joined the Conservative and Unionist Party.[5] As a business member of the Sussex divisional Conservative and Unionist Association, he frequently shared meetings with Lord Zouche about the third Home Rule bill: the threat of violence in Ireland was more menacing than anything industrial unrest or civil disobedience in England might unleash.[6]

Not to be outdone by Harry's involvement in the way the nation was governed, Connie became a member of the Women's Social and Political Union (WSPU) and as a middle-class reformer stepped out on a public campaign to Brighton along with the redoubtable Mary Hamilton, the Corbett sisters and an estimated 700 other suffragettes in a public show of disgust over the Asquith government's forcible feeding of women on hunger strike and also to agitate for the vote.[7]

Given how busy he was, it is surprising to find that Harry, with his irrepressible energy, was becoming a well-thought-of member of the British College of Psychical Science (BCPS), one of the country's earliest known centres for psychical research.[8]

It was at the college in 1914 that Barbara McKenzie, wife of the founder, James Hewat McKenzie, first asked Price to take charge of the photography in a seance meeting with the spirit photographer Mrs Irving.[9] At one sitting Price secured an 'extra' in the shape of a hand, which he claimed could not have been produced by normal means because of the strict conditions in which the photograph was taken. There is some confusion over the date of the meeting, since Paul Tabori wrongly gave it as 1924, either because he had not found the earlier letter from Barbara McKenzie or because he deliberately suppressed it, knowing that it flew in the face of Harry's carefully controlled life story.

In the course of the next few years Price's great ambition to set up an international laboratory where psychical research in Britain could be placed on a proper scientific footing would come to fruition. Although the eventual creation of such a laboratory was a product of his restless mind, it was far from being an original idea. The BCPS had taken the lead in investigating psychical phenomena just a few years after the foundation of London's Society for Psychical Research, which in 1882 had begun exploring the muddy waters of telepathy, hypnotism and the survival of the soul. Various universities and research bodies across Europe had also been testing supernatural phenomena in the way Price had wanted to since the turn of the nineteenth century.

The germ of the laboratory idea was sown by meetings with spiritualists, the McKenzies and other friends, acquaintances and casual conversation; but, as we shall see later, Harry was particularly influenced by that heady mix of international fame and fortune, unknowingly aided and abetted by a rival spiritualist organisation to the BCPS, the London Spiritualist Alliance (LSA).

Harry may well have entertained happy thoughts of greater worlds to conquer than simply working for Edward Saunders & Son and the odd bit of journalism here and there, but whether he decided to establish, as he claimed to have done, that symbiosis of medium and scientist that existed before the First World War is unsubstantiated in any available correspondence or journalism in his meticulously kept records. In fact, until the early 1920s, when he at last found his place in the verbose world of psychical research, he had been fully occupied at the BCPS as an ardent pro-spiritualist rather than a sceptic.

His way of life in Sussex and London may have been simple, but it was not such as to cut him off from social contact with those he knew or wanted to know. Nor did it preclude regular visits to the theatre to see leading performers such as Maxine Elliott in Mrs Henry de la Pasture's *Deborah of Tods*, or the French actress Sarah Bernhardt starring on the London stage in Edmund Rostand's *L'aiglon* at the Coliseum in Charing Cross Road.[10] The Edwardian London of the great hotels, brightly lit restaurants and gentlemen's lounges of the Royal Societies Club at Burlington House was the wonder of the empire. It was a hedonistic, chaotic, restless society. Harry was living a full and rich life, so free of money worries that he donated a painting of the Salopian sporting eccentric John Mytton, then valued at over £300, to the National Portrait Gallery.[11]

There were frequent visits abroad, sometimes with and sometimes without his wife. With Con (as Harry called her) he went mostly to Paris, but on his own or with other companions, both male and female, he travelled to Germany and Scandinavia to discover novel trends and witness fresh miracles of faith or simply to unwind. The names of his travelling companions at this period have sadly not survived. He did not speak or write of them much, and whatever clues there were in his private correspondence have long disappeared from his personal archive thanks largely to the casual way people were allowed to inspect documents at the University of London Library – and in some cases take papers away with them – before stricter conditions were imposed.

But soon this world of contentment would be shattered. For several months newspapers in Britain had been reporting that the crumbling Austro-Hungarian Empire had decided, after the assassination on 28 June of Archduke Ferdinand, to take action against Serbia, which was suspected of being behind his murder. But even after the assassination at Sarajevo, the mood had not changed to one of especial menace, and no fresh crisis had developed: it was a period of relative calm. It seemed impossible that other parts of Europe would become involved in what was thought to be an old sparring match between two well-entrenched sides. During the weekend of 25/26 July Harry and Connie remained of the same mind and went, as planned, on their holiday to France.

On the afternoon of 2 August the game changed significantly when German troops entered Belgium. A British declaration of war became virtually certain and France decided she should begin an immediate mobilisation of troops.

On the same day the Prices apparently witnessed the dramatic death of the first person of the war to be killed in France. This changing moment in Franco-German history happened as they were approaching a viaduct over the small leafy town of Pontoise, approximately 8 miles from Paris, near the spot where Camille Pissarro had painted his wonderful image of La Valhermeil a year before Harry's birth.[12]

According to Harry's doubtful testimony, the train in which he and Connie were travelling slowed before the viaduct and had barely stopped when, peering out of a window, Price saw a man carrying a parcel, which was later found to be a bomb: 'He had barely crossed the rails when a shot rang out and he fell screaming by the side of the line. He was dead. It appears – as I learned later – that he was a German spy with instructions to blow up the bridge. I often think what would have happened to us – and him – had he succeeded.'[13]

Other dangers intruded on their return journey. A public notice warned all foreigners to leave Paris at once, but, as only two trains had been laid on to take them, they were jam-packed with nervous passengers. The Prices left their luggage behind and just managed to get on the boat at Dieppe when supposedly a demented French artilleryman made a desperate dash for the gangplank, hoping to get away from a war that would ultimately cost his nation five million lives, until the rifle butt of a guard floored him.

Harry and Connie returned to England to be reminded that on Monday 4 August everything had changed with astounding speed. When the war began, Harry was 33, young enough to be called up, though his first action on arriving home was not thinking of how he could help the war effort but how to collect the insurance money on the cabin trunk he had mislaid in Paris. When the excitement over his missing trunk had died down, he turned his thoughts to what he could do in this terrible new European crisis. He had been told that he was unfit for military service (he had been classified C3) and that he should occupy himself on the Home Front.[14]

At first, according to his autobiography, he tried to interest the Royal Flying Corps with his knowledge of photography and photographic filters for reconnaissance work; but nothing came of this, and he could only fume that the photographs he had taken along to show the RFC at Farnborough were never returned to him: 'They are probably adorning the walls of some official's home, and should he ever see this, I hope he will return them,' he puffed in his memoirs.[15]

In another version of this failed episode, however, written at the time he joined the ASPR as Foreign Research Officer in the 1920s, he wrote that he had 'helped to improve the filters by the Royal Air Force in taking aerial photographs'.[16]

Instead, it was to be Lloyd George's response to the 'Shell Scandal' in early 1915 and his idea of increasing the supply of arms by recruiting extra light engineering firms to manufacture munitions that finally handed him his niche in the war effort and a reserved occupation.

I was asked whether I could undertake the manufacture of shell fuses. I said I would. I enlarged my workshop and employed a man and a boy, and got down to the job.

In my workshop we made No. 101E graze-fuses, complete from the castings. The three of us finally attained an output of nearly 1,000 fuses a month. This may not sound very high, but considering the very fine and accurate work required; it was quite good – with our modest equipment.[17]

As if Price were not busy enough already, he claimed that he embarked on another career when he was recruited in March 1917 to take charge of a night shift at the factory of Grimshaw, Baxter and J.J. Elliott Limited, clockmakers in St Ann's Road, Tottenham.

> I had entire charge from 8 p.m. to 8 a.m. and there were some hundreds of employees. Our principal work was the making of the clockwork mechanism for fuses and parts of the Mill hand grenade.
>   We had occasional 'air-raid warnings' and when an 'alert' was telephoned to me, I had to march the staff – especially the girls – to the crypt of a nearby chapel. I saw more than one Zeppelin brought down in flames. I remained at the Tottenham factory until the end of the war.[18]

Many of his anecdotes described how he had helped Britain through the depressing days of war, how this developed the engineering skills that stood him in good stead for when he later founded his psychic laboratory and workshops. But even a quick reading of Harry's account brings suspicion. There is scant detail of the time of year when he began churning out fuses, the hardships this brought, and no emotional feelings about war and the turning point of the loss of national innocence; his tally of 1,000 fuses a month seems impossible for a home workshop simply because it would have been too labour-intensive (there were ten milled sections to one brass fuse), and there is no description of the people he shared his onerous workload with. Seemingly, the only conclusion to be drawn is that he deliberately set out to underplay his invaluable and heroic contribution to building up the nation's arsenal.

Until, that is, one begins to look under the surface of the story. All factories turning out munitions for the Allied war effort had to be regulated under Section 4 of the Munitions War Act 1915: a complete list of the country's controlled establishments is contained in a 127-page booklet held at the Imperial War Museum in London. And of the 4,625 firms producing munitions and other materials for the war, none was based in Pulborough, nor did Harry Price or any member of his family run a factory producing armaments. In fact, Sussex had just six controlled establishments and only one of these was commissioned to manufacture the Mills bomb. This was Allen-West in Brighton. We are told in *The Allen-West Story*, a green, cloth-covered booklet published to mark the firm's golden anniversary in 1960, that during the '1914–1918 hostilities, a nucleus of staff, supplemented by largely untrained overage and "C3" men, were steadily engaged in making munitions, including the 106 Fuse, the Mills bomb, a spring-loaded bomb thrower and the famous Stokes Mortar shell'.[19]

It was most likely here that Harry was handed a smock and, along with other unfit, untrained and over-age men got down to making armaments. Nor is it true, as earlier Price biographers maintain, that Price worked as a night-foreman making munitions for Grimshaw, Baxter, and J.J. Elliott.

According to James Taylor, the respected historian at the Imperial War Museum, the firm never received a commission to make weapons; moreover, the Mills bomb did not use a clockwork mechanism to trigger its explosive. It seems, therefore, that Harry spent the majority of his agreeable war in Sussex, quietly working in Brighton. He had no need to travel to London for work, since Edward Saunders & Son ran on a skeleton staff as the British government had restricted the output and supply of paper, becoming the chief buyer of this important raw material.

The war itself had a profound impact on spiritualism's landscape during a period when death was a feared and frequent visitor to families, and the private tragedies, whose details we can dimly perceive even after all this time, led many to look upon it as a source of solace and hope.

On the battlefields and in the unsanitary trenches, fearful men, who minute by minute faced being annihilated, rapidly prayed to their God for deliverance and in scores of incidents saw visions of angels protecting them from death. Other soldiers brought back the famous image of medieval archers leading them on against the enemy.[20]

Sir Arthur Conan Doyle, one of modern spiritualism's greatest evangelists, wrote that the war had changed everyone's state of innocence:

The deaths occurring in almost every family in the land brought a sudden and concentrated interest in the life after death. People not only asked the question, 'If a man die shall he live again?' but they eagerly sought to know if communication was possible with the dear ones they had lost. They sought for 'the touch of a vanished hand, and the sound of a voice that is still'.[21]

Price later tried to take credit for Doyle's full conversion to spiritualism in 1915, saying he 'rather turned to me for support . . . he thought that my investigative and scientific work for psychical research would somehow endorse his opinion that every phenomenon was the work of spirits, a view I do not share, and for which there is little evidence'.[22] In fact, Doyle's proselytising mission, which was long in the making and which would absorb him for the rest of his life, was triggered by the respected physicist Sir Oliver Lodge, the leader of the new spiritualist revival; and the hope of life after death intensified for Doyle when his son Kingsley, his brother, his two brothers-in-law and two nephews were killed in the trenches.

Like many eminent men of his time, Sir Oliver – in Doyle's view 'a decent solid man' – believed that the possibility of an afterlife should be open to investigation. His lifelong interest began in Liverpool in 1883 with experiments in telepathy, and three years later he introduced Conan Doyle to the subject. In 1884 Lodge had joined the SPR, not because he believed in the subject of psychical research but, as he noted in his autobiography, because he had 'found a series of facts that were unpalatable and mainly neglected by scientific men, and felt them worthy of attention'.[23]

His championship of spiritualism, fixed in the public mind with the death of his youngest son, Raymond, who was shot and killed in Flanders in 1915, progressed with his belief that his son had communicated with him through a clairvoyant, the subject of his enormously popular book the following year, *Raymond or Life and Death*.[24]

Price complained that the proof of the 'return' of Raymond was not comparable 'with the standard of evidence that Sir Oliver would have demanded from one of his own students who claimed an important discovery in the field of physics',[25] a statement that he would have done well to remember before reporting some of his more bizarre cases.

The war had also created an underclass of street-sellers and gypsies who haunted the boats at Southampton and trains at Victoria, selling lucky charms, medals and amulets to the thousands of numbed troops coming home on leave. Letters of immunity, grim, cardboard-backed paper prayers, were pressed into the hands of superstitious servicemen and their relatives. Phoney clairvoyants, thriving on poverty and disaster, offered seances to deprived families. Paul Tabori stated that it was partly Harry Price's intervention that led the military authorities to 'stamp out this damnable trading on the most sacred emotions of the bereaved'.[26]

This is a ludicrous suggestion, since Price was virtually unknown outside his immediate circle.

But letters of immunity did indeed find their way into Price's huge collection of war souvenirs, as did pieces of Zeppelins and various other German commodities, such as bullets, grenades, trays of chocolate, false teeth and a rather eerie frayed portion of a toupee said to have been all that was left of a German general as he took a direct hit from a British shell at the battle of Mons. When the idea of the Imperial War Museum was mooted and a public appeal launched to start off the collection, Price sent in a list of items that he had first put on display at the Home Life Exhibition in Brighton.

After the war, Price rejoined Edward Saunders & Son, then based in Park Royal Road, as sales manager, earning a pitiful farthing (a quarter of a penny) on every pound of greaseproof paper parchment he managed to sell.[27] In his spare time, he began mixing with magicians and show people, but not until 1920 did he join the Magic Circle and the SPR, encouraged by William Baggallay, both organisations representing a life that seemed far more glamorous, mysterious and powerful than anything he had experienced before.

Around this time he was still writing contorted, heavy prose for the *Public School Magazine* and the *Magazine of Magic*, where one of his features in the March 1921 issue, headlined 'Mornings amongst the Cobwebs', tells of his innate love of books.[28] He also branched out into writing for the staunchly conservative *John Bull* magazine. His first article, a sparring piece about the unfairness of a disputed 1826 election in County Meath, included a long diatribe against Roman Catholics, usefully flagging his Unionist leanings.

At the Magic Circle Harry began to make countless valuable contacts, such as Dr Eric John Dingwall, an anthropologist who later became director of the department of psychical research at the SPR and whose honorary job as keeper of exotic and rare books at the British Museum earned him the nickname Dirty Ding. He was to prove an important touchstone in Price's career as a psychical investigator. Another valuable acquaintance was the smooth-talking British Jew Will Goldston,[29] who in the early 1900s was the motivating force in British modern magic and ran the theatrical and entertainments department of A.W. Gamage in Holborn, the capital's most famous department store. He was also the publisher of *The Magazine of Magic*.

In the course of his career Goldston published forty magic books, some of which he fashioned with a Brahma lock so that only buyers and chosen gazers could know the book's mysteries. Harry was a contributor to several of these books, including *More Exclusive Magical Secrets*,[30] first published in the early 1920s.

Goldston's position as a professional supplier to professional magicians guaranteed that he knew everyone in an industry famed for its tight friend-ships, and when he acquired, to the Magic Circle's disdain, a strong and persistent need to leak secrets, he set up in 1911 a rival group for magicians called the Magicians Club, which he invited Price to join in 1921. The offer was enthusiastically accepted and Harry moved in to support his friend, six months later becoming the club's honorary librarian, remaining a member until his premature death in the late 1940s.

A year earlier, Goldston had introduced his friend to the American escapologist Harry Houdini, who was then touring Britain and at the height of his career. The meeting was a twinning of minds.[31] Houdini and Price soon found that they shared a deep interest in collecting magic books and an attachment to psychical research.

Behind the exuberance of Houdini's friendship was a deep curiosity and purpose; Houdini realised that Price was a rich source of information, and one of the few men in Britain capable of procuring books for his collection. He also knew that there were not many with the skill, knowledge or patience to deal with his notoriously short humour and pomposity; but perhaps the most striking parallel was that both of them flagrantly lied about their places of birth, invented academic honours and manufactured tall tales about their lives.

It was Houdini though, rather than Price, who had the better knowledge of vaudeville mediums, having worked as one early in his career. He was also a recognised celebrity, and had the greater amount of money to spend enriching his half-mile-long library. Price was a long way behind in this respect, and his prospects only began to improve in 1922 after his exposure of the spirit photographer William Hope and the publication, along with Eric Dingwall, of the facsimile book *The Revelations of a Spirit Medium*.

Could Houdini's and Price's egos work smoothly and closely together? Their relationship began excellently, with a warm and frequent exchange of letters written in mutual confidence. Houdini persuaded Harry to join the American Magic Circle and set about helping his friend make business and social contacts in the United States, a country that Price would never visit.

Over the next twelve months Price would be the main repository of Houdini's news, prejudices and opinions. It is easy to see why Houdini felt so at home with Harry. Books and the probing of spiritualism were the two mainstays of their lives, and although Houdini was telling newspapers on both sides of the Atlantic that 'My mind is open, I am perfectly willing to believe,' he was a steadfast debunker of the possibility of contacting the dead. As if to emphasise to Houdini that he was of the same mind, Price took up offers from the BCPS to examine mediums sure of their own unimpeachability, analysing the Austrian poltergeist medium Frau Sadler, whom he was to retest years later, as he did the famous Ada Emma Deane, a spinster of 58 who lived at 151 Balls Pond Road in Islington.

Ada Deane's psychic career was the subject of much criticism and suspicion owing to her peculiar habit of keeping photographic plates in her blouse, a mysterious process she called 'magnetisation', expecting that her own energies would twin with those of the spirit world, an eerie 1920s version of speed dating. In early 1921 Colonel Dr Allerton Cushman, Director of the National Laboratories of Washington, had a sitting with Mrs Deane. He claimed that after the seance his own photographic plate contained a striking portrait of his daughter Agnes, who had died the previous year. From this moment on Ada's diary was full with social obligations and sittings.[32]

However, within six weeks of Cushman's claims, a certain Adeline Perryman was writing to David Gow, editor of *Light*, the spiritualist weekly, claiming Mrs Deane had faked photographic plates of her and her father. Just as she was going to take them from her, Ada had allowed her ginger tomcat, Salty, into the room, 'which jumped on the plates and smashed them to little pieces'.[33]

Gow hurriedly ran a story, which set in motion a shift of opinion against Ada, and shortly afterwards the *Daily Sketch* published the news to their mass readership, which in turn spurred on the Occult Committee of the Magic Circle to investigate her claims.

The Occult Committee, or OC, was a mysterious bunch of men selected from the Magic Circle to investigate strange and supernatural feats and root out fraud.[34] They recruited Harry to test Mrs Deane's claims. Their published report lifted the veil, telling the world that her 'extras' were no more than pictures cut out from popular periodicals. Harry felt that his part in her downfall (he had written the original unpublished assessment of her) was obscured, smoothed over with awkward tact, which prompted a falling out with the committee's chairman.

But it was far from the end for Mrs Deane, who fell again the following year when she published a photograph taken on Remembrance Sunday 1922, during the two minutes' silence at the Cenotaph in Whitehall. Her photograph showed a hazy procession of men lingering above the crowd. The *Daily Sketch* published the images as genuine, then retracted the claim after the Topical Press Agency recognised that her picture of 'spirits' contained many of England's first eleven national football side; they were a little slow in defence and torpid in attack, but they were still breathing.

Since there was no law to stop spirit photographers making money, a whole slew of mediums scented the possibility of making a profit out of a gullible public simply by pasting heads on to photographic plates and then taking a photograph of their subject in the normal way. The most famous of these was William ('Billy') Hope, a former docker,[35] who at the beginning of his photographic career worked at a dye works near Pendleton, a run-down district of Manchester. Hope, 'a niggardly, coarse-mouthed man' according to the *Illustrated London News*, sensibly gave up his job in grimy Pendleton after discovering that a photograph he had taken of one of his fellow workers showed up a figure of a diaphanous woman who was later identified as his friend's sister, who had died many years before.

Inevitably, newspapers reported these phenomena, the feeding frenzy attracting all sorts of mediums to Hope's door. One of these, a Mrs Buxton, who had set up a circle of eight friends to pray for God's gift of spirit photography, invited Hope to live with her and her husband in Crewe. With Billy Hope at its helm, the Crewe Circle, formed the very year that Hope discovered his gift, brought about a radical shift in spiritualism, convincing ordinary people that a gifted observer could peer into another dimension.[36]

Unfortunately, none of the earliest images taken by the circle exists today. The glass plates were broken up or discarded, lives and deaths forgotten because, initially, the circle respected the rites of the Roman Catholic Church, which it believed would see the pictures as idolatrous. But this standpoint was soon to change when the Venerable Thomas Colley,

Archdeacon of Natal and Rector of Stockton, near Rugby, joined the group six months later: from then on the circle began to shout and rave about its discoveries. When Colley died in 1912 Hope and Mrs Buxton moved around Nantwich in Cheshire before finally settling in London. It was here that they re-established the Crewe Circle under the patronage of the British College of Psychic Science.

While Hope was a talked-about celebrity, there were as many doubters of his talent as there were believers. As early as 1909 the *Daily Mail* set up a committee to examine his photographs, speedily concluding that they were fakes. The main sceptics, however, were the SPR, led by its august president Sir Oliver Lodge, who had been trying to obtain an interview with Hope since before the First World War. The SPR had failed to make any headway because strained relations between them and London's various spiritualist organisations proved impossible to shake off. The society saw itself as operating on the side of reason and wanted nothing to do with the spiritualist movement, which it considered vulgar and naive in accepting spirit phenomena without question.

Hope was well aware that staying one step ahead of his doubters shortened the odds of his risking sudden exposure before a public who had been mesmerised by his feats of tapping into an invisible world.

To finally expose Hope's trickery, the newly appointed research officer of the SPR, Dr Eric Dingwall (who had recently returned to Britain from a spell in the United States) realised he needed someone with intimate spiritualist connections. He first thought of the conjuror William Marriott, but quickly dismissed him since he had tested Hope before and had come away from the Crewe Circle with a spirit 'extra' even though the photograph was taken under strict test conditions.[37]

Harry Price was then suggested as the man for the job. A fully paid-up member of the British College, he was trusted and liked by the McKenzies and anticipated no problems in getting Hope to sit for him. However, worried that the experiment might impair his relationship with the BPCS, he introduced James Seymour, a member of the Magic Circle, as the experimenter.

By January, McKenzie had agreed to Harry's request to bring along a friend to experiment with Hope. All this was unknown to the assistant secretary of the college, who wrote to Price as though he was just another interested sitter:

My dear Mr Price – I enclose particulars of an experiment offered you with the Crewe Circle. If you decide to take this, kindly confirm as soon as possible. The fee for non-members is £2 2s 0d to be paid on confirmation. You should provide a half-dozen packet of ¼-inch plates for the experiment, Imperial, or Wellington Wards are considered preferable.

Mr Hope gives every opportunity to the sitter during the experiment, but he will not undertake tests and will use his own camera.

Nothing is guaranteed but good results can be assisted by sitters keeping the plates in their environment for a few days.

If you wish, you are at liberty to bring a friend to share the sitting if they are sympathetic.[38]

The sitting was postponed a couple of days later as Hope contracted flu, but was rescheduled for 24 February at 10.30 a.m. This gave Price and the SPR valuable thinking time.

Price was able to visit the works of the Imperial Dry Plate Co. Ltd at Cricklewood, one of the best manufacturers of photographic glass plates in London, to try to devise an infallible test for Hope. He discussed in detail with Miss Newton, the secretary of the SPR, his method of entrapping Hope:

I have spent the morning at the works of the Imperial Dry Plate Co Ltd Cricklewood, discussing and trying out various tests by which we can invisibly mark the plates, which will be handed to Hope.

We have decided as the best method that the plates shall be exposed to the X-Rays, with a leaden figure of lion rampant (the trade mark of the Imperial Co) intervening.

The centres of each set of four plates will be treated, so that when the plates are placed in their proper order, the full design will be seen. This is to safeguard against the allegation that some of the plates may have been missed in the marking.

Any plate developed will reveal a quarter of the design, besides any photograph or 'extra' that may be on the plate. This will show us absolutely whether the plates have been substituted. I am also thinking out other safeguards that may help us.[39]

On the morning of 28 February Price and Seymour arrived at 59 Holland Park and, after a short stumbling service of hymns and prayers for divine guidance, the two investigators followed Hope into his studio. Here Hope invited Price to open a packet of plates that he had brought with him, the invisibly marked plates from the Imperial Dry Plate Co. As Hope took a plate from Price's hand, Harry watched his movements very carefully, which was not easy in the semi-darkness of the room. Price claimed that he saw how in a quick smooth movement Hope took 'a half turn, two or three paces from the light, put the dark-slide in his left breast pocket', then, apparently, pulled it back out again. Price, unable to see if Hope's eyes flashed an anxious, accusing look, sat down for his photograph to be taken in the normal way.

The sitting over, the Crewe Circle invited Seymour to develop the plates. Waiting a few minutes for the blurry image to sharpen, Seymour realised that the dry plate brand trademark was not going to appear. He had developed one plate that showed Price on his own and another with 'a charming female form looking over his shoulders'. Fearing that, if challenged, Hope would destroy evidence of his work, the pair thanked the Crewe Circle for their time and jubilantly headed back to the SPR where a stenographer took down Price and Seymour's evidence. That afternoon, Price, Seymour and Dingwall headed to the studio of photographer Reginald Haines.

The photographic plates, according to Price's own testimony, were 'independently developed' to show what part of the Imperial Company's trademark had been retained. Of the two plates Price and Seymour took away with them, neither showed the heraldic lion branding, and they appeared to be of a different thickness, whereas, according to the Imperial Dry Plate Co., all had been cut from the same piece of glass. This was unassailable proof that Hope had cheated.

The society was in no great rush to publish its findings, since to go public on such matters was something of an anathema for the vast majority of its members, with the result that the news was only trotted out four months later, in the May edition of the SPR's *Journal*.

The official report created instant pandemonium when it went public, becoming an immediate worldwide sensation and giving Harry his first taste of celebrity. The general verdict was that he and the SPR had secured a great victory, though the poor public was confused when Hope went into hiding and refused to answer his critics.

Hope's sponsors, including Sir Arthur Conan Doyle, went on the defensive. There were two theories about the incident as far as the spiritualists were concerned, and both hinged upon the idea of the SPR doing their utmost to destroy their faith.

One was that in the twenty-four days between the plates being delivered from a friend of Harry's in Pulborough (Charles Haines) to the SPR's headquarters in Tavistock Square someone had tampered with them – 'a fatal blot' according to the creator of Sherlock Holmes – or the SPR had paid someone to conceal the truth.

A few days after the exposure was publicised Conan Doyle received an anonymous parcel containing a photographic black plate marked with the 'lion rampant' allegedly switched by Hope. The plate was wrapped in the headed paper of the British College of Psychic Science with an anonymous note saying what the glass plate contained. Doyle understandably wondered who could have known that this still undeveloped plate was a marked plate – sight alone could not have identified it as such. He passed the plate to *Light* magazine so that its legitimacy could be tested.

At a meeting in the magazine's offices in September, Colonel Cushman, Dingwall, Price and David Gow exposed the plate. It showed up the Dry Imperial Company's trademark. Having finished the test, Gow decided to publish the findings in the Christmas edition of *Light*. Harry, though, had other ideas. He devised a classic spoiler by phoning the news through to *Truth* magazine, *Light*'s main spiritualist rival, who duly revealed the fraud the following week.

Gow was justifiably furious. He made it clear to Harry that the magazine was 'extremely concerned at what we consider a flagrant breach of etiquette committed by you in imparting information that is to appear in our Christmas number. We are amazed that you should have made any public statement connected with it.'[40]

Yet Harry was not going to be nagged, pestered or bullied into abandoning his strategy of talking to the press and, it seems, was unworried by Gow's threat of 'informing our Council of your actions'. Soon after this incident he published the SPR report as his own pamphlet, calling it *Cold Light on Spiritualist Phenomena: An Experiment with the Crewe Circle*.[41] His aim in reprinting the work (with a decidedly clownish cover of a man in a death shroud) was to give 'the public a useful lesson in the observation of alleged psychic photography'.

Houdini claimed that he had beaten Price to the testing of Hope by a few months, but had not thought to tell anyone. Desperate for evidence of fraud,

Alexander McKay Stewart, a Scottish magician friend of the escapologist, sat with Hope and after the sitting found a 'clean shaven face' had manifested itself just above his own in the photograph; he then reported his findings back to New York.

James McKenzie, the founder of the British College of Psychic Science, claimed McKay Stewart had done no such thing, stating 'I do not know anything of Houdini's sitter you mention,'[42] thereby opening the stunning possibility of Houdini telling a lie to protect his ego.

Many questions about this experiment remain unanswered. For example, Reginald Haines, the independent photographer, was in fact Price's shady friend from Pulborough, Charles Reginald Haines, who added credibility to his archaeological finds and who left the village in a hurry shortly after Charles Praetorious had exposed Harry's archaeological prowess as fraudulent. In the intervening years, Haines settled as a photographer near the LSA's head-quarters in Kensington.

Notwithstanding accusations of swindling, Hope agreed for his unearthly powers to be tested again after finding that when the SPR test was repeated, 60 per cent of the Imperial Company's glass photographic plates showed no signs of the rampant lion when developed.

James McKenzie told Harry that there would be ten conditions surrounding the new test. Among these, six members of the Magic Circle's Occult Committee were to be allowed to spend twenty-four hours searching and sealing the room where the experiment would take place; they were invited to make a full body search of Hope; examine his camera; supply the photographic plates; and have full control of the investigation.[43]

Yet the SPR decided it had all the evidence it needed and turned down the college's offer of help, a gesture that attracted much criticism from Conan Doyle, himself a member of the SPR, who thought the underhand way of conducting the test was 'all in shocking taste'. Doyle believed Price to be 'an innocent victim of an elaborate private joke', urging him as 'a brother spiritualist' to withdraw his Cold Light booklet from public sale.[44]

For a decade afterwards the aggressive war of words between the sceptics and the disciples was to rage on, inflamed by Price on the one side and Conan Doyle on the other.

4

HARRY AND THE REVELATION

These were exciting times, and it was impossible for Price not to feel that he had been put on earth at just the right moment. In an interview towards the end of his life he maintained: 'I felt I had joined the SPR at exactly the right time so I could make such a difference to psychical research.'[1]

In the first feverish weeks after the Hope exposure, Harry girded himself for another burst of publicity when he announced, with Eric Dingwall, his intention to re-release *The Revelations of a Spirit Medium*, a comprehensive do-it-yourself guide to fooling the credulous, which revealed to the public just how mediums managed to mesmerise them.[2]

The original *Revelations* had been published in America in 1891, but had long been out of print; and mediums had bought up any copies they could find and destroyed them, so very few had survived. Fortunately, Price had two copies languishing on his library shelves, and allowed one of them to be sacrificed so that a facsimile edition could be produced. He and Dingwall added notes, an extensive bibliography and a glossary, together with an introduction.

A few reviewers found the new publication obscure and a little esoteric. *Light*, which described Price as no more than 'a private individual', criticised Dingwall for republishing a book that mocked spiritualism. However, if *Light* was slightly sour, the mainstream press found it a sensational exploration of fraud. With its cartoonish cover the publication was not destined for obscurity; indeed, its editors were making a deliberate bid for the attention of a new generation of the curious.

The *Magazine of Magic* described Price to the uninitiated as 'an exceedingly clever conjuror of the new school [of magic]. He is very good and very original but we certainly believe that he knows more about the history of magic than any other man in the world with the exception of Houdini.' It might be argued that this tribute was scarcely unexpected: Goldston knew Price, of course. However, no review could have been as unstinting in its support as the one by Harry's friend Houdini, who wrote in the *New York Times*, 20 August 1922:

If any one is seeking information merely from an educational point of view, or if desirous of a reputation as a so-called medium, the work as republished will serve admirably. It may also be regarded, as a double-edged weapon to protect against deception practiced by any medium making use of any method described therein; although a deviation from any method used by a medium may nevertheless still deceive the most astute investigator, and much more so, ordinary mortals.

It was certainly helpful to Price that the twenties were a fertile literary period and that new and interesting books, even if they were reprints, emerged with a frequency that now lends the era the aspect of a golden age. Although the book was not in itself of literary significance, its contents kindled the public imagination and the edition sold well. It also cemented the friendship between Price and Dingwall.

The pair got on well, had common interests in conjuring, book collecting and the alleged psychical phenomena of the seance room and found their collaboration in preparing the book extremely rewarding. Dingwall was impressed with Price; later he remembered him as a true iconoclast, somebody whose standards and style he thought he could trust. He saw him as a man of immense energy, with an exceptionally keen and ingenious mind, clear-sighted, enterprising and single-minded, but dismissed his claim that he had been actively engaged in psychical research for twenty years, because he was 'too fresh and he did not seem to know very much about the scientific side of psychic phenomena'.[3]

Dingwall took comfort in the fact that Harry was an agreeable character to have around, believing that if he were to have opportunities of seeing genuine psychical phenomena he might develop into a researcher of great ability. That chance came in spring 1922, when Dingwall asked Price to accompany him to a series of sittings with the medium Willi Schneider, in Germany, whom Dr Albert von Schrenk-Notzing, a noted researcher, had been testing.

It was a late call from Schrenk-Notzing to the SPR. In a letter to Dingwall dated 17 May 1922 the Honourable Everard Fielding, joint honorary secretary of the SPR, wrote to confirm the arrangements of the trip:

The following is from a translation of another very illegible letter from Schrenk received today about your visit.

'I have received your letter and agree with you entirely. If Mr Dingwall likes to come to see Willi's phenomena, I am very ready to show him.'

He does not say anything about Price, although in my letter I asked whether he might accompany you. I am writing to him today and will revert to that point, but meanwhile, as everybody seems now in agreement that you should go, I hope that you will make ready.[4]

The first set of seances, carried out at Schrenk-Notzing's mansion flat in the Max Josefstrasse in Munich, were a resounding success. Willi had confounded even the most hard-bitten sceptic with his phenomena. Schrenk had demonstrated how Willi's trance personality altered. He claimed to be somebody else, the mischievous girl Lola Montez, a one-time mistress of Ludwig I, the blind king of Bavaria.

Although incapacitated with ropes and dressed in a one-piece seance robe dotted with luminous pins (designed so that observers could see his outline in the dark), Willi moved and touched objects even though a gauze screen cut him off from them. First, an accordion played a short tune: a nebulous shape in the form of a hand appeared to handle the keys. Then a handkerchief knotted itself, a tambourine rattled, and ectoplasm, that creamy white strangeness, dribbled out of his mouth.

For the first time in the history of mediumistic research, 100 scientists signed an unchallenged statement that they were completely convinced of the reality of 'telekinesis', the movement of objects without contact, and ectoplasmic phenomena.

In the SPR *Journal* of June 1922, the council announced that a paper about Willi's powers, 'Psychical Phenomena', would be read by Dingwall at a private meeting of the society on 13 July 1922. Dingwall duly reported his findings, illustrated by a variety of lantern slides. Price stared ahead, silently operating the lantern and allowing Dingwall to describe the remarkable things that had taken place.

Harry's response to this wonderment was to write a flowery semi-academic article for *Light* magazine with the hopeful title, 'Convincing Phenomena at

Munich'. The first paragraph read as though he had seen himself doubting Dingwall's surprise invitation.

> It was with mixed feelings that I accepted the invitation of Mr E.J. Dingwall, the Research Officer of the SPR to accompany him to Munich in order to witness the phenomena alleged to occur through Willi Schneider, the boy medium and protégé of Dr A. Baron von Schrenk-Notzing, who had kindly arranged sittings for us.

Although the *Light* article was clearly a gambit on Price's behalf, it also showed his intransigence – he published it again, virtually word for word, in *Psyche*, the influential successor to the *Cambridge Magazine*, which occupied a unique place for over thirty years as a journal of general and linguistic psychology.[5] Dingwall considered the article to be flagrantly double-edged, pointless, unfocused and so far removed from the truth that few would recognise it. If these articles were unashamedly flippant, perhaps Harry knew that, given the traditional disciplines of the SPR, he would inevitably be snubbed for a time. In the event, this article and the publicity he received from the Hope exposure were responsible for ruining his chances of further progress within the society: a lifelong tussle of mutual distrust had begun.

Dingwall's essential objection was that Price displayed all the signs of being a difficult colleague and a wholly impossible confidant; and besides, a partnership, he pointed out to Price after a thrilling row, was a partnership. Shortly after the publication of the *Light* article, Dingwall addressed the issue in ink, asking Harry for a response which he seems not to have made. Then the second article appeared in *Psyche*; now a trifle fed up, Dingwall sounded a jaundiced note in a letter:

> We all have to learn and had it not been for me you would never have had the chance of coming to Munich to see Willi. Things are very difficult, and I was glad to find somebody who had a certain amount of time and knowledge of magical devices.[6]

In his reply of 2 April Price batted aside his true feelings and wrote a single-line admission, saying 'It was certainly down to you that I went to Munich.'[7]

However, the themes in both the *Psyche* and *Light* articles were at some variance with the truth and when they were expanded on some years later in

Price's autobiography, Dingwall had disappeared from his account altogether, as had the SPR:

During the early part of 1922 I had heard a good deal about the alleged marvellous phenomena that a young Austrian boy was producing for Baron Schrenk-Notzing at Munich.

I learnt that savants from all over Europe were being impressed with the marvels they had seen – and with the conditions under which they had seen them – in Schrenk's seance room. Imagine my delight, when Schrenk invited me to witness these things for myself. 'You are a great sceptic; you know all about mediumistic trickery; come to Munich and if Willi is tricking us, tell us how he is doing it.' So I went.[8]

The trip to Munich proved to be Price's mainspring to the world of grown-up psychic science; and so by circumstance, rather than by aptitude, he gained a comfortable berth for his talents. The seance had overshadowed any previous display of supernormality, convincing him of the existence of strange untapped energies and, along with Dingwall, he signed a statement stating that he was convinced by Willi's otherworldly ability.

Price acted on this remarkable reversal of almost everything he had been saying and thinking for the last two decades. It is a useful reminder not only of his ability to be persuaded, but how divided he was within himself: even when apparently most comfortable with his beliefs, his elastic mind flexed towards whichever way he thought would give him most direction and attention.

The manifestations of power, which, according to Harry's own version of Willi's seance, had included a misshapen hand (technically known as a pseudopod) that appeared and slowly disappeared, came as such a surprise that they compelled him to study the upper end of psychic phenomena and not merely the amateurish splendour of the vaudeville acts he had witnessed in his youth.

Price was increasingly asked to submit material to newspapers and magazines, but he realised that his biggest drawback was his writing style. Although readable, his work did not have fluency and its pace was all wrong; it was regimented, sallow and hollow-cheeked. But then something made him experiment – probably the writing of Conan Doyle. Price coveted Doyle's confidence, agile intellect and his solid, precise way of speaking to his readers. Surviving letters from Doyle to Harry show that for much of the time the couple enjoyed an amiable relationship, and Doyle frequently sent Price hints on how to improve his essays and reports. Almost imperceptibly at first, Price's writing voice changed. His original intention of keeping to a discursive, newspaper style slipped away, and he began to talk to his readers with conviction and a certain breathlessness, as if he were giving a fireside chat. Ornaments no longer fell over, they flew across the room 'as if by an unseen hand'; bottles were 'hurled'; bells did not just ring, they rang paranormally; people whose heads could not be clearly distinguished in poor light, or at a distance, were described as 'headless'.

Price began to dramatise and juggle the basic facts of all that happened around him, while at the same time he tried to raise funds from compliant spiritualists to finance his own investigations. This new outlook led him to spend hours assiduously cultivating friendships, and sometimes he would just sit, half listening to some minor debate, half wrapping his mind round the backgrounds and appearances of different people.[9]

These friendships, such as his contact with Doyle and Houdini, gave him continuing context for his ideas and what he wanted to become involved with. He was ruminating, feeling his way, absorbing the atmosphere around him, nudging towards the decisions he had to take. If Dingwall thought he was ahead of himself, Price certainly did not. He now knew he had an instinctive gift for writing and sensationalism.

In September 1922 Harry gave his first lecture on psychic phenomena to the LSA and later to audiences in Hove and Brighton. The idea behind 'The Limitations of Fraudulent Mediumship' was to show how easy it was for a skilled conjuror and magician to dupe a body of onlookers. He discussed Victorian curiosities such as colourpathy, the zoological photograph, thought waves and the cotton bandage test.

The latter had originated with the vaudeville medium Anna Eva Fay, whose father was a manager of the American magicians, the Davenport brothers. Anna, a friend of Houdini, had once entranced audiences worldwide with her mediumship, and although many people thought her a cheat, she baffled the scientist Sir William Crookes, who went all dewy-eyed when he tested her, calling her 'a fascinating little blonde'.

When the spiritualism craze faltered, Anna turned to mind-reading and escapology. Behind a screen, this small, dashing woman was tied to a post. On a table next to her was an assortment of objects including a bell, a rattle, a tambourine and a glass of water. As soon as a screen was pulled in front of her the tambourine would come spilling over into the audience, then the bell would ring, the rattle turned and finally the screen itself would be pushed over by the 'spirits' howling to be set free, while Anna, still bound by hands and feet, and minus the glass of water, would appear sweating, exhausted.

Price revealed that all Anna had done was simply slip the cotton bandages she had been tied up with and, with her free hand, throw items over the partition, gulp down the water and push over the screen. A sharp jerk on the bandage would restore the ties to their original place. Harry was able to show how easy it was to imitate her act, but so too had a popular book published nearly fifty years earlier called *Magic No Mystery*, edited by the author and magician W.H. Cremer.

In some lectures – marathons that lasted for three hours or more – Price mocked Crookes, Doyle and Sir Oliver Lodge. He recited the story of how, when Lodge was shown a spirit photograph of an alleged Red Indian spirit guide, one which matched exactly the head of an Indian that appeared on the cover of *My Magazine* of October 1920, he said that the public should not jump to obvious conclusions because 'we do not know how the photograph had been obtained'.[10]

This new enterprise opened up a new world for Harry, which he successfully repeated up and down the south coast over the next few years. He must have pondered over his relative fame at times like this, and asked himself how it had come about.

It is hard to overstate the impact of the Willi Schneider seance. A wide psychical vista opened that day. It had been Price's epiphany, a moment of revelation in which he suddenly gained a great insight into both himself and the world. His part-time fascination had suddenly become purposeful, and for the first time since his dismal failure with archaeology he truly felt at home with a subject.

Late that summer he was deeply involved with plans to bring forward an idea that had been maturing in his mind since his return from Munich. He contacted an old acquaintance, George Wright, then general secretary to the LSA. In a letter dated 7 September 1922 Harry said he was determined to find a vacant room where he could test mediums without interruption. This statement – the earliest known mention of his ambition to start a laboratory in Britain – alone scotches his well-worn and readily accepted argument that he had thought of the idea because something 'had to be done to combat the machinations of the horde of charlatans who were battening on the bereaved, the credulous, and the uncritical. To this end, I decided to establish a laboratory in London where the miracle-mongers could be tested and the genuine medium encouraged.'[11] In truth, his creative mind had been triggered by the visit to Schneider.

My dear Wright

    I think I told you some time [ago] that I was looking for a fair-sized room that I could equip as a Laboratory and Seance Room for the study of and investigation of mental and psychical phenomena.

    I am wondering [whether] it would be possible to utilise a room at the LSA for the purpose of setting up a seance room upon the lines of Schrenk-Notzing's. Since my return from Munich I have been determined to secure an apartment somewhere in a sympathetic environment that could be used for the serious and systematic development of persons with alleged psychic gifts.[12]

The council duly considered Price's letter, thought it was a good idea but had to reject it since their offices at Queens Square were stuffed with papers and boxes, all floors filled to the ceiling. Deciding it was not enough to wait in the shadows, Harry took his offer to the British College of Psychic Science.

Because the BCPS already had, in Conan Doyle's words, 'a very valuable laboratory', they dismissed Price's idea, but did provide him with a room where he tested various mediums, including the spirit photographer Mrs Irving, over a period of fifty seances, which took a year to complete.

It was around this time that Dr Albert Schrenk-Notzing became Price's confidant, helpmate and benefactor. Not only was Notzing the best-known psychist in Germany but also, like Harry, he was a skilful self-publicist and colourful impresario; but there were rumours about his probity and whether his most famous charge, Willi Schneider, had really done everything unaided and by natural means. Certainly, Willi never produced work of such intensity outside Schrenk-Notzing's apartment as he did inside, though few took up the challenge with the rather overbearing German. He was a man who inspired either intense affection or great loathing. 'He is heavily built and tall and seems to look at you a bit blearily thorough his monocle, and is a very difficult man to get to know,' said one frustrated interviewer.

Notzing, from a poor background, was a gifted scholar. After studying medicine he graduated to Nancy, in France, to study hypnosis, and later became known as one of the world's leading proponents of hypnotism as a means of psychotherapy. He specialised in sexual pathology and linked this in to psychic phenomena. As a result of his fortunate marriage to Gabrielle Siegle, daughter of a wealthy industrial chemist from Stuttgart, he was able to devote his life to psychic research, studying telekinesis and teleplastics, or ectoplasm.

His early work included testing naked mediums, who were 'stripped of all possibilities of hiding places'. Photographs show the young French medium Eva Carrière producing ghosts much as William Hope had done. Notzing noted that at one seance Eva produced a strangely shaped object on her head; but, glancing at photographs of the seances, the object bears a strong resemblance to one of the grey-coloured felt slippers she generally wore during experiments.

Harry had no difficulty in believing Eva's materialisations to be genuine. 'Eva is supposed to do her tricks by regurgitation. Personally I do not believe anything of the sort,' he said in a fawning letter to his mentor after two professors at the Sorbonne in Paris had pronounced her a fake.

Given the vast amount of publicity and adulation Price gave Notzing and his experiments with Willi, it was inevitable that he would upset certain factions within the Magic Circle, who held the view that magicians should not become involved in public displays of support for the spiritualist movement, since this was seen as damaging both to their dignity and to the established system of reserve.

The spiritualists, in turn, claimed Harry had not discovered the new but confirmed the old. They had detected a streak of insecurity beneath Price's aloof posturing and saw that his views on spirit photographs had matured, raising speculation that he would come out of hiding and fully embrace their beliefs.

In the August 1923 copy of the ASPR's *Journal*, headlined 'The Conversion of Mr Harry Price', the editor, the Reverend Dean Frederick Edwards, wrote gushingly:

Mr Price has been converted. We say this with not the slightest intention of being facetious. Mr Price is to Great Britain what Houdini is to America – the expert in the case – and since there have been some awful frauds in the manufacture of phenomena, the services of experts in trickery have been badly needed.

Indeed, many benevolently have given up in despair, thinking it was all a question for the police. Heretofore Mr Price has been very much of Houdini's mind; but he has found something genuine at last. . . . The story of this adventure has been variously told, but nowhere so interestingly and with such detail as by Mr Price himself in the April number of *Psyche*, the British Quarterly Review of Psychology.

If this all sounds contradictory then that is because it was. Harry discovered he was able to represent all sides of the argument while managing to stop just short of incoherence. He had inherited from his father the ability to be able to talk in various registers as well as holding dear beliefs without actually believing too much of anything as long as there was the slim chance of getting an audience and the possibility of setting up a rival camp of psychic research to the SPR. Price was not the wealthy man myth-makers claim. Whatever has been said in the past of his unlimited income is entirely untrue. His main source of income throughout his entire working life came from Edward Saunders & Son, perhaps enriched by a pound or two out of Connie's purse and an oblique diversion of funds from rich patrons. He realised early on that he needed to pirouette on a large groundswell of support from well-off spiritualists to try to achieve his goal. His inconsistency allowed him to grow more radical in what he said, and so subsequently he was able to agree with both believers and sceptics.

But he had to prove himself. It was his ambition, and that of many psychical investigators around the early 1920s, to be the first to discover a genuine medium and to win a prize put up by the *Scientific American* magazine, which had sprinted to cash in on the very profitable notoriety of the Hope case.

By December 1922 the magazine had promised $2,500 to the first medium to produce an authentic psychic photograph and other phenomena – the aim was to see if anyone could prove that the supernatural existed. The magazine set up a committee made up of the psychologist Professor William McDougall, the physicist Dr Daniel Comstock, two psychic investigators, Dr Walter Franklin Prince and Hereward Carrington, the *Scientific American* magazine's associate editor, Malcolm Bird, and Harry Houdini.

The prize now become Price's obsession, and early the following year, according to Harry, while travelling back from London to Pulborough on his usual afternoon train, he had the most extraordinary stroke of good fortune to meet Stella Cranshaw, an auxiliary nurse, originally from Woolwich, who was travelling to Horsham in Sussex on her way to visit her sister. It was a meeting that would change his life, that of the young woman involved and that of 1920s psychic science.

Price told his readers that Stella had run out of reading material and had asked him if she could borrow his copy of *Light* magazine, with its uplifting tagline, 'Whatsoever doth Make Manifest is Light'. As he handed it to her he asked about her interest in psychic matters. Stella told him she was not particularly interested in psychic phenomena, though she was aware of unexplained random events happening around her. Strong breezes blew across rooms, she said, especially when she was near flowers. Items would move independently away from her when she stretched out her hand towards them and at other times raps and occasional flashes of light would occur.

Price found the 21-year-old 'very pleasant and tractable' and natur-ally was intrigued at finding someone who could be his passport to fame and fortune. If we are to believe him, she encouraged his curiosity, apparently happy for her psychic powers to be tested by a perfect stranger in a dark room, locked from the inside.

A far more likely explanation of how Harry met Stella is found in a letter to him by the spiritualist Mercy Phillimore written at the end of 1922. It shows that the Phillimore family and the Cranshaws had been in and out of each other's lives for some time. Among the daily hum of everyday life, Mercy tells Harry about a young woman and the strange things that had been happening to her:

Her mother joyfully regards Stella's natural ability. It is rare to find someone who has yet to be 'tested' and I think I could persuade the L.S.A. Council to pay her fees if she agrees to be tested. You would be the natural choice of 'experimenter.'

It is impossible to work out exactly how Harry came to meet his favourite medium, but in his own introduction to his pamphlet on her phenomena,[13] *An Account of Some Original Experiments in Psychical Research*, he wrote that it was 'my good fortune, in the early weeks of 1923, to be put in touch with a young lady who was thought to possess psychic powers, but who had never been under experiment'.

He altered his story after he had gained a modicum of fame, and the train journey was substituted for the banal truth. A short time after meeting Stella, Harry mentioned his find to Eric Dingwall, who was understandably excited at the news of an untried medium. When he was told that sittings had already been arranged at the LSA Dingwell's ballooning thrill rapidly deflated, but Price offered a belated consolation prize, telling him he was more than welcome to become of a member of the circle that would examine Stella's gifts.

It is well known that Dingwall abhorred the LSA (indeed he loathed all the spiritualist organisations), and wrote a letter condemning his friend's actions as 'a frank betrayal of psychical research'. Harry replied that while he admired the methods of the SPR he was certain that the society's 'cold, critical and academic methods' would deter the new medium from sitting at all. 'I have already promised you that when the phenomena are fairly and absolutely established, you will have ample opportunities of investigating her.'

Whatever happened between them was patched up when the first series of seances began on 22 March 1923 at 16 Queensberry Place, the headquarters of the LSA, where communications to earth were to come through Stella's control from a dead child known as Palma.

At first little happened, until a table was seen to levitate and a thermometer registering the room temperature dropped by as much as 20.5 degrees. In the next seance a heavier table raised itself completely above the heads of the sitters and then two of the table legs broke away with a percussive noise, which was followed shortly afterwards by the tabletop breaking into two pieces while the remaining support disintegrated so that, according to Harry's testimony, 'the whole was reduced to what is little more than matchwood'.

At the fourth sitting on 12 April Stella reported visualising a copy of the *Daily Mail* of 19 May, which carried in large capital letters the name 'Andrew Salt'. She felt a boy was falling or tumbling over, and a man kneeling over him was 'pouring a white powder out of a bottle or tin which he was giving the boy'. None of the sitters recognised the name and no importance was given to it until the 19 May edition of the paper was published. To everyone's amazement, the whole of the front page was taken up by an advertisement for Andrews Liver Salt with the logo 'a tin kept handy always makes for health and happiness in the home'. The ad showed a boy in tears having spilt a tin of the salt, and a figure of a man standing over him.

Enquiries made by Price, who added authority by pencilling at the bottom of the letter that he was 'member of the SPR etc', to the makers based in Newcastle upon Tyne, found that until May the advertisement had not been published. The *Daily Mail* apparently confirmed this statement, adding that until about three weeks before the trailer had appeared in the paper, and two weeks after the seance of 12 April, the manufacturers were to use a commercial showing Abraham Lincoln and had not talked to the paper about the final ad. In a letter to Price dated 7 June 1923, the advertising manager of the *Mail* said he was impressed and 'quite convinced by the evidence [Price had] submitted'.[14]

By now, Harry and Stella's relationship had blossomed outside the seance room. All that intimate placing of knees between legs, the endless holding of hands and the close contact of limbs over limbs in a darkened room had branched out into something much more sexual. It was around this time that he began slipping an extra 'e' on to Stella's surname. There was now a private understanding between them. After the beginning of May 1923, her name, in his eyes, became Cranshawe, and if she saw anything wrong with this, she did not complain. From the wording of her surviving letters to Harry, it is easy to see that there was something hidden in the background of her seemingly innocent queries.

My dear Harry

I am awfully sorry to have to disappoint you today.

I have wondered several times if you have gone away yet. I did not write before because I did not know what to do.

You promised to let me know when and where you were going and as I have not heard I have come to the conclusion, you are still in London.

Well, dear, I enjoyed my holiday very much indeed . . . I believe I was a wee bit sorry to come back. It is (Lowestoft) an ideal place for a holiday. Well, I shall look for a letter from you very soon, from wherever you are.

Goodbye, Lots of love

From the beginning of June Harry had begun corresponding with Malcolm Bird of *Scientific American* with the express intention of sailing Stella across to the United States to win their prize of $2,500.[15]

Perhaps you will let me know what sum you would be prepared to allot her for her trip, and the approximate duration of the experiments. In the experiments carried out in the last few months, I have personally borne the expenses of her development, and have just concluded my original contact with her.

Of course, Bird did not suspect Price's statement, and wrote back that he was keen to invite Stella and would refund Price his money. Before meeting Harry, Stella had worked as an assistant nurse for ten hours a day, and, although she had a boyfriend, Leslie Deacon, it was a humdrum existence. Now she was offered the opportunity to see America, and she jumped at the chance.

Price though was not happy. Saunders would not offer him extended leave, so he was concerned that Stella would be out of his sight for several weeks with little contact and there was always the possibility that she might be 'stolen' from him. He looked around for someone to act as her chaperone, at last falling on Mercy Phillimore; but the ordeal ended when anxiety overtook him: he encouraged Stella not to go because she was so inexperienced. By chance, Stella was not fit enough to travel for a good part of June and July and complained that she 'felt queer', with frequent stomach problems – which sounds for all the world as though there were bigger problems ahead than either she or Price had expected.

In the midst of all this excitement, Price accompanied Eric Dingwall (who had attended the tenth Stella seance in June) to the second International Congress for Psychical Research in Warsaw. Any enmity Dingwall had felt towards Price seems to have evaporated as they travelled together to Poland with two other members of the SPR, May Walker and Beattie Simmonds.

In Warsaw Price saw and tested Anna Pilch, met Fritz Grunewald, whose presentation on the 'rapping' medium Anna Rasmussen was a set piece of the conference, and conducted worthless experiments with a medium named Jean Guzyk, who once produced a supposedly perfect materialisation of a human face, alive and speaking, and the displacement of heavy objects. By the time Price analysed his gift he had been revealed as a fraud for many years. Price also considered testing the chubby-faced Canadian Mina Crandon, otherwise known as 'Margery' the ectoplasmic Vesuvius, whose mediumship was becoming a cause célèbre. The wife of Le Roi Goddard

Crandon, a distinguished surgeon and well-respected figure in Boston, Mina's seances produced raps and music seemingly from invisible instruments, which then graduated to voices from her dead brother Walter. It was under his guidance that teleplasmic hands, like misshapen Danish pastries, came creeping out of his sister's navel and vagina. The distorted hand was warm to the touch, contained bones and felt skin-like. But Dingwall and the SPR had first call on her, and Margery's genital emissions would escape Price for half a decade.

On his return from Poland Harry set about persuading Stella to give more sittings. The offers were flooding in to him, but, as ever, space was short. The SPR had offered to split fees to test her, and Sir Arthur Conan Doyle offered Price a room at his flat in Westminster. At first, this young pliable girl was content to go along with any suggestion her mentor made, but suddenly, on 17 September, a week before his coins were stolen from Pulborough church, she froze him out of her life and became angry with him: 'please do not meet me at lunch times, because I would rather you did not'; and instead of sending her 'love' signed her full name with a 'yours sincerely', while future letters began with the frigid 'Dear Mr Price' rather than 'Dear Harry': Price had clearly upset her deeply in some way. It could be that Harry had made Stella pregnant and pushed her into having an abortion. Since he could not explain to Connie his urgent need for money he hit on the idea of staging the robbery at St Mary's. Her see-saw moods of love and hate for Price are a classic sign of some sort of trauma.

Further problems came in the shape of the SPR's research officers, Dr Woolley and Eric Dingwall, who thought that the major drawback of Harry's experiments was, unlike almost all other researchers, that he did not circulate an account of the medium's work post-seance. Instead, he endorsed his experiments by writing down the attendees, without checking whether they had agreed with his conclusions, and thus suggesting that the group had cheerfully agreed with his version of the facts. Dingwall was also suspicious that instead of using practised and experienced observers to sit in on most of Stella's experiments, Price had found an eclectic bunch of spiritualists who were willing to believe whatever they saw and were told.

Although the chain of sitters differed from one sitting to another, they regularly included Mercy Phillimore, Miss Gallon, the daughter of the ghost story writer Tom Gallon, the medium Eileen Garrett, George Wright, who had been sacked from the LSA after its council accused him of stealing books from its library, and Jonathon Stainer KC. David Thomas, the managing editor of *Light* magazine, was also a regular, as was a Mrs Pratt, the married sister of Charles Reginald Haines. 'If genuine, how was it possible that a man of Mr Price's knowledge should not have taken the opportunity of conducting a properly controlled series of experiments instead of the kind of demonstrations that he was holding? If fraudulent, Mr Price himself must have been in the fraud,' Dingwall said of one seance.

Whatever the exact reason for Dingwall's scepticism, in response Price invented the telekinetoscope, an impressive-looking piece of electrical equipment that was really a telegraph key in a brass saucer, connected to a red pea lamp which in turn was covered by a bubble of soap, shrouded under a tightly sealed glass shade. The point of the telekinetoscope was that it was supposedly fraudproof. To light the pea lamp normally required breaking the shade. At one seance where the red light came on, Dingwall, his head perched between Stella's legs because there was a shortage of chairs, witnessed the dizzy sight of an opalescent object like a piece of macaroni marching across the lino to meet him before it vanished into the shadows as quickly as it appeared.

By that October tensions between Price and Stella showed in the way their relationship spluttered to a halt. Though she tacitly agreed to another term of seances at the BCPS, which would have earned her £4 (£160 in today's values), she sat for Price only one more time before sending a formal letter terminating all contact with him:

> I am very sorry I had to disappoint you all last Thursday, but I have decided to give up the sittings altogether.
> You see I am now engaged to be married and had the sittings been entirely business it would have been different, but under the circumstances it is not fair to either of you, if I see you again.[16]

The fact that she ended her commitment to Price so abruptly has fixed the idea that it was her impending marriage to her fiancé that forced her hand. This, as Priceologists have been none too slow in pointing out, ruined the fragile relationship between the sitter and tester, and robbed psychic science of a great talent. What has been missed though, in the rush to exonerate Harry in what, even today, is seen as his shining moment, is Stella's pointedly emotional statement that 'if it had been entirely business it would have been different'. Her decision to marry Leslie Deacon meant she no longer wanted contact with Price simply because the emotional tug-of-war would have been too difficult to deal with. It was better, in her mind, to halt any association with him.

Cool in his response, Harry's reply is laden with his usual euphonious language, complete with the perverse use of the added 'e' to Stella's surname:

Dear Miss Cranshawe

We are sorry that our experiments have to come to an end, but hasten to congratulate you upon your engagement, and trust that you will be very happy in the future.[17]

Price's account of why the sittings with Stella stopped is fictionalised here, and bears no relationship to what actually happened. In private, he was no more forthcoming, writing to Barbara McKenzie of the BCPS that Stella had become 'a reactionary. She is too tired to take the sittings at the College. Her work interferes with her mediumship.'[18] Following this letter, Harry was invited by the disappointed Mrs McKenzie to give a full account of his sittings with Stella in the college's *Psychic Science* magazine. He reported that:

The number thirteen proved 'unlucky' as far as we were concerned, for after this seance Stella informed me by letter that she decided not to continue the sittings. Her employment fully occupied her time, and she said the sittings made her feel tired, which is more than probable.

Mrs McKenzie was so impressed by Harry's write-up of the Stella experiments that she posted it to the former editor of *Psychic Science*, the well-connected psychical researcher and spiritualist Frederick Bligh-Bond (who was also the gifted but eccentric archaeologist of Glastonbury Abbey, who famously consulted long-dead monks to pinpoint the famed 'Loretto' Chapel). Bligh-Bond was now living at Gramercy Square in New York, and having left the UK following a lawsuit, he passed Price's manuscript to the ASPR, which subsequently published it in their *Journal*, to great acclaim.[19]

The ASPR, the largest group of psychic researchers outside Europe, were so impressed with Price's experiments that shortly after his article was published

Harry claimed to receive a letter from a multi-millionaire named J.R. Gordon, a pivotal member of the Board of Trustees, asking him to accept the post of Research Officer and move to America. Flattered and somewhat amazed, Price suggested that they should discuss the offer when Gordon paid one of his biannual visits to London. Determined to persuade Harry to accept his offer by any possible means, Gordon invited him to spend a couple of months at his luxury home on Riverside Drive in New York. Apparently Harry reconsidered the offer but in the end he turned it down: 'much as I appreciated the research work that was waiting to be done in America, I could not possibly sever the ties that bound me to the old country . . . as events proved it was a wise decision,' he wrote.[20]

It is extremely unlikely that Gordon offered to employ Price as Research Officer in America. There are no letters from the American in the huge pile of archives at Senate House at the University of London and, equally indicative, there are no records confirming the offer at the ASPR in New York, though he was offered the honorary post of Foreign Research Officer, which he accepted.

Employed as an agent of change, Price was commissioned to write for the society's *Journal* at a rate of $5 a page. Soon he was encouraging prominent European writers, including his mysterious friend, the now Dr Charles Reginald Haines, to contribute to the ASPR's monthly magazine.

Price was handed expenses of around $250 a year (not the £250 that he claimed), which now equates to a modest £2,500; but it did not last long. More importantly, the ASPR was a convenient channel for him to publicise news of happenings in Britain, and many of these were first reported in the American magazine simply because he could charge the society $5 a page for first use of his story.[21]

Soon after his appointment, Price established a close working relationship with the evangelical Reverend Dean Frederick Edwards, and with Malcolm Bird, the Society's Research Officer, the job Harry claimed he had been offered. Edwards hailed the Stella report as 'by far the most important document the Society has published in years' and wrote a letter saying the entire world should be thankful 'for putting the genuineness of the physical phenomena of mediumship on such a firm footing'.

Stella stayed out of touch with Price for two years, until, largely thanks to approaches made by Mercy Phillimore, she decided to start the sittings once more, writing to Harry at the Royal Societies Club in St James's:

'I thought it best to send this letter to you at your club,' and thanking him for taking an interest in her again. In fact, Stella would sit for him thirty-two times in 1926, and despite the outrageous schedule of seances, they still had time for each other. In one highly personal letter to Harry, which finds her mulling over their last meeting, Stella recalls she enjoyed their day out 'but it was spoilt by your unhappiness and I blame myself for it. I am so sorry.'[22]

Her role in his life has not been fully explained and it is certain there was more to their relationship than has been recorded. Had there been any intention on Stella's part to leave her fiancé after the possible abortion, she may have regretted it; in later years she was stung by Price's casual, selfish behaviour. Evidence of this comes in correspondence to Mercy Phillimore in May 1929, soon after Stella had accompanied Price to a sale of furniture at 1 Chesham Street in Belgrave Square. While there, the pair met up with a gaggle from the LSA: Mercy Phillimore, Lennox Kay and the Alliance's treasurer, Captain A.A. Carnell.

Carnell was hoping to buy various lots to augment the Alliance's library. Price was there to add to his own rising collection. He told Carnell, within earshot of Mercy and Stella, that to save time he would do the bidding throughout and settle the money owing later.

But the plan did not work out: just as the books the LSA were interested in came up for auction, Harry turned to Mercy and Carnell and advised them to go into an adjacent room to check that the books he had successfully bid on were safe. When they returned to the saleroom, they found that books they wanted had been bought by Harry. Naturally enough, they expected him to hand them over and asked how much they owed; only for Price to rudely deny any deal and say the books were his.

Writing from her home at 30 Thorold Road, Bowes Park in London, Stella asked Mercy how she possibly could 'forgive HP as you have done. I envy you having such a sweet nature. You say I remained calm – well that was only because it was not my quarrel. If it had been, the little Irish blood I possess would have boiled, but I am pleased you have become friends again if it makes you happier.'[23]

The affair became more extraordinary when Mercy Phillimore returned to the LSA after the weekend. Still stewing over the way Price had treated her she went straight up to his rooms intending to have it out with him, but inexplicably, instead of a grandstanding row, Price beguiled her into forgetting about the whole episode.[24]

Except for this brief outing to the book sale, it seems that Harry's contact with Stella dwindled to a relationship that existed in snatched meetings; and then, in 1932, she vanished from his life altogether. The chapter was finally over, and he accepted it more readily than if Connie had found out and his marriage had ended. What emerges from Harry and Stella's relationship is the question of whether any of her phenomena were genuine and, if they were, how much was invented and embroidered by Price. Stella's innocence has always represented an integral part of her appeal, and this in turn has increased belief in her abilities as a medium. But it is precisely this virtue that allowed Harry to smuggle in phenomena such as the Andrews Liver Salt advertisement, a dangerous, one-off episode.

Because of Harry's snaky ways one has to ask whether he found the information from his numerous sources or invented facts to support his claims. The most obvious tools lay at his feet. As well as selling stationery, Edward Saunders was also a printing house and undertook print services for newspapers. Also, most of the scientific instruments used in the Stella seances were either made or devised by Price. If you add to this the couple's close relationship and the way in which Price signed off the sittings regardless of what other people's opinions may have been, the statistics appear doubtful in the extreme.

There is other evidence, too: Price used the classic magician's trick of misdirection in seances. In one letter, Mercy Phillimore wrote to him that she 'quite realised your reason for varying light . . . but I think you could arrange to have one definite degree of light all the time to avoid the constant change', and once she felt that when he got up to read the graph, 'there was a distinct feeling of disturbance'.[25]

More importantly, Price knew that his rate of success or failure with Stella would determine his future as a psychical investigator. The whole series of his first great experiments can be seen a promotional tool in persuading people that he was the man to take over the SPR's mantle.

As his fame grew, Price turned out for glitzy charity fêtes in his home village. At one, held at Coppice House in Pulborough, he offered crystal scrying as a sideshow, hopeful that he could enlist the use of angels and tempt from them advice on improving a person's state of health, or what they should do if they had debt problems. Price even offered a limp form of marriage guidance ('via the crystal') for 2s 6d.

He was becoming a new kind of public figure in an age where psychical opinion was no longer conducted by leagues of mad-eyed zealots, but had generated a star system of its own. He realised after his successes in journalism that if he was a competent enough writer he could put whatever he liked in print as long as it was halfway believable.

As he became better known he also became impervious to risk, taking deliberately calculated steps to settle old scores, challenging magicians he did not like while making numerous assurances about his importance to the world of magic and psychical investigation.

By July 1924 his opinion about the existence of the supernatural was fixed firmly enough to challenge at least one magician who had taken a public stand against psychical phenomena. Nevil Maskelyne, the elder son of John Nevil, the lionised chief of British magic and the cunning brains behind the penny in the slot toilet machine, had written a feature for the *London Magazine* in February 1923, attacking the way in which fraudulent mediums played on the emotions of the bereaved. It was this rather innocent article that precipitated the outbreak of hostilities.

Maskelyne explained how many people had suffered at the hands of frauds and charlatans and pointed up the good work Harry Price had done in unmasking William Hope. He went on to add that his brother Clive could produce 'spirit photographs' and duplicate everything that a medium could do in a well-controlled seance. With these words of praise in mind, Price, perhaps remembering the way the Occult Committee had ignored his help in snaring Ada Deane, was commissioned to write a raging open letter showing passionate hostility and strong resentment for *Light* magazine, something which he hoped would ingratiate him with the LSA and Conan Doyle.

He argued that it seemed 'the fashion for professional conjurers to gibe openly at all mediums – fraudulent or otherwise – and ridicule the world's most learned scientists in their efforts to determine the laws governing psychic phenomena and in their honest endeavours to elucidate the mysteries of the human mind' – notwithstanding the fact that he had done just this to Hope only a few months earlier.[26]

Price's article included the far-reaching claim that most magicians, including Will Goldston, 'took psychical research seriously, and, if not Spiritualists, they at least were not complete sceptics'. 'I was once as great a sceptic as yourself, Mr Maskelyne, before I took the trouble to investigate honestly the subject and sift the evidence for myself. This means time of course, but isn't it worth it?' he scolded. Towards the end of the letter he pompously advises Maskelyne to 'cultivate a more serious attitude towards the whole business of psychical research and to study the literature on the subject'.

The letter won plaudits from the LSA's ruling council, delighted by this new champion of spiritual research. David Gow, who had once browbeaten Price for his lack of morality, added a note explaining to the uninitiated who this upstart was:

> An amateur conjurer of very wide experience. Starting as a sceptic, he has investigated the different types of psychic phenomena with an unbiased mind, and has reached the conclusion that they are realities and not the compound of fraud and prestidigitation as suggested by certain magicians and conjurers.

However, the row did not spill over into a sparring match, even though Price hammered Maskelyne mercilessly in a second censorious article. Then, in a vehemently antagonistic piece for *Light*'s 1925 Christmas number, Price opened a third salvo, audaciously stating he was writing to the Maskelyne family 'more in sorrow than anger – as the fond parent said when he carefully laid his son and heir in a convenient position across his knee'. Exquisitely pressing the matter home, he demanded mockingly of Maskelyne:

> Can you lower the temperature of a sealed room, containing fifteen persons, twelve degrees in an hour? Could you make my handkerchief (with every stitch visible) casually thrown at the base of a bright red electric lamp, dance around the room like a moth round a candle? Could you materialise a half-formed hand and arm, under the same red lamp, with the medium controlled as a vice?

It was a full 360-degree twirl: instead of him whipping up disillusion against the spiritualist camp, he was working as a propagandist for their cause, which was received with great enthusiasm, particularly by Doyle, to whom Price had sent an advance copy of his last feature before it was published, no doubt wishing to extract a heartfelt approval, an approbation he later received: 'Your excellent article soon to appear in *Light* shows that you are a fair man in your judgement of psychic phenomena. Is it not a question now whether we can find some means by which the Hope controversy can be settled in some honourable fashion?'[27]

Price's response to Doyle's letter was conciliatory. Wisely using his own letter as a vehicle to champion mediums in whom he believed, he moved far away from his original position as a sceptic and began to press exorbitant claims, even going so far as to recant his feelings about Hope: 'I have always thought Hope had genuine powers and recent cases had strengthened that view,' he confessed.[28]

On the face of it, this was an astonishing volte-face; however, it is a story that needs to be treated with caution, since Price knew how much depended on the favours Doyle could offer. (And he eagerly pointed out that his booklet *Cold Light on Spiritualist Phenomena* was no longer in circulation.) Doyle was understandably pleased with Price's progress as an assumed believer, and over the next few months the two men exchanged a number of letters about the Hope affair. Sir Arthur pleaded and Harry Price resolutely assured him that when the opportunity presented itself he would repair the damage or retract his earlier statements. Doyle behaved with astonishing decency in deciding not to report Price's remarkable change of mind about Hope's powers to the press – though had he done so, Price would probably have lambasted him for his change of mind.

The conversion of Harry Price may well have been at the back of Doyle's upright mind, and Doyle's wealth at the forefront of Harry's; but when he asked the author to write a preface for his book on Stella Cranshaw, Doyle demurred. 'I have written such a number of prefaces to psychic books in the last 3 or 4 years, that it has become a little absurd, and I have to lay off.'

The incessant and feverish barrage of open letters to Maskelyne had been triumphant for Harry, his finest moment of publicity. It had increased his profile in the circles where he needed to be seen and read, and it minted new affluent friends. Yet even before this latest success had been scored there was a move of incipient disaffection in the SPR's ranks towards him. The opening of a seance room at the society's headquarters in Tavistock Square in February 1924 must have proved a further maddening moment. Harry had been a member of the society for four frustrating years. He had helped them in one of their greatest exposés, yet he had not been rewarded with a place on the committee, nor a position on a research group. He knew that his boom time with the society was already fading, and some years later he wrote, perhaps a little exaggeratedly, that 'the knives have been there from the moment I joined'.[29]

The SPR's ruling council was a closed circle of academics who came from backgrounds higher up the social ladder than Price, and was dominated by members closely related to each other by marriage. The council had come to loathe Harry for his defence of spiritualism, his incendiary journalism and his hiding away of mediums they wished to analyse.

Eleanor Sidgwick, the widow of the SPR's founder and daughter of the 2nd Lord Salisbury (she was also honorary secretary of the society from 1907 to 1932 and a cousin of the prime minister, Arthur Balfour), made it plain she did not want him on the council or on any of the society's committees, since he was 'not a gentleman' – a late-nineteenth-century euphemism for someone who could not be trusted – besides which, he lacked the distinction of a university degree. He did not possess the intellectual rigour psychic science demanded from its researchers; he was rebellious and unprincipled – he was simply out of his depth.

Realising it was impossible to succeed against this level of antagonism, Price approached the LSA, and in a letter to Mercy Phillimore, now general secretary of the Alliance, reiterated the offer he had made to George Wright:

> I have already some hundreds of pounds of equipment. The work we did with Stella C[ranshaw] has created great interest in all parts of the world . . . I think the possession of such a room by the society would materially further the influence of the Alliance, especially as the psychical researchers of today are more than ever inclined to accept the spirit hypotheses as the basis of the phenomena common to both Spiritualists and their non-Spiritual opponents.[30]

The LSA was keen to back his idea, and recruit someone seen as a celebrity to the spiritualist cause, but again lack of will prevented them acting on Price's offer.

A year later, after a few shambling niceties, Price floated the idea for the third time, a week before the Alliance council meeting.

Still in the role of a man who has the money, skill and expertise but lacks the essential gravitas, he is anxious that the LSA Council sees the prospect of the laboratory 'as a constant source of wonder':[31]

The two London organisations which already have facilities for experimental work are (for reasons well known to us) quite useless to the ordinary student of our subject. It having been decided that opportunities for the study of physical phenomena be offered to the members of the LSA, it is obvious that the title of the association must be amended so as to include some reference to its wider activities.

I suggest an ideal title: The London Spiritualist Alliance and the National Laboratory of Psychical Research and that a 'director' or honorary director (as at the Institut Metapsychique) to be appointed at once.

Switching to begging-bowl prose, he said the laboratory 'will fill a want, long felt, and will interest a great number of students who do not hold with the alleged commercialism of the BCPS or the aloofness and frigidity of our friends in Tavistock Square. By the way, I notice that the SPR are going to hold discussion meetings once a week!'

The day after the LSA's council had sat, on the morning of 13 February 1925, the much-anticipated letter from Dawson Rogers, the LSA's solicitor and company secretary, landed on the doormat of Harry's pleasant home, Arun Bank in Pulborough. How his body must have panted! Rogers wrote that he was delighted to confirm the post of Honorary Director of what would be called the National Laboratory of Psychical Research (NLPR) and with it a seat on the LSA's Council.[32] The breakthrough was complete: all the strenuous string-pulling had paid off and at last he had acquired a new status. In his reply, written on St Valentine's Day 1925, Harry accepted the position with great keenness, hoping the new department would be 'of considerable benefit to the Alliance'.[33] Though his post was not a funded one, Price instinctively knew that the NLPR was going to be his lifeline and his regular route to prominence with the public.

In April steps were taken to plot the direction of the National Laboratory and to decide on its terms of reference. A short news item in *Light* on 4 April snappily sketched out the news for the faithful: 'A number of gentlemen have decided to form a National Laboratory. An inaugural meeting will be held at the Royal Societies Club in St John's Street, on 25th April 1925.' In all, nine prospective members, including Dennis Bradley, Dr Robert Fielding-Ould, a former medic in the army, and Arthur Findlay OBE, cousin to the magician James Findlay, met to distil the group's objectives,

which Price optimistically called 'a milestone in the scientific investigation of
the paranormal'.

It was here, at a club with so many eminent members of orthodox
science looking down on them, that the committee concluded the laboratory
would 'investigate in a dispassionate manner, and purely by scientific
means, every phase of psychic or alleged psychic phenomena'.[34] It
was carefully emphasised that full and frank cooperation was planned
with similar research bodies throughout the world. At Tavistock Square the
SPR's Council was predictably frosty towards the news of the founding
of the laboratory, believing it would be a populist flash, while others,
including Sir William Barrett, the SPR's ageing founder, thought it
was an excellent idea 'since it is impossible to expect the SPR to cover the
whole ground of investigating psychic happenings'.[35] Lord Raleigh, a free
thinker and one of the last intellectual giants of the Victorian era (he was
a world-famous experimental physicist who had discovered argon – and,
incidentally, was the brother-in-law of Eleanor Sidgwick), congratulated Price
on his new post, which came at 'a great and interesting period in
our lives'.[36]

But the SPR still had its polemicists who argued, not without reason, that
Price's strategy of paying mediums encouraged them to cheat. His reply was
that they had a job to do and 'there are things we do not understand, and
Science to its eternal shame is making little attempt to understand them'. He
related to the *Morning Post*, with great solemnity, the brave steps the
laboratory was about to take:

> We will be un-embarrassed by useless or obsolete traditions, free from
> extraneous influences and with no obsessions as to what is or is not
> possible in psychical research.
>   The Council of the Laboratory hopes to present to the General Public
> authoritative reports of its experiments, which will carry conviction.[37]

Two hundred and fifty members immediately paid one guinea to get the
organisation through its first year. Its workings were unashamedly based on
the French spiritualist Institut Metapsychique. Within the space of two years,
membership increased to 995 members – almost a bigger membership base
than the SPR – with 150 life members paying £25 (the equivalent of £900
today) for the privilege. The LSA was soon able to buy its long awaited

headquarters at 16 Queensberry Place, so the bright, shiny National Laboratory of Psychical Research now had a home.

Very quickly, however, and for reasons that are not exactly clear, it was decided that it would be better if the National Laboratory was turned over to a reviewing council and was quite separate from the LSA. This was exactly what Price had wished for. Not only was he the laboratory's director but chairman of its investigating board too.

Psychic science was taking precedence in Harry's life over the selling of paper bags, though in a letter to a colleague in 1925 he was still wildly enthusiastic about his friend's idea of a London-wide paper bag convention: 'I am interested in what you tell me about the Bag Convention and it will work only if every wholesaler is in it. For instance the Wholesale Co-Op will not be interested in it, surely? They are our greatest competitors concerning pastry bags,' the stepchild of non-orthodox science warned. He was now a psychic scientist who sold paper bags and confectionery wrappings in his spare time, not a salesman who hunted ghosts in his spare time.[38]

During the short period that elapsed between the inaugural meeting of the founders of the laboratory and the organisation moving into 16 Queensberry Place in January 1926 Price was invited to step into Sir Arthur Conan Doyle's shoes on a lecture tour of Copenhagen – an interesting switch of personalities, one might think. Doyle had been booked to appear at various venues in Denmark, but at one seance a spirit guide had warned him that a cataclysmic disaster was impending; his life was at risk if he travelled, so he dropped the idea, asking Harry to go in his place.

Price's first task as he arrived in a bitterly cold Copenhagen was to open a psychic exhibition at the Metz Tea Rooms in the Ostergade, the Danish equivalent of Carnaby Street in London. The exhibition had been formed by Johannes Jensen, the president of the Danish Society for the Promotion of Psychic Knowledge, a Scandinavian version of the SPR. For years Jensen had been collecting weird objects connected with mediums and psychical research. The exhibition would tour to London later that spring – although of course this is not how Harry saw it nearly two decades later when he made out that Jensen had suggested that he should bring the Copenhagen show to London. In truth, the bazaar and psychic fête, which had taken months to prepare, was devised by Doyle and Mercy Phillimore. The exhibition attracted curious happenings from the moment Price walked into the hall.

Iltyd Nicholl, the future father of Kenneth Nicholl, the graceful right-hand batsman for Middlesex and England cricket teams, claimed to be a target for a variety of apports (the spontaneous appearance of solid objects) including an 'African native's leather apron' that had been forwarded from nowhere 'by easy stages', the only example of psychic hire purchase. At another time, he was on a bus travelling to Piccadilly when a tea urn mysteriously appeared on his lap.[39]

When he came to remember these incidents in his autobiography Price scoffed at the 'large collection of apports that had barged their way through solid brick walls and closed doors'. There were spirit writings and drawings and autographs of spirits; slate writings in Greek produced by the conjuror-medium 'Dr' Slade; portraits of spirit guides and controls executed spontaneously at various seances. 'It was a pathetic sight to see how some of these visitors took at their face value these "shocking examples" of fake, credulity, and self-deception.'[40]

These in fact were the raw materials from which he had penned the glowing foreword to accompany the show:

It is a great honour that I introduce this Exhibition to the great public whose ridicule of, and apathy to, psychical research have been the means of retarding progress in the science . . . No one – however sceptical – can regard the mass of material brought together at this Exhibition without coming to the conclusion that there is a strong prima facie case for very serious investigation.

'The observer who will not admit this is not honest,' he thundered, adding that it presented 'the opportunity of studying under one roof the records of famous psychics and psychists from the time of Mesmer (1778) to that of "Margery" (Mrs L.R. Crandon of Boston USA) whose phenomena are the wonder of the civilised world'.[41]

The rest of the year was busy for Price. In June he and SPR member May Walker visited Vienna to attend more seances with Willi Schneider. Through a misunderstanding, and quite unexpectedly, he was invited to lecture on psychical research at Vienna's university by the physicist and undercover psychic tinkerer Professor Hans Thirring. The lecture took place before a large and dyspeptic audience, which included the clubbable figure of Dr Fritz Wittels, a German psychoanalyst, journalist and academic who wrote a number of articles for British and American magazines in the 1920s on subjects such as 'why women bob their hair' and 'why men fascinate'.

Vienna was the precursor to the most important event of the year, the Second International Psychical Congress, held in Paris. Enormous public interest in the congress had been sparked off by the debate on the possibility of contacting Martians. This was an area of which Price had a little understanding, but a few weeks before the congress a City of London solicitor, Henry Mansfield Robinson, wrote to him about an amazing invention of his that he claimed could contact any life form in the solar system:[42] 'My chief work is telepathy by which I have succeeded in getting in touch with Martians by an instrument I have invented called the Psychomotormeter and in the Martian language through a floating trumpet and through trance.'[43]

Robinson arranged for a medium, Mrs St John James, 'a small, busy woman' who insisted on wearing a monocle and bright ribbons in her hair, to visit the National Laboratory to prove his point. He added: 'I have arranged with the Martian Lady Oomaruru telepathically to come and talk and she is very pleased at the idea of being treated with scientific seriousness and will recite a short poem of her own composition. I have also invited along a very civilised giant, and a Martian savage bushman to speak Martian to you.'

Other mediums were involved, including the conspicuous figure of Charles 'Fatty' Madoc, who arrived at the NLPR with a large amount of copper wire, bottles of assorted chemicals and insulators to try his luck with the ruling council on the Red Planet. Madoc explained that his astral body only contacted Mars when he was in the correct orbit. He had to wrap himself in copper wire then sit in a wheeled hipbath of chemicals before slowly manoeuvring himself around the laboratory until he found the right position to go into a trance, rather like a human satellite. He reeled off a detailed account of Martian life, people and animals, their hopes and fears and what they lived on – then he burst into tears on hearing from a Martian friend that his pet donkey had died.

A year later Price began to explore the possibilities of communicating with Mars by means of a huge beam of light. He travelled to an observatory on the Jungfraujoch in Switzerland to arrange for a test site to be established, believing that the nearer the planet the beam was, the greater the chance it would be seen by aliens. He approached the lighthouse engineering firm of

Chance Brothers, who offered to build special lenses and arc lights that would produce a massive beam of light equivalent to 15 billion candle power. But the project was scuppered because of the cost – some £6,000 (approximately £230,000 in today's terms).[44] Unable to raise that sort of cash from wealthy spiritualists, interested scientists padded away, and the plan was shelved. Price so enjoyed his adventure, though, that he wrote frantically for assorted psychic weeklies including *Two Worlds* and the *South American Psychic*.

If his relationship with scientists and Conan Doyle was at last on the up, his friendship with Houdini was decidedly on the wane. Towards the end of December he wrote to Houdini warning him, in couched terms, that he had written an article on his beliefs for the February 1927 issue of *Light*. Unaware of the nature of *Light* magazine, Houdini thanked Price for his kind thoughts, fully expecting the article to wax lyrical about his abilities; instead, it was a measured attack. Price made out that Houdini's defence of scepticism did not represent a commitment to what he said in private. In other words, he accused Houdini of lying to his public:

> My friend, Harry Houdini, the famous American 'escape' artist, has more than once been credited with psychic powers by means of which he is supposed to form some of his miracles.
>
> Though Houdini would be the last person to pretend to powers he does not possess, he has confided in me the fact that there have been occasions when he has been helped in his performances by some unseen and unknown force; an intangible 'friend in need' which has rescued him from many an awkward dilemma.[45]

While the hard facts of this piece were far from being news (Price was merely echoing what Sir Arthur Conan Doyle and John Hewat McKenzie had said on previous occasions), he was coming from a different angle. A close confidant of Harry Houdini's had come out in public and was within a breath of accusing him of admitting that he had psychic powers.

Price wrote the article because he needed to court spiritualist opinion and to keep both Doyle and the BCPS on side in a year where they had provided money for sittings with Stella Cranshaw. However cruel and barbed the writing, he knew that Houdini had little influence in Britain, was hated by the spiritualists and would be no help in setting up hoped for experiments.

Unsurprisingly, Houdini became standoffish and broke off writing to Price for over a year until he sent 'HP – it sounds like the sauce' a signed copy of his fiercely anti-spiritualist book *A Magician among the Spirits*. It was his seminal work, his 'monument' he called it. Price was stunned by the book's poor quality and decided to review it for the SPR's *Journal*. The review was to be another assault on the American's professionalism, but to save face he asked the society to print his review anonymously, without a byline – a rare example of Harry's timidity over-taking his vanity:

> Though Houdini's knowledge of psychical research may be most profound, he has successfully hidden this from the reader of *A Magician among the Spirits*. And the historian of the future who has to refer to 'impartial results of many years of careful study' (see advertisements) will deserve all the pity he gets.
>
> Students of the 'nu speling' will find many choice examples in *A Magician among the Spirits*. We read of Eva C. and the Villa 'Carmine'; Mlle 'Tomchick'; and Mr 'Baggley' etc etc. The author informs us in his introduction that he doubts 'if any one in the world has so complete a library on modern Spiritualism' as Houdini. What a pity he did not make use of it!

It was a vicious, uncompromising attack, but the review was typical of Price's quick, capricious, sceptical mind, and frankly there was little he could have said to recommend it, riddled as the book was with errors and poor grammar, despite the fact that much of it had been ghosted for him. In professional terms, Price had no cause for regret. Indeed, there was no stopping his attacks on Houdini, a development underlined by the sniping tone of his 'International Notes' column for the ASPR's *Journal* in December 1927, in which he wrote:

> According to the *Birmingham Gazette* for September 16th Houdini cabled a $10,000 challenge to the Spiritualists' Congress assembled in Paris, offering to expose any medium the Congress cared to send over to America. The fact that the challenge arrived two days after the Congress had dispersed is by the way.
>
> Without disparaging Houdini's powers as an observer or detective, it is only fair to call the attention to the fact that all the mediums he has

exposed have been either known frauds or tricksters, whose 'phenomena' would hardly deceive a schoolboy – very small beer indeed for such a great magician.

The relationship with the American could not have been helped by the fact that by now Harry was on social terms with Conan Doyle, that the great and the good were fascinated by his work, that he was receiving plaudits from all spheres of the spiritualist movement and that the press delighted in his acquaintance. Price, the supreme peer-chaser, now had a start in the world of psychic science and realised that he no longer needed Houdini's wavering friendship.

5

THE BLONDE AND THE CAUSE OF BAD BEHAVIOUR

Lucy Kay was the slim, blonde daughter of a prominent spiritualist and a white-collar commercial clerk. She was born Violet Lucy Kaltenbach in Germany in 1902, but her father Maximilian changed the name of the family to the anglicised Kay in the late 1890s, following anti-German sentiment provoked by alarmist stories in the British press about Imperial Germany's dreadnought programme and the strong possibility of the country being invaded by moustached men with spiked Pickelhaube helmets and jackboots.

A beautiful 24-year-old, a lookalike of the American novelist Anita Loos, Lucy was working as a model and was preparing for a show in Paris when her mother, Lennox, invited her along to the public opening of Price's National Laboratory on Saturday 26 January 1926. It is not clear how she and Harry met, but by the date of the open evening of the laboratory – and presumably through various meetings and correspondence, some of which still exists – there had been a great advance in friendship. When she set eyes on him that Saturday he was, in her own words, 'a harassed man', as host to hundreds of visitors who were keen to see the new wunderkind in action.[1]

Taking stock of their surroundings, Lucy and Lennox busied themselves looking around at the various beakers, retorts and instruments in the pristine, film-set laboratory.

The upper floor exhibited all the nauseous instruments of the time, including an X-ray machine, an electric marvel used for examining mediums' stomachs to see if they had swallowed tissue paper or the ubiquitous cheesecloth that would later be swagged around wire coat hangers to reappear as cadaverous shapes.

There was also a seance area, a chemical and physical laboratory stacked with large tins of red, green and yellow sulphide of zinc, the slightly radio-active chemical used to make luminous paint, a darkroom to develop photographs, a library, an office and a workshop.

There was also a gloriously ramshackle museum with odds and ends of mediumistic contraptions, many of which had been used to conjure up arcane phenomena. The curios included a string of Madame Blavatsky's pearls, a well-worn pair of trousers spotted with luminous paint, a trick-laden stool and a bunch of psychic roses – thornless, of course. In one corner stood a locked cabinet containing an assortment of mediums' photographs cross-indexed with confessions of their trickery; a Mrs Monica Edmunds claimed in her signed confession to have contacted a good number of dead English aristocracy and royalty, including Charles II.

The laboratory's bookshelves, alas, were rather bare, since the bulk of Harry's library, complete with phoney heraldic bookplates, was on loan at Tavistock Square. When the SPR decided to return the books to him 'for reasons of space', they formed a large part of his interior design and gave the rooms 'a homely feeling', so that visiting mediums would feel at ease among the wires, valves, chemicals and cables of an Edwardian seance room.

In the rush of people that night Lucy casually mentioned to Harry that the laboratory must be a lovely place in which to work. It was an idea that must have stopped him in his tracks and made him pause for thought. Clearly enchanted with Lucy, he offered her a job as his secretary and librarian there and then, brushing away the small problem that he had no power to appoint employees for a position that in reality took up very little of his time and created little work. This aside, for the next five years Lucy would be, as she put it, 'secretary to this newly born stepchild of orthodox science from which so much was expected'.[2]

For Lucy, Harry was a supremely charming and amusing man – when his air of diffidence vanished – and, despite the persona he sometimes cultivated, he was not an insular person. But he was very tight with information and it is intriguing to note that his second secretary, Ethel Beenham, once said that it was several months before she realised that he was a married man, so one can only guess how long it was before Lucy knew about Connie sitting at home in Pulborough twiddling her thumbs.

David Meeker, Lucy's son from her second marriage, says his mother was in awe of Price. 'Her eyes used to light up whenever she mentioned his name.

She was in admiration of him, always trying to mention him in a conversation.'[3]

Since they worked closely together their relations had to be amicable, but within a short span of time the friendship developed and matured. In her regular correspondence with Harry Lucy was intermittently light-hearted and needy. 'I do not feel able to love anybody,' she wrote to him at one point.[4] For his part, the relationship with Lucy allowed him to entertain much more in London, usually at the Royal Societies Club, to air his own prejudices in confidence, and to note the gloom and glories of his calling.

For a secretary Lucy Kay enjoyed an extraordinary amount of freedom away from her job, with regular cruises to Egypt, the Mediterranean, Sri Lanka (then Ceylon) and America, where she visited her distant relation, who would later find fame as the Nazi propagandist Frederick William Kaltenbach, or Lord Hee-Haw. Wherever her ship docked, there would be letters from Price waiting for her at each port. In one reply she takes flight into a flirty openness that must have sent Harry's heart racing: 'My dear Lord and Master, do I dare expect another [letter] from you when I land,' she wrote to him from aboard the 20,000-ton SS *Orama* on its way to Australia in 1926, barely five months after being caught in his web.[5]

While Lucy was away, Price contrived to make friends with as many members of the press as he could. Turning on the full force of his salesman's charm, he told them that their readers demanded more stories about psychical research. 'It is so interesting to a very large number of people that the papers fall over themselves in trying to get copy,' he wrote to a friend.[6] From experience, he related well to the press and had a natural talent for placing propaganda. He now set himself the task of establishing a better dialogue with all areas of the media, where before there had been pretty much none. It was a world away from the cold-blooded, disciplined business of the SPR.

The Times, still a parochial noticeboard for the Establishment, generously described Harry as a 'mixture of Professor Richet of Paris, Professor A.M. Low, Captain Clive Maskelyne and Sherlock Holmes – with just the faintest perceptible dash of Sir Arthur Conan Doyle'.[7] The middle-market newspapers, the *Daily Express* and the *Daily Mail*, shared *The Times*'s triumphant story, calling Harry 'a man deserving to be called a scientist'.

This indulgence helped the NLPR to match the SPR's call on the nobility, and Harry was soon able to handpick his own titled gallery of figures from across the psychical swathe. The Scottish advocate Lord Sands (Christopher Johnston) took the post of honorary president, with Pamela Adelaide Geneviève, Viscountess Grey of Falladon, heading up a roll-call of leading European enthusiasts, researchers and parapsychologists, including the formidable Schrenk-Notzing and the equally quick-tempered Eugène Osty, director of the Institut Metapsychique in Paris, both of whom took up positions as vice-presidents. The only task of the honorary corresponding members seemed to be to keep the laboratory up to date with interesting mediums they wished to investigate. Finally, there was a research council.

In all, the NLPR boasted twenty-six officers and two members of staff who, according to the membership application form, were prepared to ask weighty questions about the meaning of life and the spiritual extent of the world. They had all independently 'investigated and were absolutely convinced of the reality of mediumistic phenomena (both physical and mental) for which a normal explanation cannot be found'.[8]

What the great and the good brought with them was authority, credibility and international status. This, in turn, enabled Price to attract the patronage of the ASPR and to ask J.R. Gordon, the American shipping magnate, to become an honorary vice-president of the laboratory – and thus the ASPR's only European outpost.

The broadening of Price's psychic career brought a new excitement into his life, and by March 1926 he could bask in the laboratory's glory, which even then was becoming more and more his private and idiosyncratic vehicle, even though not much work was being done to discover the quick and the dead.

For most of the week Price was a commercial traveller, earning approximately £500 (in the region of £20,000 today) a year. He dressed in a well-cut suit and tie from Austin Reed or Simpson's, but each Wednesday from 10 a.m. to 5.30 p.m. and each Friday from 10 a.m. to 12.30 p.m. he threw a white lab coat over his flannel knockabout suit, tailored by Pope and Bradley of Bond Street, and became a scientist, aping the way other enthusiastic amateurs had mapped out their own worlds of research and discovery, presenting the world of academia and the public with a new and exciting discipline: Price saw himself as a modern-day Paracelsus, that fascinating Renaissance magician, part scientist, part alchemist, part father of modern chemistry.

He wanted to be able to elucidate everything and explain it in a way that left no room for further discussion. The laboratory was where he hoped his career would be marked by solid accomplishments; it would provide the living world with major breakthroughs from a world no one understood.

According to Kathleen 'Mollie' Goldney – a member of the SPR, at first an admirer of Price, then an enthusiastic lover and later still a reluctant detractor – the NLPR had an expectant and indulgent party air to it. On holiday from India in 1926, where her husband was in business, she visited the laboratory for the first time and thought of it as an imperial outpost: 'it was always full of people. From Journalists to retired colonels, everyone liked going there.'⁹ It was a typical product of the new discrimination after the First World War, the new leitmotif of British psychic investigation; it had a refreshing egalitarianism, one that rose above fashion, class and intellect.

Now the laboratory itself was established, Price's mind focused on launching the magazine, the *British Journal of Psychical Research*, or the *Journal* for short, published under the skilful editorship of Mrs Francis Leaning, a former reporter with the *Manchester Guardian*. This was a move guaranteed to upset the SPR, which issued a magazine of the same name. Taking no chance that the average reader would flick through the pages of their newssheet without seeing a notice condemning the laboratory, the SPR published a bold editorial, written with what must have been commendable restraint:

NOTICE: Concerning 'The British Journal of Psychical Research'
    On account of a danger of confusion we think it right to point out that a new association calling itself the National Laboratory of Psychical Research and publishing an official organ styled *The British Journal of Psychical Research* has no connection whatever with our society. It is regrettable that names should have been chosen for this new association and its publication likely to lead to misunderstandings especially abroad.

The new publication, however, was unlikely to cause confusion. The *Journal* had a deep carmine cover with white letters in bold relief, and, for its debut edition, a photograph of Stella Cranshaw on the front. 'Its exterior is so cheerful that one would instinctively select it from among a number of periodicals presented to one,' Harry cooed in his International Notes for the ASPR in June, before extending another rude gesture towards the SPR:

It is hoped to make the contents as bright as the exterior, many psychic periodicals, and journals being written in a manner which bores the reader through their deadly dullness. An article can be accurate, scientific, detailed, and convincing and yet be written in a style both interesting and bright. A good example of what I mean is to be found in Sir Oliver Lodge's article on dreams, which he wrote for the *Strand Magazine*.

But besides the article by Lodge, there was a short history of the Stella Cranshaw mediumship, 'some interesting personal psychic experiences by Susan, Countess of Malmesbury and a plea for accuracy by the present writer', worded as if to prove that the *Journal* was emphatically not a repository of one man's views. Price spoke confidently in the magazine about the basis of scientific research and how he would make psychic science comprehensible, where before abnormal phenomena had been analysed and the results shut away for years on end; and even eminent science magazines such as *Nature* were, thanks to him, beginning to show interest in the subject.

Nature's editor Richard (later Sir Richard) Gregory hesitantly asked Price to navigate him through a seance: 'I must see things and understand things first-hand before I can form any opinion whatever on them. I should find it most difficult to accept as real any phenomena about which I can read only.'[10]

The day the National Laboratory began its voyage into sailing the well-trafficked routes of the paranormal, the distinguished psychic investigator Lord Charles Hope asked Price if he thought he would be the one to discover the key to the age-old mystery of immortality, by then a quest that had reached legendary proportions. That, Price replied piously from his chemists' kingdom, would be the ultimate test of his laboratory – as if he was set to unlock the secrets governing the universe.

It is no exaggeration to say that the launch of the newfangled National Laboratory caused a whirl of excitement throughout ordinary homes in Britain. Spiritualism still held thousands of people in its grip, television had yet to arrive and many Hollywood films around the interwar years were dosed with the fantastic and the horrible. Ghosts and haunting were a staple diet. Price's insistence on demystifying the practice of professional psychic investigators was new; it brought much-needed understanding of the occult into people's lives. Even in its first few months, the NLPR was changing the culture of psychic research. No longer was it an academic, lofty and almost impenetrable subject but something of wide public appeal.

Stirred with emotion at Harry's new endeavour, and perhaps realising what sort of danger it might court, Conan Doyle pleaded with him to leave the 'spiteful teasing and ignoble sport of medium baiting' alone, and said the way forward was to give a medium the benefit of a defence before condemning them in public.

When Price returned to writing to Houdini in mid-October it was to refute an attack on the American's integrity by an Austrian magician called Ottokar Fischer in the magazine *Das Program*. The publication had pointed out that, acting as Price's interpreter at a lecture, Fischer told the audience that Houdini had falsified information against Mina Crandon because he secretly believed in her mediumship. After taking Houdini aside and giving him a literary shaking, Price scolded him for not verifying information with him first. 'I puzzled my brains thinking what I had said concerning you, and your letter supplies the answer . . . Fischer had no right and no justification for making the remarks you said.' Letters reveal that Price knew exactly what Fischer had said in German, because Price had said it in English first.

It is most likely Houdini never had the time to read Harry's reply. He died aged 52 on 31 October 1926 at the Grace Hospital in Detroit, Michigan. He was taken there suffering from a burst appendix complicated by peritonitis after tempting a student at McGill University in Canada to punch him in the pit of his stomach.

The process of Price's great exploration into psychic phenomena began when he tested George Valiantine, a celebrated American medium who bore a strong resemblance to G.K. Chesterton's popular Father Brown. Valiantine was brought over to London in the winter of 1927 by the society tailor, playwright, author, spiritualist and patron of the NLPR Dennis Bradley. Harry thought Valiantine was a good mimic and a particularly valuable conjuror, but was unsure of his talent as a communicator with the spirits.

A small businessman down on his luck when he first heard discmbodied knocks on his hotel room door, Valiantine had held Americans in rapture for years and had nearly fooled the *Scientific American* magazine into handing him their prize – until Houdini, who had hidden himself in the seance room where his countryman was giving a sitting, declared him the rawest of fakes.

When Valiantine arrived for a tour of Britain, dozens of celebrities, wooed by Conan Doyle's fanatical advocacy, attended his seances. At one sitting in Bradley's home in Kingston, Surrey, the author P.G. Wodehouse, who had

attended Valiantine's seances two years before with the *Daily Mirror* editor
and photojournalism pioneer Hannen Swaffer, brought along two more
neophytes, the writer Dennis Mackail and Baroness de Kakucs, to witness
what would prove to be a lively night of bobbing tables and spirit watching.[11]
As the lights went out a stifled noise came from a trumpet (used to amplify
the spirits' tiny voices), which then sailed through the air – it was marked
with luminous paint so that the levitation could be seen in the dark. Next
Wodehouse and his friends heard a war whoop by Black Foot, one of
Valiantine's Red Indian controls, then a small voice tried to speak to
Wodehouse saying it was his grandfather, but it was so muffled 'that no
identity could be established'.

Later on in the seance the Victorian critic and playwright William Archer
came through and told the author of *Heart of a Goof* that 'on the other side
literature still goes on' and that he was continuing with his craft because
'writers on this plane are helped by those on the other side'. A short while
later Confucius was in the room: though he had died in 479 BC, Bradley was
adamant that the speech from Valiantine's spirit guide, White Hawk, was by
the Chinese philosopher.

Later that year Bradley made a recording of Valiantine's thin, 'rather flute-
like voice', though his optimism was crushed in 1931 when he discovered
the extraordinary coincidence that Valiantine's big toe print was exactly the
same as the late Sir Arthur Conan Doyle's thumb print, which the American
claimed had been passed on to him from the other side. Price, on the other
hand, thought Valiantine 'good, but not very'. At one seance the Italian
composer Arditi came through and said a few simple phrases, which Harry
found unconvincing: 'they were nearly as insensible as the traditional "The
pen of my aunt is in the garden."'

Following his testing of Valiantine came Harry's first big investigation,
which turned out to be much more serious than the dozens that were to
follow. Eleanore Zugun had become known to the British press as the Devil
Girl of Romania, and Harry's own telling of her tale shows how painful and
disturbing life must have been for this uneducated peasant girl of 11.[12] She
was victimised by the equally uneducated and deeply superstitious people of
her own village of Tapau in Northern Romania, who believed the Devil could
mould himself to any shape or size and split himself into a million particles,
each one as dangerous as the other – it is easy to see why innocent people
spent their lives in asylums, battling against myth.

Eleanore's troubles began when someone smashed the windows in her parents' house. Suspecting witchcraft, they called in a local priest to exorcise the house. The priest marked with a cross the stones that had flown through the glass and tossed them back into the river, only for them to reappear inside the house the following day. For the villagers there could be no other explanation than that Eleanore, wilful and troublesome, was responsible. The villagers believed she had been seized by Dracu, the Devil, with the result that the commotion became so great she was forced to move in with her great-grandmother and cousin in a neighbouring village.

On her way there Eleanore found a coin and picked it up. She showed it to her older cousin, who warned her that according to old Romanian superstition all lost money was the Devil's money. Shrugging this off, and desperate for a treat, Eleanore spent the money on sweets and ate them alone. Finding out about this, her great-grandmother passed the word on that this selfish act was the Devil's work, and, following the customs of the day, hounded her into an asylum at the request of her family. As her story broke across Europe, it was picked up by Professor Fritz Grunewald, a Berlin mathematician, engineer and psychic researcher who decided to discover more about her.

He interviewed people connected to what was fast becoming a modern fable, managed to convince the teenager's father to release her from the asylum and was about to take the girl to Germany when he suddenly dropped dead. (Price valiantly added a dramatic lustre to the mundane in a later account by saying that the German's body 'lay in the hall of his flat in the Spandaerstrasse for twelve days before it was discovered', neglecting to say that the 41-year-old German was vastly overweight and had been suffering from heart disease for some time.)

On Grunewald's death, Eleanore was again at the mercy of a venomous crowd of villagers, and hated and despised by her family, who regarded her as nothing more than a pestilence. But she was rescued by Countess Wassilko-Sereki, a minor member of the nobility, a keen devotee and writer on the supernatural who was then living in Vienna.

The Countess took Eleanore to Austria and eventually adopted her. She maintained that Eleanore's problems were the result of incest and domestic rape, but stopped at naming a suspect. Whether this was speculation or an allegation by Eleanore she refused to say. She concluded that the teenager's strongest phenomena occurred around the time she was due to menstruate each month; Notzing, superstitious to his fingertips, attributed the phenomena to the full moon.

Invited to examine the case by his friend Professor Hans Thirring, Harry's first meeting with Eleanore was at the Countess's 'charming flat in the Josefstadterstrasse' on 1 May 1926. His first reaction when he saw her was full of contradiction. At first he extolled her as 'an intelligent, well developed, bright girl with a sunny disposition', then, in the next sentence, disagreed with himself, saying he found her to be 'more like a girl of eight, her shyness, her extreme fondness for simple toys, her simple games and childish ways'.

As the Countess and Harry watched the girl play with a toy gun randomly firing plastic balls around the room, one of the projectiles separated into two halves. Just as Wassilko-Sereki was about to snap the ball back together, a steel stiletto paperknife came from a doorway. Narrowly missing Price's head, it hit a door and fell on the floor. 'I instantly turned around and a minute investigation revealed nothing – and no one – that could have projected the stiletto.'

Back at the Countess's home each morning and night, Price claimed to witness greater trouble from what he presumed was a poltergeist. Soft toys bounced up and down, cushions slid slowly off chairs, spoons fell off tables, bite marks and stigmata appeared on Eleanore's body. He commented: 'After each of these phenomena, I examined the room, the furniture etc, but everything was normal. . . . I reiterate that there were no wires, threads, spring releases, rubber bands, compressed air tubes. Well, I was much impressed by what I had seen,' and though he did not explain why the Countess might be hiding a compressed air tube and presumably a generator under her soft furnishings, he invited her to accompany Eleanore to Kensington to take part in a series of experiments at the National Laboratory as part of her grand procession through Europe, where she demonstrated the phenomena to a host of savants, some professional, some worryingly amateur.

In London, the Countess read out a prepared statement telling assembled pressmen that her teenage charge had said 'The Devil has come with me to London. The Devil is very pleased to come to London, for he hopes to find plenty to do here.' Eleanore was immediately set to work.

At a welcoming event, paraded before guests at Queensberry Place who included members of the Magic Circle, the Honourable Everard Fielding, Edward Heron-Allen, William McDougall, Harvard University's eminent professor of psychology, Julian Huxley, as well as staff from the London mental asylum, Eleanore was given a tin clockwork cat to play with. Now, for the first time, the phenomena around her changed.

As she was winding up the tin toy, something hit her on the head. Price, closest to her, picked up the object and saw that it was a white magnetic enamelled letter 'L' which he recognised had come from a noticeboard in the reception area, four floors below.

After telephoning reception and discovering that no letters had disappeared from the board, his party made their way downstairs to investigate. In a tone of breathless excitement he added that:

Upon checking the unused letters we found that one was missing – the letter L. Only three persons in existence knew where the unused letters were kept. One of these was out and the other two, the typist and a youth employed in the library were actually in the library when the letter appeared in the laboratory.

It was a mystery worthy of his champion Sherlock Holmes. In Harry's stubborn view no one could possibly have had access to the letters because the box in which they were kept was known to so few people. He encouraged readers to make no allowance for the fact that both he and Lucy Kay worked late and could easily have cheated, seeking to impress an entourage largely made up of leading lights of the SPR.

Clephan Palmer, a staffer for the *Daily News*, disputed Price's telling of the event, saying that the letter dropped from the ceiling, bounced on Price's shoulder, and then tumbled to the floor. But Price disarmed the supposition that anyone was cheating and threw out another theory, probably a red herring, that 'there are theories that because the letter is magnetic it might have had some affinity for the girl, but I think this story is fantastic'.

If he was sanguine about the theory of magnetic letters sticking to her skin he was positively hawkish about her scratch and bite marks and the sudden appearance of stigmata. These were unaccountable, he told the *Daily Sketch*, and her injuries seemed to result from control from an alien and evil power.[13]

The last day of Eleanore's stay in London ended with her meeting a group of people that included the spirited populariser of philosophy Cyril Joad, the Head of the Department of Philosophy and Psychology at Birkbeck College,

London, and Professor Richard Tillyard, a New Zealand biologist. The meeting was interesting, but nothing outwardly unusual happened until both men travelled home by train to their respective homes. While reading a new book he had bought that day Joad found that some of the pages had been left uncut. Taking out his penknife he discovered to his surprise that the knife was tightly banded with a metal letter 'C', just like the letter 'L' Price said had fallen on Eleanore's head. It was so tightly welded to the knife that he only managed to remove it later with a hammer and chisel. Tillyard had a similar experience as he was reading a copy of Professor Julian Huxley's *Essays of a Biologist*. Again, pages of his book were uncut and taking out his pocket knife, he discovered that it had been encircled by a metal letter 'C', rendering it unusable.[14]

Price could not explain this extraordinary coincidence, though W.H. Salter, a member of the SPR's Council, caustically remarked that it was such a strange coincidence 'that Dr Joad and Professor Tillyard should both have experiences so strikingly familiar on the same occasion. Difficulties and discrepancies such as these are the despair of the psychical researcher.' Harry, on his part, continued to ponder over her bites, rashes and stigmata, putting them down to an obsession: 'we tried to eradicate it without success. The painful weals, teeth marks and scarifying that she experienced were more than a match for our logic.'

After London, the Countess and Eleanore took in various other cities, such as Berlin, Nuremberg and Munich, where they visited leading parapsychologists, and while in Munich, the EMELKA film company recorded a documentary about her. When the tour ended, Eleanore, now largely unwanted, found her problems decreased and soon disappeared completely. She stayed with the Countess for one more year, before she was bundled back to her homeland, where she began work as a hairdresser.

In time, her story was re-examined. Psychiatrists very quickly diagnosed her to be suffering from an acute psychological disorder, largely brought on by the accusations and paranoia surrounding her from a young, impressionable age; also, and by coincidence, her skin was hypersensitive. In this Price had been partly correct, but it was nothing to do with anything of a psychic or supernatural nature. Independent investigators found it difficult to explain how various letters of the alphabet followed Eleanore around – curiously, only while she was at the National Laboratory under the director's control.

Just after Eleanore had left London, a mighty row blew up in the pages of *Nature* magazine following a lecture at the NLPR by Dr Richard Tillyard, who maintained that 'scientific men were afraid to study psychical research because they would be persecuted by their colleagues'. We can detect Harry's fingerprints on this statement – it was a phrase he had used often in the past to excite opinion in the press. When A.A. Campbell Swinton, the television pioneer and Fellow of the Royal Society, wrote a meaty letter to *Nature* accusing Price of concocting stories that had nothing to do with psychical research and of calling his research body the National Laboratory of Psychic Science so that it should be confused with the National Physical Laboratory, Price, apoplectic with rage, responded by claiming that Swinton was guilty of a 'lack of intelligence or gross carelessness. Both organisations are engaged in an endeavour to increase the sum total of the world's knowledge by scientific means.'

It was an argument that would rumble on for several months, and led to much resentment towards the NLPR. Harry eventually bowed out by disclaiming any responsibility for inviting Tillyard to speak, although of course he had.

If there had been ups and downs that year, at least the laboratory had been kept busy. Occult lectures, one of which was chaired by Britain's foremost counsel, Sir Edward Marshall-Hall KC, were sold out, but in the early part of 1927 it saw virtually no activity, and experiments had drawn more or less to a halt. Investors and members of the council were getting itchy feet and they looked in vain for evidence of psychical phenomena moving forwards. Price knew he had to keep the impetus moving, and eventually came up with a crafty counter-intuitive piece of marketing.

He decided to give the public a kind of studio theatre. It would be a performance of frank sensationalism worth witnessing as an event in itself, irrespective of whether anyone believed in what was being promoted; and it all centred on a rosy-cheeked farmer's daughter from Devon.

In 1792, following her mother's death, Joanna Southcott, a Baptist, was seized by a mystical fervour and began to pour out spite towards the ungodly in the form of tracts. These were turbulent years in Britain. The French Revolution had electrified British observers over the Channel and for many it looked like the end of 2,000 years of Christian civilisation. In a society where most drew their entire frame of reference from the Bible, political events appeared to be the realisation of the Book of Revelation. These biblical warnings saw people focus their attention on the prophets, and Joanna became the starting point of this new time.

She had travelled to London at the invitation of the engraver William Sharp, and published religious pamphlets with the similar stark warning: if the country dared to ignore her visions it would face an apocalyptic doom. In 1813, now aged 64, the prophetess told her public she was pregnant with a new messiah called Shiloh.

Expectation and Joanna's girth grew, but fatally, after a gestation period of eleven months, she fell ill with depression. Though some of her followers became disillusioned, the inner core never lost their faith, believing Shiloh had been born as Joanna had suggested, on Christmas Day in the afternoon, and that the baby had gone to Heaven, to save him from the Devil.

After a short illness, Joanna died at four in the morning on 27 December 1814 – ironically, the day the Christian Church celebrates the life of St John the Evangelist, author of the Book of Revelation. Her followers waited three days for what they thought would be her undoubted resurrection before turning her blackened, putrefying body over to the Royal Physician, Dr Reece, for a post-mortem. He discovered her pregnancy was nothing more than dropsy, the abnormal swelling of the body because of water retention; her followers buried her at St John's Wood Cemetery in London.

Southcott left a legacy of sixty-five published works as well as manuscripts and letters. God had also commanded her to keep some of her writings secret in a 'simple box, nailed and bound with strong rope', with the instruction that it could only be opened at a time of dire national emergency, and then in the presence of twenty-four bishops of the Church of England – the number of the twenty-four elders mentioned in the Book of Revelation.

After the First World War a vicar's wife recruited twelve female apostles and founded the Panacea Society, a sort of Maidens of the Lost Ark Society, who campaigned for the real box's opening, but failed to convince twenty-four bishops of its importance. Almost every newspaper in Britain had its own version of an 'eerie scene in a London room' when the box was supposedly found in Hammersmith. Opened in the presence of a paltry five witnesses, it was found to contain a copy of the New Testament, a wisp of silvery hair, a piece of old, torn parchment bearing a document allegedly written by Joanna, and a brass medallion.

A few years later a group of Cambridge University students taking part in a rag-week stunt attempted to open a box in front of a surprised public; but this was clearly a hoax.

That was the last anyone heard of anything resembling the true article until a slightly damp 'bulky-metal-bound walnut coffer' was mysteriously deposited at the National Laboratory on the morning of 28 April 1927, together with a letter written two days previously on Carlton Hotel headed notepaper.

Price wrote that the first time he saw the box was when he arrived for work one morning and Lucy Kay had yelled out, 'Joanna Southcott's box has arrived!' The box had had a curious journey to the address in Kensington. According to Harry, 'a gentleman of the name of Mr F' (he refused ever to reveal his identity) had been staying at the Carlton Hotel and had the previous day left for New York. In a letter addressed to him, the mysterious Mr F set out the box's unsubstantiated history.

After a couple of routine sentences explaining how difficult it had been to dispose of the box, Mr F claimed that he had employed two servants, both of whom were the children of a woman named Rebecca Pengarth, who had served as the sole companion of Joanna Southcott from 1798 until her death in the spring of 1814. On her deathbed Joanna had entrusted the box to Rebecca and exhorted that it should 'be opened only in the time of dire national need and in the presence of twenty-four bishops but only if they had recognised the box's importance'.

Rebecca had sworn an oath that in no circumstances would she allow the box to be opened except under the required conditions. Fifteen years after Joanna's death Rebecca married a Welshman named Morgan, by whom she had four children, the last surviving being John, who died in 1925 aged 81. John, Mr F's old family retainer, had inherited the box from his mother. On his deathbed he insisted that Mr F should take it and do what was right with it. Breathing his last, he managed to utter the immortal phrase, 'Don't forget the bishops.'

As Mr F had decided to emigrate and never return to Britain, he naturally decided the only resting place for his inheritance would be the NLPR. According to his letter to Price, which no one else ever saw, Mr F conveniently wanted neither publicity nor thanks, and definitely no correspondence.

Harry examined the box and, certain that it bore all the hallmarks of authenticity, validated Mr F's claims. Of course, this flew in the face of all logic: no one had heard of the mysterious Rebecca Morgan (née Pengarth), the box was quite unlike the 3ft original, which weighed 156 pounds compared to Price's 12 by 9in matchbox which tipped the scales at a diminutive 11lb. For a man of keen critical faculties he was oddly blasé about the box's statistics.

Nevertheless, within fifteen minutes he had knocked out a press release telling the newspapers of the find and his decision to have the box both X-rayed and psychometrised by a leading trio of mediums including Eileen Garrett, Stella Cranshaw and the trance medium Claire Cantlon. *The Times* stated that the 'proceedings that followed were not without excitement and interest'. If anything, the newspaper underplayed the event; scientists and reporters were agog to see what the box contained, and had besieged the laboratory.

On 28 June Price wrote a letter to Rachel Fox, the then president of the Panacea Society, setting out his intention to open the sealed box at 8 a.m. at the Hoare Memorial Hall in Church House, Westminster, on Monday 11 July 1927, since

> the Council . . . believe this is a good opportunity of disposing of all existing Joanna Southcott boxes and they therefore extend a cordial invitation to your Association to have the so-called 'Great Box' opened at the same time. A similar invitation is, by public advertisement, being extended to all owners of Southcott Sealed Boxes.

Clearly, Harry was hedging his bets. It is not hard to see what he was up to, since having the original box would have created more mayhem than the shadowy Mr F's totem. He hoped all eighty bishops and three archbishops from England and Wales would answer his call to show up, dressed in purple, at Westminster Hall even though his council had 'a natural reluctance to violating the definite wishes of a dying woman no matter how misguided', and therefore preferred to 'open the box in circumstances as nearly as possible in accordance with her dying injunction'. Only the elderly suffragan Bishop of Grantham, Dr John Hine, decided to go along, 'just out of curiosity', while the suffragan Bishop of Crediton, realising that there was some fun to be had, sent his 35-year-old son, the Reverend Trefusis, a curate, in his place.

The finale on 11 July was a playful rival to Armageddon. There had been violent thunderstorms and torrential rain that day. Fingers of lightning flashed around Westminster and the power cuts across London plunged the city into darkness at least three times. Such eeriness did not escape the *Evening Standard*. The scene in the City, it wrote, was a 'most remarkable one as darkness developed'.

The ceremony had aroused extraordinary interest among the public and the world's press, so much so that the adverse weather did not stop a large turnout. The opening was presided over by a youthful Professor Archibald Montgomery Low, physicist and inventor of the vibrometer, who made a humorous remark on mass psychology and the madness of crowds, with special reference to the 'particular form of lunacy known as the Southcott movement'.

Edward H. Hunt, a member of the NLPR and the LSA, gave an hour's lecture on Joanna Southcott and her sealed box of prophecies, despite the booing and jeering from the hostile faithful, who had paid a 3s 6d entrance fee for the privilege.

Finally, at 9 p.m., an hour later than planned but in plenty of time to catch the later editions of the next day's newspapers, the metal bands on the box and the wax seals were broken. The elderly Dr Hine delved into the casket and handed each item to Harry Price, who described the objects with the enthusiasm of someone reading out the FA Cup fifth round draw.

In what *The Times* described as 'an atmosphere of humorous scepticism' the bishop handed Price a strange medley of bric-a-brac: a rusty horse pistol, a dice-box, a bead bag containing several coins, a puzzle, a pair of earrings, a printed diary from 1715, a dusty copy of Ovid's *Metamorphoses*, two religious pamphlets, a Jubilee Medal of 1791, a thin booklet called *The Remarkable Prophecies and Predictions for the Year 1796* by Don Johannes Gautier, followed by numerous other items of absolutely no use in saving a nation from peril. The audience was in hysterics, and the Bishop of Grantham was moved to utter: 'I have always been interested but it is not very illuminating, is it?' As reporters rushed away to file their story, thus ended the well-staged sensation of the year.

Mary Robertson, a Southcottian historian, wrote a letter to the liberal *Daily News* a day after the event saying that the opening of the box 'with its absurd contents, should not receive any serious consideration from the public. . . . Joanna's box is made of "common wood", is not ark-shaped, bears no mother-of-pearl escutcheon, and is of a peculiar construction in that it is threefold – the original, that of Joanna being in the centre.'

Even a cursory glance at Harry's claims should suggest that without detailed information, identity and provenance no one could intercept Mr F or follow up his story. It is an implausible tale that has been taken seriously for nearly eight decades, but then so was his claim that someone robbed him of his silver ingot and gold coins. Price was the person who benefited most from this palpable fake, of course. He had drawn the world's press to the front door of the NLPR; he had a sly nod in the direction of the Southcottians, whom he dismissed as a bunch of swivel-eyed fools; his reputation, after the opening, soared above the more disciplined psychic researchers who were willing to take painstaking care and put hours of laborious study into their investigations.

The biggest insight into the stunt came from a hint Price himself gave his readers: 'The public has always been fascinated with mysterious boxes: one has only to possess a box with a history and one immediately becomes a headliner. If it happens to be a locked box, so much the better. Several boxes have created sensations.'[15] As for the Southcott faithful, they believe that the real Southcott treasure rests in Bedford, where at 8 Albany Road (which they say is built on the original Garden of Eden), in a house close to local amenities and within easy reach of local schools, a box awaits the Second Coming of Christ.

6

BEHIND THE SCENES AT QUEENSBERRY PLACE

Helped by the enormous exposure of the opening of his fake Southcott box, Price was commissioned to write a series of articles for the *Sunday Chronicle* on a range of psychical issues; what he actually wrote, however, turned out to be scathing attacks on spiritualism – an extension of his lectures about the credulity of Sir Oliver Lodge and Conan Doyle.

If 1927 had been a year of happiness and success for Price, the tables would turn rapidly in 1928, a year of uncertain happenings and hidden transforming forces.

In one of his *Chronicle* articles, he mentioned the husband-and-wife team of Mr and Mrs Thompson, two Wild West materialising mediums who had fooled Sir Arthur Conan Doyle into believing that his mother, Mary, had appeared at one of their seances; and how, at a particularly emotional moment, Doyle had rushed forward, embraced her and begun to babble about how much he missed her.[1] Soon realising that his mother was a good foot taller than the spirit in the room, Doyle composed himself, realised the seance was nothing but a poor display of adult-sized puppets and angrily banished the Thompsons from his life. Naturally, this was something of a sore issue for him, and he later called the duplicitous couple 'palpable humbugs'.

On seeing the *Chronicle* article Doyle wrote Price a stinging letter of rebuke, saying he should never make any mention of the Thompsons in his writing or talks.

Harry replied that he did not; all he had done in his lectures was show his audiences a photograph of Mr and Mrs Thompson, rally against commercialism and proclaim that mediums should keep themselves free from human vanity and the desire to show off.

Contemporary press cuttings of Price's lectures put a more malign spin on this episode. The *Brighton & Hove Herald*, under the headline 'Mediums and their Ways: The Wiles of the Wizard', wrote:

The audience listened with keen interest to descriptions of how famous slate-writing mediums and 'materialising' mediums perform their feats. The latter class of medium has a horror of being gripped. In this connection, Mr Price related how police officials unmasked some American mediums who pretended to 'bring back' Sir Arthur Conan Doyle's mother. Among numerous articles discovered were a black silk cloth for imitating a coat, phosphorescent buttons, a trumpet and a 'spirit piano' – a clever mechanical device.

Two weeks after this piece appeared Doyle criticised Price for his negative stance on mediums and spiritualism at a London reception in honour of Johannes Jensen. The speech was reported in the next day's newspapers and incited Harry to retort with a calm letter to his hero, saying that his articles in the *Sunday Chronicle* had not been anti-spiritualistic: 'On the contrary I have gone out of my way to placate the Spiritualists who are my very good friends.'

Doyle ignored this 'shambling guarantee' and in his response emphasised the part Price had played in the fall of William Hope and the slur he had brought on Hope's twenty years of splendid work. In a crescendo of anger, Doyle further accused Price of denouncing Mrs Deane's artful footballers photograph. 'These offences are the more serious because you and your Laboratory are, in a sense, the guest of a Spiritualistic body.'

Clearly upset and believing he was becoming an increasingly mocked part of the occult landscape, Doyle instructed the LSA's solicitors to look over the National Laboratory's tenancy agreement to see if there was any way in which they could expel Price from his rooms. The lawyers soon reached the conclusion that although the NLPR's tenancy contract 'was a most unsatisfactory document' nothing could be done to cancel it and that Price should be allowed to keep his rooms at Queensberry Place.[2]

There the matter rested until *Light* published another of Doyle's letters singling out Price's penchant for writing spiritualist black propaganda. The dispute became more spiteful still in August, when the *Revue Metapsychique* carried a full report of one of Harry's lectures in Paris that again mentioned the Thompson couple.

Usually a passive, thoughtful man, Doyle could contain his anger no longer, and spat an instruction to Mercy Phillimore to call the attention of his council to the fact that Price was attacking

many of our mediums in a most gross way. Among other things, he repeats a story against myself, which he knows to be a lie for I have already contradicted it when he told it before. The object of a page or so of the article is to hold me up to clumsy ridicule.

I suggest that every possible means shall be adopted to get rid of Mr Price as a tenant. The mere fact that he acts in such a way would, I should think, offer a legal reason. I feel strongly upon the subject – indeed my own position as President demands such an action . . .[3]

Harry too went on the attack. 'Your letter to *Light*,' he told Doyle, 'is full of, to put it very mildly indeed, spiteful inaccuracies.' He went on to state that in future he would read out the story about Doyle and his mother at his lectures, letting his 'audience judge the matter for themselves', which represented a climb-down of sorts.[4] Then, in a later letter, he waved a literary fist at Doyle, taunting him that 'even your own followers regard most of your doings and sayings as a joke'.

The LSA publicly requested Price to stop 'the unseemly battle' between Doyle and himself and threatened to 'look very carefully' at his rental agreement. But what they said to him and among themselves was entirely different. Dawson Rogers, the LSA's fashionable liberal lawyer, who in his day job got involved in all the sensational cases involving attacks on the Establishment, told the LSA early on in the affair that 'to raise legal questions of tenancy based upon the perverted policy or lack of taste on Mr Price's part might . . . be best avoided'. They simply had to stick it out in the hope the two protagonists would find common ground or that something might come along to take their minds off the matter.[5]

They did not have long to wait. On 16 June the LSA was raided by the police, who arrested Mrs Claire Cantlon, one of the three mediums who had psychometrised Joanna Southcott's box, on charges of necromancy. They also handcuffed Mercy Phillimore, and charged her with aiding and abetting Mrs Cantlon. It was an unprecedented scene. Twenty police officers armed with truncheons barricaded the doors of Queensberry Place as if they were raiding an American speakeasy. It was the first time the police had raided a recognised spiritualist society; and it would be the last. It also capped the long saga of spite between Sir Arthur and Harry Price.

The police raid so angered Doyle that he switched his mind to helping the two defendants in the case – one of the strangest of the twentieth century and one that shocked the normally sedate gatherings of spiritualists, who saw it as an attack on their faith, and who elicited a wave of public sympathy after accusing the police of entrapment.

Detective Inspector Walter Burnaby of Scotland Yard had been anonymously tipped off about the activities of a fraudulent medium. He investigated the accusation by sending in two plain-clothes policewomen, Inspector Lilian Wyles and WPC Violet Ritchie, together with a civilian. They each had a sitting with Mrs Cantlon, who consequently gave them 'ideas of their futures'.

The Home Secretary, William Joynson Hicks, prosecuted Cantlon under Section 4 of the Vagrancy [fortune-telling] Act of 1824, which stated that 'every Person pretending or professing to tell Fortunes, or using any subtle Crafts, Means or Device, by Palmistry or otherwise, to deceive and impose on any of His Majesty's subjects . . . shall be deemed a Rogue and Vagabond, within the true Intent and Meaning of this Act'.

The show trial was heard at Westminster Police Court over three days that sticky summer, on 11, 18 and 24 July. By mid-morning on the first day the road outside the court thronged with people clamouring for space inside. Both defendants entered a formal plea of not guilty, though Mrs Cantlon later pleaded guilty to a technical offence under the same act.

The stipendiary magistrate William Oulton heard from Cantlon's expensive defence counsel Peter Bullock KC (provided by Sir Arthur Conan Doyle) that she had not been telling fortunes but simply relating back images she had seen; she had been in a trance and therefore knew nothing of what she was saying or what was happening around her – a truly dazzling defence. In outlining their evidence, the prosecution heard that all three witnesses had had fruitless sittings with Mrs Cantlon, who repeatedly asked them leading questions throughout each seance.

Inspector Wyles informed the bench that Mrs Cantlon had related that her spirit control, a 400-year-old Red Indian called White Chief, had described 'the spirit of a little boy named Alec or perhaps Eric who had his white rabbit with him'. Then, in a loud voice exactly the same as her own but using the full extent of her lung power, she described an old man of noble appearance named William, also an aunt, Ellen or Eleanor. Inspector Wyles had no aunt, alive or dead, answering to the name or description given, and did not recognise the old man. Wittering on and desperately casting around for names, in a voice described in court as one 'which might be used by an amateur actress attempting to play a French part', Mrs Cantlon's spirit guide asked Miss Wyles what her sister looked like, only to be told she was an only child. Next Mrs Cantlon told the policewoman that she was getting a 'man with a large nose. It could be your husband. He is a tall, dark man, with blue or hazel eyes. He is temperamental and Irish and you have recently parted? Do not worry about this because you will be soon reconciled to each other. He was so pleased about the baby.'

In a terrific piece of underplay and to loud guffaws in court, Miss Wyles told Mrs Cantlon, in what was fast becoming a fiasco of a sitting, that she had said, 'I am afraid White Hawk is quite wrong there, because I am single and there are a large number of babies in the family. He must be very mixed up.' After a long silence, Mrs Cantlon asked the policewoman if she had ever had a pipe burst on her. Then, after a further silence, she asked the time and told the witness that her power was going and she had to stop for tea, though she could give her another ten minutes if she liked, but finished anyway and rushed off for a cup of Earl Grey and a bun or two.

Sir Arthur Conan Doyle and Sir Oliver Lodge mitigated on behalf of the defendants but could not excuse Mrs Cantlon's spectacular flop of a seance. Doyle lost no time in launching a tirade at the police, protesting in court that they should not be employed upon such a matter, especially as their activities took the hateful shape of agents provocateurs.

The trial took a more confusing route when the stipendiary magistrate allowed Sir Ernest Bennett, a Labour MP, lawyer and vice-president of the LSA, to sit with him during part of the trial to explain mediumistic terms and jargon. In delivering judgment Mr Oulton, with a healthy sense of humour, told the court that:

Three witnesses have testified to the telling of the future by Mrs Cantlon by occult means.

Mrs Cantlon has pleaded guilty; Miss Phillimore has pleaded not guilty. I may say at once that I am of opinion that both defendants are guilty. I give Mrs Cantlon the benefit of the doubt, as she believed she was under the control of this defunct Indian chief, but I should strongly advise Mrs

Cantlon to get rid of a disembodied spirit who wants to know the time when the hour of lunch or tea approaches.

The summonses in both cases will be dismissed under the Probation of Offenders Act, and the costs (£30) will be apportioned: £20 for Miss Phillimore, £10 for Mrs Cantlon.

Price offered no comment on the Cantlon case until some time after the trial; and when he did he was careful to feign an unconvincing indifference.

We do not know the identity of the person who tipped off the police, but the timing of Mrs Cantlon's arrest and the police raid was so opportune that it is hard to believe that Price was not responsible. He certainly had both motive and opportunity, and there can be no doubt that he was ruthless and devious enough to follow his plan through. He had much to gain in a year when the LSA had threatened to take away his cherished laboratory.

Barely a week seemed to go by without some new development to bring Harry renewed difficulty; and when things seemed at their blackest, Lucy Kay amazed him by announcing that she was pregnant. There are plenty of signs that Lucy knew who the father of her future child was, and although we cannot say for certain that it was Harry, letters and strong circumstantial evidence, such as blandishments of large sums of money, make him the obvious candidate.

Despite the fact that well-meaning gossips would undoubtedly have spoken of the pair's closeness, Lucy kept the existence of her baby secret all her life. She never spoke about the affair to anyone but close members of her family, and her third son, David Meeker, only discovered his half-brother's existence while researching his mother's life. In an age when the mother of an illegitimate child was denigrated and shunned, this was a story that had to be hushed up. Harry and Lucy both recognised that it would be impossible for her to care for her son, whom she had named Ian, and so application was made to the National Children's Adoption Agency to find a suitable foster family.

Naturally, Harry was asked to give a reference. When the Association's secretary asked his opinion as to whether Lucy was a suitable mother, he wrote back that 'despite her present circumstances I have always found her to be a moral person'. As Ethel Beenham, his second secretary, was typing out the reference (Lucy was on maternity leave), Harry turned and told her that 'the son of Colgate toothpaste is the father of Lucy's baby'.[6] It is a most unlikely suggestion, but if the toothpaste heir was the father, it makes no sense that later in life Lucy never mentioned him in any of the intimate letters she sent Price and why she continually hung on to Harry for money. Happily, the baby boy later found a family life with a Harry Trent and his wife, who lived at 46 Shrewsbury Lane, in Plumstead.

It is a measure of how fond he was of her that Price altered the spelling of Lucy's first name and surname, so that from the middle of 1929 her name changed from being Lucy Kay to Lucie Kaye. The extension that once appeared on Stella Cranshaw's surname now appeared on that of his new girlfriend.

In the midst of this turmoil, Harry still managed to explore the realms of the occult and publish volume one of the NLPR's colossal *Short Title Catalogue*, a 422-page jaunt through his library. Its main purpose, he whimsically claimed, 'was to assist the serious investigator in detecting psychical imposters, at the same time enabling him to recognise a genuine phenomenon if and when he sees it' – but it is hard to see this encyclopedia as anything more than a gigantic excuse to illustrate the contents of his library, at no cost to himself.

Among the more fantastic cases of suspect phenomena he examined around this time were the haunting of a girl's pram in Hampstead and a 19-year-old woman named Dolores who 'apported' a set of false teeth. There was also the case of the American medium Amy Smith, who produced a mouthful of foamy white ectoplasm, which smelt strongly of peppermint, before being sick. Always willing to go that extra mile in search of the truth, Price said he exactly reproduced the effect by chewing half a tube of toothpaste, though there was no mention of whether he used a tube of Colgate.

The most prominent reported haunting that year was the less than mysterious case at a small villa in Eland Road, Lavender Hill, Battersea, which the press had uniquely dubbed the Battersea Poltergeist Case. The story was some months old when Harry first investigated the violent disturbances at the house. He already knew that the rackety owner of the villa, the 86-year-old invalid Henry Robinson, had been moved to the local rest home at the request of his 27-year-old son Frank. Henry had lived in the house all his life, as had his son and three daughters, Lillah, Kate and Eleanor, who still lived at the house with her 13-year-old son.

The police had been called to the villa on numerous occasions, usually because windows at the back of the property had been smashed – some of the activity was blamed on a nearby convalescent home that was largely inhabited by men who had served in the First World War.

Harry paid his first visit to the house on 9 January at 9.30 a.m. to join the family at breakfast. Armed with his portable ghost-hunting bag – containing soft felt slippers, measuring tape, screw eyes, a hank of flex, an assortment of batteries, flash bulbs, notebook, string, chalk, flask of brandy, bowl of mercury, bandages and surgical tape – he found that a mysterious aggressive force had hurled a variety of objects through the windows obliterating china ornaments in the front parlour. He noted the damage in red, blue and black pencil, and returned to the laboratory.

Later that same day he made his second visit, along with a reporter from the *Evening Standard*. There had also been 'great activity amongst the furniture': chairs had marched down the hall in single file and then bunched themselves together on the dining table, making it difficult for the family to eat a meal. Objects had been thrown about both inside and outside the house with terrific force. Pieces of coal, potatoes, pennies, stones, red-hot cinders, lumps of sugar and soda came down in showers. An investigating policeman had his helmet knocked off by a piece of coal and subsequently arrested Frank Robinson under the Lunacy Act, detaining him in an asylum for several days for his own safety, since he was suspected of starting the phenomena.

This came as a surprise to Harry: after all, he told the *Standard*, the house was a typical poltergeist haunt and these upsets 'were quite out of the reach of any human agency'. He was certain that there was some connection between poltergeists and puberty and the mysteries of sex, which enter largely into poltergeist doings:

All the available evidence points to the fact that Poltergeists prefer little girls and girl adolescents to boys – the ratio is about 95% to 5% respectively. Though we know there is this connection, we cannot explain it.

He also believed that poltergeists were attracted to soap.[7]

It was after reading this theory that the *Daily Express* rang to ask Price if they could let a medium named Miss X, 'the daughter of a well-known professional man', search the house to see if she could work out what might be causing the disturbances. Miss X made her search, and, feeling cold and miserable, she gave up and returned home. In the next few days Henry Robinson died. His family sold the house and suddenly the haunting ceased.

Several people, particularly investigators from the SPR, were convinced that the haunting was the work of the Robinson family, though William Salter, in his book *Zoar or the Evidence for Psychical Research Concerning Survival*, pointed to 'a freelance investigator'; in other words, Harry Price.[8]

In public at least, Harry was satisfied that the disturbance was caused by the family having suffered a severe shock that had somehow sucked them into the vortex of a violent poltergeist disturbance. Thanks to the systematic way Price kept most of his correspondence, however, a letter in his archive shows that in private he was of a different opinion altogether. In a letter to the theologian Sir Arnold Lunn – who had read about the case in Price's *Confessions of a Ghost Hunter*, a book he reviewed for the Catholic weekly *The Universe* – he revealed that the Robinsons were trying to move their father out of the house in order to sell it; but, he continued, 'unfortunately, I am permitted only to write nice things about people'. It was acceptable in Harry's mind to invent anything he liked, so long as it was uncritical.[9]

With little happening at the National Laboratory to greatly occupy him, and short of cash, Price recognised that a closer relationship between the NLPR and an organisation that was sympathetic to his work would be really useful to him; the problem was, how should he go about it?

7

THE GRATIFICATION OF
PERSONAL SPITE

It was clearly time for the National Laboratory to find a new way of going forward. Harry thought he had found a solution in trying to offload his entire library of 16,000 books to the British Museum, a deal that came unstuck only after the museum realised they had half the titles already and proposed to sell off the duplicates – the bibliophile Price refused.

There was a pall of gloom hanging over the top floor of 16 Queensberry Place in 1929 as Harry set about writing an article for the laboratory's *Journal* that he hoped would go some way to repairing ruined friendships.

In the January/February edition he had written a long feature headlined 'A Plea for a Better Understanding', with the sardonic subtitle, 'A Seasonable Effort to Repair Some Shattered Friendships'.[1] There were diagrams showing how the world's fifteen leading psychic societies related to each other, and coloured circles to show how serious the various bodies were in accepting the supernatural, and whether there was a lack of trust between them – the darker the shade the more untrustworthy, in Harry's slanted view, the organisation.

He was penitent: he had done some things wrongly, but he also castigated the laboratory's doubters. The world of psychical research was increasingly competitive, he claimed, and had to change to survive. The golden age was over.

The atmosphere of mutual tolerance was helpful in that it allowed some researchers to share research data, but there were too many separate bodies chasing the same mediums, the same patrons and the same money. Price made the automatic assumption that if the NLPR did not take the lead and administer the remainder of researchers, psychic science would ultimately die.

Seemingly forgetting his seasonal message of goodwill, he painted a most unflattering portrait of what was happening in the sectarian world of his hidden discipline:

I wonder how many of my readers are aware of the number of squabbles, petty jealousies and open feuds that are taking place amongst those investigating psychic phenomena.

Quarrels, backbiting, lawsuits, sharp-practice, scandal mongering, the gratification of spite, these things are rampant, to the detriment of the science of psychical research and a paralysing drag on the wheel of progress . . . there is evidence of jealousy, snobbery, cupidity, amazing credulity, personal spite, inordinate love of self, the desire for kudos, private quarrels and mutual criticism are some of the causes for the friction.

Harry dismissed the notion that the cause of this upset had anything to do with a collision of religious beliefs; all the problems, in his eyes, were the result of poor communication. One anonymous organisation (undoubtedly the SPR) had made him very cross because they had failed to deliver a promised lecture; another had tried to notch up a victory against him, but he had retaliated with rather more success. The article castigated all but three researchers. Those who escaped the literary axe were Lord Charles Hope – 'because I am not aware that he is at loggerheads with anyone – except perhaps a few mediums of doubtful reputation' (and at that stage Hope was paying for the majority of the laboratory's experiments) – Dr Eugène Osty, Director of the Paris Institut Metapsychique, and Harry's friend and mentor Albert Schrenk-Notzing, who had died from acute appendicitis shortly after the *Journal* was published.

In the same edition Harry penned a peculiar article about how he had visited the catacombs of St Agnes and St Calixtus at Rome in September the previous year. He and Lucy had gone to Italy at the invitation of Dr Emilio Servadio, editor of the psychist magazine *Luce e Ombra* (Light and Shadow), and while there Price arranged for the 'luminous wonder of Naples', Pasquale Erto, to visit the National Laboratory later that year.[2] A chemist by profession, Erto was one of the very few mediums to appear completely nude in the seance room, and was famous for producing sparks that at times shot out of his rectum. On later analysis, the sparks were found to be caused by Erto hiding iron filings up his backside, which he sometimes managed to rather painfully ignite by vigorously rubbing his buttocks together.

When he first appeared at the laboratory Erto (or Eric, as Price preferred to call him) tried to undress Harry as if in a trance, but mercifully stopped when he started to unbutton his trousers. Soon after, he went into a deep trance, which did not reach its climax until the room was in total darkness. Then, according to Price, he immediately began to 'groan, moan, gasp, growl and hit a chair with great violence, hit himself and bark like a dog, roar like a lion, choke as if suffocated, mutter ma-ma-ma-ma-ma, shout, shriek and scream'.[3]

Erto's usual manifestations of famous entities, some of which included an intriguing meeting between a naked Pope Leo III and Charlemagne at Paderborn, never materialised. Instead, there were sudden sharp flashes of light, pinpricks of luminosity – some observers even saw flames licking around the Italian's body. Just as Harry was to subject him to a close examination with a 2lb magnet the medium fell to the floor and began another session of moaning and writhing. When he finally stopped, now sweating profusely, Price made a sweep of Erto's body using the metal lure, but found no evidence of trickery.

Arriving at the laboratory the next morning, Price claimed to have found the floor sparkling with a dusting of ferro-cerenium (used as the flint in cigarette lighters) which, he said, 'formed a very unsatisfactory ending to a very spectacular seance'. He had come to the conclusion that 'undoubtedly the man was a showman but not a medium. He returned to the land of sun, sin and spaghetti, where I understand he is still scintillating.'[4]

Before their Italian sojourn, Lucy Kay had written to Price asking if they could visit the Basilica Agnese Fuori le Mura at Via Nomentana, where St Agnes's headless body is buried. After the event, Harry could not help but turn the visit into the story of how he had used an anonymous local clairvoyant to test the emanations of millions of Christians who were buried there. In his usual breathless style he described the medium as being 'in a state of ecstatic exaltation' and was amazed to hear of her visions and her account of St Agnes's life, which was completely at odds with the traditional view held by the Catholic Church – it was almost spiritualistic in its context. The medium told the couple the exact spot, by the side of the Via Appia, where St Agnes had buried a chest full of golden ornaments, and which only awaited finding by a lucky archaeologist.

This low-cost tourist farce and the plea for repairing broken friendships were written largely to appeal to the LSA and Conan Doyle before Price approached them with his idea of forming a partnership.

To help the matter along, Price had intimated his belief that survival after death was proved by his curious trip to Rome, but he was cautious about putting the statement in print, a point which Sir Arthur focused on when he wrote to Mercy Phillimore asking if 'Mr Price would be prepared to put in black and white his statement that he now accepts Survival as being proved'.[5]

The word back from the Price camp was the curious 'he thought he might', but that he would not want to 'rub it in', though he went so far as to repeat his belief at a private lecture he gave to the LSA in March. Doyle thought the issue of disclosure was a major sticking point, but realised there was substantial room for manoeuvre. In the event, the terms of the new agreement were that Price would surrender his title of Honorary Director of the NLPR. He would no longer be the publisher of the *Journal* but would continue as Research Director of a new research committee, a group headed up by Doyle. The proposal went to a special subcommittee in mid-April, but was turned down, perhaps not surprisingly given Price's recent truculent behaviour towards the organisation's president.

Sadly, these events were to spell the end of the laboratory's principal magazine. The fact that the plans were so quickly discarded suggests Price had never seen them as part of a grand plan he would adopt if the LSA refused him. This is also supported by the fact that after the death of Schrenk-Notzing Price travelled to Munich to conduct a seance with Rudi Schneider, Willi's brother. The seance took place in the apartment of Karl Amereller, who was both Schneider's employer (he worked as a mechanic) and had designed various electrical controls for Schrenk-Notzing's experiments with mediums. There and then Price offered Rudi a contract to appear in a series of six exhaustive tests at 16 Queensberry Place, which dismisses the thought of a quick handover to Paris.

Price had had several sittings with Rudi before Notzing's death and said he had two aims in inviting him to Kensington. One was to settle once and for all the genuineness of his mediumship. Rudi had been analysed any number of times by European and American psychical researchers before his visit to London, and most viewed his gifts as debatable. The second was to inform the press, which, Price later claimed, managed to rescue 'the science from the mire of charlatanry in which it has been wallowing for generations'.

While in Germany Harry wasted no time in courting the blonde, blue-eyed psychologist Gerda Walther, Notzing's former personal assistant and now Rudi's chaperone, persuading both her and Dr Hans Driesch, professor of philosophy at Leipzig University, to take up unpaid posts at the laboratory.

Walther was a useful contact, having a wide network of friends, which included noted academics such as Sigmund Freud, Edith Stein, Carl Jung and Martin Heidegger. Like Walther, Driesch was an enthusiastic supporter of Price's attempt to adopt psychic phenomena as a new science involving psychology, and backed his idea of thinning out the number of quasi-psychical organisations. In a heartfelt letter congratulating him on his campaign, he wrote in praise of Harry: 'You are absolutely right! It is a real nonsense that all the various societies are quarrelling with one another rather than working together in true co-operation.'[6] In response, a rather obsequious Price replied: 'If you do not come to the rescue of psychical research in Germany, I do not know who will.'

On arrival at Liverpool Street station on 10 April the 20-year-old Rudi and Amereller were met by Lucy Kay and a phalanx of newspaper reporters and photographers. Price, the compulsive communicator, wired the Press Association with news of Rudi's visit to London. Henceforth Rudi was expected to act in a way that Harry thought fit for public consumption: any medium he used had to contribute something to keeping the NLPR in the media's gaze, whether it was a simple quote or a press conference.

Back at the laboratory Price had been busy developing an electrical control system to improve his method of medium control. The new apparatus was fastened to a chair with a rope. The sitters would sit hand in hand and foot to foot, wearing electrically wired gloves and socks connected with a red light indicator. If the circuit broke a signal would instantly flash, thus revealing any trickery. But it was a flawed system. Archibald Low did not consider it satisfactory, saying it was liable to short-circuiting; others, including the thoroughgoing ASPR sceptic Henry Clay McComas, pointed out that Rudi might contrive to join the hands and feet each side of him, thus freeing his own without breaking the circuit.

Under these conditions Rudi, in his first seance, aided and abetted by his trance personality 'Olga', who had sought the Austrian out after his brother's powers had waned, produced discarnate 'floating, levitation, and other movements of a coffee table, a ringing of a handbell, the tying of a hand-kerchief; shaking of curtains as if fanned by a violent wind and the playing of a zither in midair; raps, knocks, and the child-like form of a snowman all showing volition and, sometimes, intelligence'.[7]

The next seance, attended by Lord Rayleigh, was a becalmed flop: Price attributed this to the sitters, who were unknown to each other, whereas what Rudi really thrived on was amicability and friendship.

To emphasise to the public how versatile an act Rudi could put on, a number of celebrities, including the actors Laurence Olivier and Stanley Holloway and the film actress Marjorie Mars, were allowed to sit in on a seance where all sorts of wonderful assorted phenomena were paraded – and which left some of them in tears. At the same time, Harry extended an invitation to the Occult Committee of the Magic Circle to investigate the young Austrian's extraordinary supernatural feats. The committee declined, however, saying if 'the phenomena proved to be normal, it is not always simple to copy the specialist'.

It was seemingly impossible for anyone to copy Rudi's acts, and Price aped the cash prize competitions of the day's newspapers by ringing the *Daily Express* and offering £1,000 (£40,000 in today's money) to any conjuror who could repeat the phenomena under similar conditions. The offer was repeated in all the London evening papers the next day, and most of the Sunday press at the weekend. But no magician took up the challenge until Rudi had departed for his home in Austria; and even then, when a 'world-famous' but anonymous magician contacted Harry, he took no further interest in the matter once he understood the conditions; and Harry declined to name him 'out of respect for his anonymity'.

Rudi returned to London that autumn and took part in an exhausting series of twenty-one sittings from November through to January 1930. The first trial seance on 21 November showed promising signs that the Austrian's power was as strong as it ever was. Dr William Brown, a psychiatrist, Wilde Reader in Mental Philosophy at Oxford and later director of the university's Department of Experimental Psychology, together with Lord Charles Hope and others, witnessed a zither slide off a table, a basket being taken from a sitter's hand and levitated; and all the while cold graveyard draughts pervaded the room.

The second seance was not nearly so successful. The Reverend Digby Kittermaster, a hard-headed priest and tutor at Harrow, observed that Lucy Kay was able to walk around the room, quite free to do anything she wished. This was a point picked up by Charles Sutton of the *Daily Mail*, who had been impressed by seeing a pseudopod, described by Price as 'something more like a paw with thick fingers and a large thumb', at one seance. Whatever the creature was, the 'hand' was almost the same as that seen at Mina Crandon's seances. Now Sutton was doubtful, telling Harry that if he was to see it again a hundred times, under any conditions, he would not admit the genuineness of Rudi.

The *Daily Mail* expressed its own collective doubts about the phenomena and called into question the validity of the National Laboratory after Eric Dingwall wrote a letter calling Rudi's sittings 'a cavalcade of burlesque entertainment'. But all this criticism aside, and amid all the excitement, William Brown, Lord Rayleigh and Lord Hope, who provided much of the cash for the tests, were sufficiently impressed with the results that they wanted to take part in further investigations.

Harry underwent a shift in self-perception. He floated the possibility that his Rudi investigations may well have contributed towards solving the riddle of man's existence. He was going to preserve the dictaphone's recording cylinders, he told the press, so that one day they 'may adorn a museum devoted to the birth of science which is destined to revolutionise, perhaps even regenerate, mankind'.

The times were changing. Although Harry was widely distrusted and unpopular, he had every reason to believe that Rudi had produced genuine abnormal phenomena while he had been at the National Laboratory. He was filled with hope that he alone was an inch away from harnessing something that for centuries had eluded the finest of minds.

PRICE AND THE PERAMBULATING NUN

As Alexander Campbell, editor of the *Daily Mirror*, spoke to his reporters at the morning news conference on 9 June 1929, he had little idea that a letter written by a desperate vicar in a forgotten corner of Essex would become the news event of that year, one which would boost the then genteel *Mirror*'s sliding sales and temporarily halt the worst financial period in the newspaper's history.

The *Daily Mirror* was regarded as something of a laughing stock by its peers – derided as 'The Daily Sedative', it was seen by some as a silly little Tory newspaper that ran quaint front-page picture stories of girls frolicking in the park, boring events in the Home Counties and brass bands playing music to insects.

Yet one of Campbell's staff had received a letter in the morning's post from Guy Eric Smith, rector of the lonely parish of Borley, which asked the newspaper's 'Question and Answers' column if it knew the address of the Society for Psychical Research, as 'unusual happenings' were being experienced in the rectory and the rector wanted them to be investigated.

Sensing a scoop, Campbell instantly dispatched the seasoned Home News reporter V.C. Wall to the hamlet to cover the story. He then telephoned the NLPR and spoke to Lucy Kay, who told him that Harry was at work but that she would pass his message on. Lucy duly telephoned Saunders & Son and gave Price the details. Harry, in turn, promised Campbell that he would travel up to Borley in two days' time; it was to be the beginning of his longest-running psychic investigation, one that has been flagged as arch fakery and yet for the last seventy-seven years trumpeted as absolute proof of life after death.

As the reader may know, long and detailed accounts of the happenings at Borley have been the subject of several books, hundreds of broadcasts and a mountain of newspaper and magazine articles. What all this suggests is that whatever happened demands to be written about; however, my intention is to beat free of the stifling myths and simply report the provenance of the present-day legend, which began when the skeletally thin V.C. Wall arrived at the tiny village on the north Essex–Suffolk border on the morning of 10 June.

Wall must have been delighted to see the immense, ugly, thirty-roomed Victorian redbrick rectory in a state of some disrepair – a quintessential ghost-story house, if ever there was one. The front door of the rectory was permanently shaded along a brick-setted area. One of the house windows was bricked up and its garden colonised by wild plants, which only managed to add to its forlorn appearance.

Guy Eric Smith, a bespectacled Bunteresque figure, and his wife Mabel were offered the living of Borley after returning from India. It had previously been offered to and refused by twelve clergymen, because the house was cold, dreary and dull. Water had to be drawn from a well in the courtyard and the roof was in such a bad condition that several of the bedrooms could not be used. Living under these conditions brought Mrs Smith close to a nervous breakdown. When appeals to the diocesan bishop brought no response, the couple decided to move out and look for another curacy; but first, they had to convince the diocese they had good reason to move.

Having lived at the rectory for less than year after the death of the Reverend Harry Bull, the previous incumbent, the couple explained to a willing-to-believe-anything reporter that they were nervous, fearful and a little confused. There had been the sound of slow dragging footsteps along the long corridors; creaking noises in the bareness of many of the rectory's rooms. Tales of ghosts and murder abounded and though no apparitions had been sighted, there was a sense of doom and foreboding about the house.

Borley Rectory had been built in 1863 by the Reverend Henry Dawson Ellis Bull, a member of a wealthy local family, and was enlarged a decade or so later, as his family, governesses and domestic servants expanded in number. When Henry died in 1892 one of his sons, also called Henry (but known as Harry to avoid confusion with his father), took over the running of the parish. Imbued by his father's tales of the legends of ghosts, pared from rich village folklore, it was not long before this Oxford-educated eccentric – who lived in the days when vicars not only believed in God and the Bible but held that cats had souls – had allegedly seen a phantom coach being driven slowly by two headless men across fields near the rectory.

The *Daily Mirror* picked up on the story and embellished it. According to Wall, Borley Rectory had been built on the site of 'a great monastery which in the Middle Ages was the scene of a gruesome tragedy'; a nun had fallen in love with a coachman and, after a steamy affair, they had decided to elope. Alas, after discovering the nun's plan, the religious members of the community lynched the coachman and a companion and the nun suffocated after being bricked up alive. Beyond rival newspapers' murmuring that the invention of coaches came long after the dissolution of the monasteries, the story stuck and became established 'fact'.

Ethel Bull, one of Henry's seven daughters, was the first of the sisters to see the fabled nun one hour after sunset at approximately 9 p.m. on 28 July 1900, a date that even today sees hordes of rubber-necking ghost hunters in this Essex hamlet. In a recording for BBC radio Ethel was happy to gibber away about how she was walking around the garden with two of her sisters after they had returned from a nearby garden party.

> They wondered why I didn't take any notice and they looked down at me, and I said 'Look there's a nun walking there!' I was terrified and so were they when they saw her – and it sent cold shivers down our backs and we simply flew up to the house. Then we saw my eldest sister, who was staying with us.
>
> She said 'Oh I'm not going to be frightened', so she came down, and when she saw the nun she made to go across the potato bed to meet the nun, and the nun turned and came as it were to meet her, she was seized with panic and simply flew up to the house.[1]

Quite unaccountably, the Bull sisters believed that the long-talked about nun had finally appeared, and they were providentially on hand when Wall arrived at Borley to add lurid detail to the Smiths' accounts of cold rooms. They told how a young servant had left after seeing an old-fashioned coach, drawn by two bay horses, gallop through the rectory hedge, sweep across the lawn and vanish into thin air. Although Wall witnessed nothing strange himself, besides mistaking the Smiths' maid for the nun (she later admitted pulling her apron over her head as a prank), he wove a ghoulish tale from the material he was given.

The next day readers of the *Mirror* gasped at the report of mysterious lights in the rectory's windows, odious smells, tapping mirrors, bells that rang of their own accord and odd groaning noises. For many, here surely was proof of survival after death.

When Price and Lucy Kay eventually arrived at Borley on the afternoon of 12 June (after first going astray in the nearby town of Sudbury), Harry told the Smiths that he represented the ASPR, to override any suggestion that they should contact the London Society, and particularly William Salter, who lived nearby. Almost immediately, a remarkable sequence of poltergeist phenomena happened. Where before the Borley stories had involved shadowy figures seen in twilight, the rectory, according to Mrs Smith, was now home to an onset of phenomena – bangs, clattering, keys were thrown, coins rained down and cats were scared to enter the house. As Mrs Smith would say later, 'We could not help being led to suppose that Mr Price was producing some of the effects.'[2]

By the evening, the phenomena had turned a corner and the Smiths invited the Bull sisters over to dinner to talk about the problems with Price, Lucy and Wall. Those few hours turned out to be packed full of incident after the Bull sisters suggested holding a seance, which produced another intense display of poltergeist activity. A 'spirit' managed to communicate through tapping on the bedroom mirror, and later a cake of soap, which had been on the washstand, was thrown so violently against a metal jug standing on the floor that it was deeply marked. Then, according to Mrs Smith, small lights appeared in the darkness. 'They were like little bluish sparks in the darkness, when Mr Price was conducting this seance. Such things never occurred before or after – apart from this one time.'[3] Price commented:

Whoever was producing the taps could not spell . . . there was great difficulty experienced in obtaining the names or messages by spelling out the alphabet. At the best of times, this method is laborious, slow and cumbersome, and whatever it was tapping, it did not appear to grasp the technique of this system of communication.[4]

Lucy, however, gave an entirely different story: 'Names were spelt out – dates given – the intelligence purporting to be the late rector himself, begging us to help him with regard to his will which in some way was being misinterpreted.'[5]

As Price and Lucy ended their stay the next morning they handed over the task of keeping watch to Wall and two mediums supplied by Lennox Kay. One of these was Charles Glover Botham, a smooth-talking, well-built Londoner in his 40s, who for a number of years had supplied Air Chief Marshal Sir Trafford Leigh-Mallory with admiring tributes from his brother, who had died on Mount Everest in 1924.

Since nothing happened that night, the following day the *Mirror*'s reporter phoned through a lighthearted piece to the paper's copy-takers, saying that the ghost had 'flatly declined to exhibit itself'. With Harry back in London, Wall ended his week by writing stories about the havoc his pieces in the *Mirror* had caused, and then departed back to Fleet Street.

It was only at the weekend that the Smiths realised the full consequences of their actions. Carloads of local people trampled over the flowerbeds, hordes of ghost hunters were banging on the doors to try to get access to the rectory, hundreds of day-trippers fuelled by locally made beer began throwing bottles through the windows – in the end the police had to be called in to prevent a riot. One enterprising firm from nearby Long Melford began running coach trips to the rectory, inviting the public to 'come and see the Borley ghost'. News organisations around the world began telling their listeners and readers about the dead walking the previously quiet lanes of this small, scattered settlement in north Essex: the story was already becoming the news phenomenon of that summer.

To the Smiths' delight, just a few weeks after the peculiar disturbances had begun they were moved by the diocesan authorities to a small house in nearby Long Melford. In mid-July, Price and Lucy returned to the rectory with Lord Charles Hope. Almost immediately small eerie demonstrations of a psychic nature took place. Price wrote in his article on Borley in the ASPR's *Journal*:

We have experienced all the usual typical poltergeist manifestations such as the throwing of pebbles and other objects . . . we received a shower of ten keys which had been extracted from as many doors in various parts of the building. Amongst the keys was a brass Romish medallion,[6] which the rector could not identify. The flight of keys was accompanied by the ringing of the house bells – apparently of their own volition . . .[7]

Lord Hope was not at all sure that the phenomena had been produced by anything other than human means. Later he wrote, with a cool, calm voice, that 'Although I did not feel certain, I left Borley with the definite suspicion that Mr Price might be responsible for some at least of the phenomena which had occurred whilst I was present.'[8]

On 25 July the *Daily Mail*'s Charles Sutton accompanied Price and Lucy Kay to Borley. Getting out of Lucy's small Fiat car, the three of them began wandering around the rectory grounds before Price made a point of looking at a broken window, supposedly smashed by earlier poltergeist activity when Lord Hope had visited a week earlier. 'Within two or three seconds of Price pointing out to me the glassless frame of this window, its neighbour suddenly smashed and another cascade of glass tumbled down. Just before this, I realised Price had taken a step behind me. I heard a swishing sound as if a missile had been thrown and then the window broke. I was a little suspicious how this had happened,' Sutton later told the BBC.[9]

The three of them then stepped inside the rectory. Lucy Kay opened the doors, Sutton examined each room with the light of a hurricane lamp and Price followed, locking each door after them. But before he did so, according to Sutton, each time there was a resounding crash as if a stone had been thrown at an object.

They then went up to the first floor, entered a bedroom at the top of the stairs and stood looking out on the lawn, waiting for the famous nun to appear. Only a peculiar moaning noise disturbed the peace, which Sutton realised was Price's feeble attempt at ventriloquism. As the *Daily Mail*'s reporter was walking down the stairs, a half-brick rolled down the staircase.

This last piece of trickery impelled Sutton to put down the hurricane lamp he was carrying, seize Harry Price by the arms and accuse him of having thrown the brick and the pebble: 'I got hold of him and found two of his coat-pockets full of stones. He stammered and stuttered but offered no excuses or explanations [but] just asked "What are you going to do?" I said I would phone in the story and set off towards Long Melford to do just that.'

After filing his story, Sutton returned to Borley to pick up Price and Lucy and drive them back to London. Both appeared sanguine when Sutton told them what he had done. In the car on the way back, Price was lighthearted, sang popular songs and encouraged Lucy to do the same.[10]

Unfortunately for Sutton, his news editor later embellished the story – so much so that the new story would almost certainly have ruined Price's credibility at a stroke. But on looking through the reporter's copy, the *Mail*'s night lawyer came to the conclusion that Price would have grounds for suing the newspaper to save his reputation, and since it would be Harry and Lucy's word against Sutton's, it was not a matter the *Daily Mail* wished to pursue; so the story was killed. Harry had escaped a fatal exposure: he decided to let things cool down a little by saying he was feeling unwell. Lucy later wrote an unpublished play, *Journey: London to Borley*, based on the incident. The name of Sutton was changed to Burton.[11] In the preamble Lucy wrote:

> After meeting Burton at the NLPR, Lucy notices Price stuffing his pockets with anything that would fit in them. Price follows Burton out of the door while Kaye stands back waiting to lock up. As Price passes her on the way out, she notices the bulging pockets and tentatively taps them as he passes. He smiles and shakes his head.

It is an interesting insight into how Price operated.

A couple of days after this incident, Charles Hope went to the NLPR to arrange another visit to the Essex hamlet on 28 July, the date the nun was supposed to walk the rectory grounds, only to get the brush-off from Lucy Kay – Lucy was in a vile mood, as if there had been a row between her and Harry. Perhaps she was angry with him for being caught cheating, or was it another argument about money matters, or her careless pregnancy? In any case, Hope reported that, 'She told me that Price had been taken ill with a heart attack and led me to understand that this had been brought on by an accusation made against him by Charles Sutton. I got the impression that Miss Kay was really very angry with Price.'[12]

Harry was now presented with a farcical situation. He could hardly go back to Borley and invent a perambulating nun and other phenomena for fear of this getting into the newspapers, which would most likely see Sutton's story appearing in print. Equally, it was impossible for him to feign a heart attack. So he stayed quiet, in the British press at least, and inexplicably lost all enthusiasm for what he called the most haunted house in England, even though he believed that the phenomena at the rectory were cyclical and that poltergeist activity would start up on the same day each year.

When Hope and his party went to Borley on the 28th they saw nothing; and as Harry told his enthralled ASPR readers in his International Notes:

> We have not yet had an opportunity of 'laying' the ghosts of Borley rectory. On the other hand, the disturbing entities have succeeded in

driving out the rector and his wife and the dilapidated mansion is empty once more.

Since I wrote my last Notes, I have visited the place three times – and on each occasion, have witnessed manifestations. But on July 28th, the day of the year when the pious nun, headless coachmen and black coach – complete with a fine pair of bays – always appear (according to legend) nothing happened.

On the contrary, the mansion (unlike the feeling experienced on other occasions) seemed particularly peaceful – much to the disappointment of Lord Charles Hope, the Hon. Richard Bethell and others of the National Laboratory who visited the house on July 28th and 29th. Perhaps now the place is again empty the haunting spirits are at rest. It is a very extraordinary case . . .' [13]

So extraordinary that Price could not be bothered to monitor or visit the house again for eighteen months. Yet he egged on reporters to write increasingly lurid and sensationalist stories, with the result that it looked as if the fast-growing legend had fallen off the back of the history lorry – a crumpled sack of historical odds and ends. Perhaps this is what he had in mind when he wrote that 'all psychic societies must number among their correspondents crazy people who waste officials' time writing silly letters, but the great majority of the lunatics . . . lived in America . . . I can only put it down to the fact that our work was reported in the United States in a more sensational form than it was in this country . . .' [14]

Years after his alleged heart attack, the author Peter Underwood, now executor to Price's literary estate, wrote in *Borley Postscript* that he had met the still sharp-minded Connie Price at Arun Bank in 1967. [15] Relating how Connie had found Harry slumped dead in his favourite chair, Underwood wrote '[It was] A great shock for her but she said he must have had some sort of heart trouble and sometimes he used to say his heart was pounding. He had not been well the whole of his last week.' This is an extraordinary statement, suggesting that Connie knew nothing of her husband's previous heart problems. It was certainly true that Lucy and Harry would lie for each other; and Connie may well have been unaware of Harry's ill health because, apart from a problem with occasional migraines, he was fit enough to investigate haunted houses all over Britain and the continent and continue his day job, selling paper bags. [16]

Still lying low, Harry now returned to his experiments with Rudi Schneider, but had time enough on his hands to invent mysterious phenomena. In a letter to Professor Archibald Low, who had joined the NLPR's investigating committee in 1928, he wrote: 'We would defray any expense in the "frame-up." Our members would much relish the experiments in inverse ratio to the disgust, which the hard-shell spiritualists would feel. This is what we want, of course!'[17]

This declaration, with its unfortunate tone towards invention – could Price have been referring to Borley, or Rudi? – shows that not everything the public read could be taken at face value: there were ornamental additions to make things seem more impressive than they really were. The letter also shows how deeply Price was disgusted by much of the spiritualist movement, though in private he was perfectly happy for members to fund his own research.

It was around this time that he considered resigning from the ASPR because it was dominated by those who believed in the extraordinary mediumship of Mina Crandon.

He told the society's Board of Trustees that if it was not 'for its fine *Journal*, with its important foreign contributors, the American SPR would have no particular reason for continuing its existence,' and threatened to give up his post as Foreign Research Officer; but his conceit was pacified by a hike in his writing fees.

And then, in October, came the cataclysmic Wall Street crash. The confidence that had held together millions of human lives throughout Western civilisation was suddenly removed. The rich became penniless, the poor became homeless. The Great Depression halted and reversed the industrial growth that had been in full flood since the First World War, and the wise began to shed unwanted responsibilities.

It was this crisis that induced Price to approach Eugène Osty and the Nobel Prize winner Charles Richet, who had founded the Institut Metapsychique in Paris in 1919, with a proposal to amalgamate the National Laboratory with the French organisation.[18] Osty had been sitting in on random seances with Rudi Schneider at the NLPR for some time, and Harry undoubtedly saw there was little point in duplicating experiments when money could be saved by performing them under one roof. According to the proposal, Price was to be awarded a position on the Institut's executive council and to have unfettered access to its laboratories and equipment. The NLPR would retain its address and title in London for correspondence reasons.

Richet seems to have given Price his tacit agreement that the NLPR, then valued by him at £7,000 (the library took up £5,000 of this sum), would be housed at 51 rue de l'Aqueduc by that Christmas.

Matters quickly reached an impasse, however, and the laboratory stayed resolutely in Britain. Osty told Price that he wished the outcome had been different, and thanked him for his offer; his committee had decided that they did not have the space and new projects had been planned requiring elaborate extensions to the already existing laboratories. Harry's worsening relationship with the SPR had undoubtedly soured negotiations. For Price, the rejection was another reason to slight the society.

THE LION, THE WITCH AND HER WARDROBE

y 1930 Harry Price was a heavily set, quietly dressed man of middle age, with a balding pate, jowly cheeks and projecting ears. He was gimlet-eyed with a mouth of false teeth stained by his habit of smoking fifty Players cigarettes a day, and puffing on a pipe in between – he was an unlikely pin-up boy for many thousands of households across the world.[1]

The huge popularity of his early investigation at Borley Rectory and his much-reported seances with Rudi Schneider had firmly placed him in the public's consciousness, though ironically he was still working at Edward Saunders to try to make ends meet. He continued to report interviews and write for regional and national newspapers, but in this time of parsimony his journalism brought in only small fees, and by the end of 1929, when he had written nearly half a million words (including contributions to the ASPR's *Journal*) he had netted only £235 (approximately £8,800 in today's money) for a whole year of relentless effort.

Yet he told *Time* magazine in America some years later that he was spending $5,000 or £1,000 a year (£43,000 today) on his investigations, the majority of which was from his own fortune, 'inherited from his family', and that he was working in his South Kensington laboratory 'every week day until 5 o'clock unless he was out on a case'.[2]

Even if this account of his spending was a huge exaggeration, which it almost certainly was, the cost of his explorations in psychic research, the lack of results and the failure to combine experiments with Paris was making him demoralised and depressed, so much so that he was advised by his spiritualist friend and accountant Edward Wood to turn the laboratory into a purely private concern.

Wood believed that by making the laboratory an exclusive members club the actual number of members paying subscriptions could be concealed, which would have been advantageous to Price since under the terms of the laboratory's lease, the more members it had the more rent Price had to pay the Alliance for the use of the premises. But a couple of days after receiving a letter from their awkward tenant telling them what he intended to do, the LSA's Council responded to Wood's suggestion with a notice of eviction.

In a starchy letter Mercy Phillimore told Price 'we cannot allow you to continue in possession except under the terms of the Agreement which you signed . . . I must ask you to take immediate steps to vacate the premises'. She casually added that the LSA would take legal steps to throw out Price and his National Laboratory unless the premises were given up within a reasonable time.[3]

Desperate for a solution, Harry tentatively approached the British College of Psychic Science with plans to amalgamate, but although Conan Doyle (a former president) had given the college a significant amount of cash to keep them afloat, the BCPS was virtually broke.

Yet for all the official awkwardness and threat of eviction, the NLPR's relationship with the LSA simmered away cordially, with vice-president Robert Fielding-Ould continuing to act as a member of the laboratory's permanent research group. One of the stranger mediums they encountered was the black-knickered Mrs X.

Price had invited Mrs X, otherwise known as Diane Hartley, to be tested after getting fed up with her letters containing mothballs and half-eaten apples, which she claimed were apports from her spirit guide, the irascible dead gymnast Arthur Russell, otherwise known as the Flexible Friend. Hartley claimed that two other spirits controlled her: Gerald, a famous violinist, and David Dorothy, a deceased civil servant with a penchant for blowing raspberries. She arrived for the seance dressed in a tight black costume and a pair of pink dancing shoes on her size 8 feet, and her appearance remained fresh in Price's mind when he came to write up his notes a few days later.

She removed her false teeth, stood in the middle of the well-lighted room and gazed at the ceiling for a few moments. Suddenly, as if lashed by a whip, she spun round and round on one foot, made sucking noises with her mouth, fell down and was up again, laughed and groaned, threw herself on the floor and tried to levitate.

Having failed, she spun round on her dorsal extremity, jumped on a table and jumped off again, roared with laughter, struck her chest and clapped her hands, curled herself up into a ball on the floor and spun like a peg-top. She then knocked her head on a table, had a terrific struggle with an imaginary person, turned head-over-heels, took an invisible something out of her mouth, and threw it out of the window, hissed the word 'finished' – and became quite normal again. All in the space of half an hour.[4]

Unimpressed, Price encouraged her to go home and rest.

Although these mediums were fun to experiment with, they were not providing him with any good news copy, nor did they provide his research council with any hope that psychic research was moving forward. Ever more desperate to make up his mind to quit his responsibilities, Price again tried to interest the LSA in taking over his laboratory, and this time used his friendship with Laura Baggallay, the wife of his old chum William, as a go-between.

In late March, after taking some time off work for a snapped Achilles tendon, he wrote to Laura saying that it was the ideal time for the societies to join forces, marketing the NLPR as he would a new fancy paper bag: 'The present time is a golden opportunity for the LSA to become the leading organisation of Great Britain . . . the new organisation should sweep the country,' adding adoringly that there was 'no other person in the world I would rather hand over the Lab to than yourself'.[5] Price wanted the traditions of the laboratory to be maintained, his property to be taken care of, and, if everything went according to plan, he would bequeath his entire scientific chattels to the LSA.

It was a generous offer, but typically there was a sticking point. The Alliance would have to drop the word 'spiritualist' from its title because, he told Mercy Phillimore, it was synonymous with credulity and charlatanism and every new society gave the word a wide berth. 'It now remains for us to coordinate our resources (and energy) and make the new organization the authoritative society.' Referring to the LSA's legions of old clairvoyants who gathered at Queensberry Place in mid-week to discuss various tit-bits of news, Price warned that they would 'have to shunt the tea-drinking cronies who assemble on Wednesday afternoons'.[6]

Price's idea of amalgamation was in fact enthusiastically endorsed by the LSA's Council, and the process took off at lightning speed; the LSA even gave way to Price's wish to move the band of old and retired clairvoyants, and his demand that the LSA drop the word spiritualist was not as audacious as it may sound. The previous year the society had recognised the trend of the popular spiritualist movement, which was turning its face away from the extravagance associated with it in every quarter, and the need for common-sense guidance and the desire to remove itself from any association with fraud and hysteria.[7]

Within days, Dawson Rogers announced that the bright, new organisation would be chaired by Lord Charles Hope – a choice intended to minimise the 'influence of Mr Price, past and future' – and the new organisation would be called the London Alliance of Psychic Science and the National Laboratory of Psychical Research, with the entirely unpronounceable acronym of LAPSNLPR. The laboratory was valued at £6,000 (or about £240,000 in today's money).[8]

In April the LSA wrote to Harry saying that everything was in place to bring about the changes at the earliest possible moment.[9] It looked as if at last Price had scrabbled his way to financial safety. The new body was to be wholly responsible for funding the laboratory; he was to be its International Research Advisor; and though he would lose control of the respected *Journal*, the publication would appear alongside a revamped *Light* magazine. The International Research Council would comprise people who had accepted the facts of abnormal phenomena and so would be drawn from bodies unassociated with the popular spiritualist movement.

Price's only wish, he told the new council, was to promote harmony and a smooth working environment. The remarkable transfer had taken just two months to come into effect, which was a tribute to Harry's ability to ingratiate himself with the LSA's Council, which he referred to as 'a very intelligent committee of men'.

The amalgamation was not expected to last; and indeed it did not. In the last week of May 1930, just as the contract for the handover of the NLPR was to be signed, Price withdrew what until then had been firm support. A day later he stressed in a letter to Mercy Phillimore that he was not so biddable that he would give up his laboratory, and, like a petulant child, maintained that he had never wanted the amalgamation in the first place, seemingly forgetting the mountain of letters and press interviews to the contrary.

Why this massive sea change? In his explanatory letter, he sneered at Robert Fielding-Ould, his former friend and colleague, who just a couple of months earlier had been unequivocally generous about him, calling him 'a highly successful and highly intelligent man – a tireless worker, one of my great friends'.[10]

Price told Mercy Phillimore that he 'did not know yesterday that Dr Fielding-Ould intended to be at our meeting, or I would not have attended'. 'When he butted in I knew that it was the beginning of the end. I should be grateful if you would kindly keep him out of my way in the future as I will not meet him again under any circumstances.'

Then, with typical bluster, he announced that the 'agreement you have handed me is ludicrous and no one but a mad man would sign it. I still want to help the LSA in particular and psychical research generally and I am willing to loan the Laboratory, the library etc, but I think it best not to be connected in any official capacity.'[11]

Still bitter and humiliated at the way the LSA had spurned his earlier offer of joining forces, Price's vengeance was complete; but it was a foolish gambit, and one that was to cause him a great deal of pain and anguish.

Against this new fallout, Harry made a formal approach to the Rector of the Board of Psychology at the Georg-August University in Göttingen, offering the same deal as he had proposed to the LSA, though in his letter to the rector his entire equipment and library had increased in value – in only a few weeks – to £10,000.

Six years ago, as a climax to a lifelong interest in psychical research I founded and equipped the National Laboratory of Psychical Research. This venture has proved an unqualified success but the time has come when my health will not allow me to give my entire time and energies at the Laboratory and at the end of 1930, I propose to close the Lab and make a gift of the equipment, library, goodwill etc to one of the universities.

In England the machinery is too slow and cumbersome. I am therefore offering the entire equipment and library to Göttingen.[12]

It is easy to see why Price favoured Göttingen and Germany above Britain and its university system. The Georg-August was a university with an astonishing pedigree: no fewer than twenty Nobel Prize winners had studied or lectured there, and it had previously staged experiments in telepathy. More importantly, occultism was so prevalent throughout Germany in the late 1920s and early 1930s that, in Price's own words, 'it seemed alive with clairvoyants, astrologers, occultists and mediums', and incomparably more so in the Weimar region than in any other area of the country, except Berlin. Here, in the German capital, where the erotic subculture was mixed inextricably with the occult, at least 20,000 believers in the mystic arts followed all sorts of strange and eclectic passions.

The German university system was developing a wide range of psychologies to deal with the problems of modern German life, but there was little funding to match the ambitious projects, and so an offer to equip and endow a department was to be seized with both hands. Even so, it took until the beginning of September for Professor Narziss Ach, an experimental psychologist and director of Göttingen University's Psychological Institute, to write to Price, accepting his 'kind and generous gift, so this important section of science should be pursued here'.[13]

In the intervening four months before Ach had answered his letter, major changes had happened in Price's life. Sir Arthur Conan Doyle, who had thrown so much confusion and resentment in Harry's way, had died. Suffering from angina pectoris, he had risen from his bed on a spring day and gone for a stroll into his garden and a short while later had an angina attack. He was discovered lying on the ground, one hand clutching his heart, the other holding a single white snowdrop. He died on Monday 7 July.

Harry claimed that despite all their differences he was satisfied Doyle 'liked me very much'. At the time of writing his autobiography in 1940, Harry was indignant that the spiritualists had almost forgotten their former supporter: 'they have not even troubled to establish a memorial to the man's memory' he said pointedly, paying him a generous tribute:

> He was a giant in stature with the heart of a child. I do not know of another spiritualist living with the same dynamic personality, driving-force, dogged grit, tenacity of purpose, fighting qualities and worldwide prestige than this great High Priest of Spiritualism possessed.[14]

In September Laura Baggallay had sensed a thaw at the LSA and implored Price to re-establish good relations; rather naively, he agreed. Although only a few sentences long, his letter encapsulates many of the flavours of the previous six months. First, he tells the Alliance that unless someone takes over the laboratory as a going concern he will be compelled to dismantle it at the end of the year, when his tenancy runs out. Next, he drops a hint about the amalgamation issue, saying there has been a 'misunderstanding', which made further negotiations impossible. 'But I am not going into this matter: this letter is to offer members of the LSA the use of the Laboratory and the equipment, under the management of your council for an indefinite period.'[15]

Predictably, the LSA rebuffed this latest overture, but, unknown to Harry, for good reason: the Alliance had equipped its own laboratory to rival his, so that now the London Psychical Laboratory (LPL) was presented as the only body to further the cause of psychical investigation in Britain.

The LSA planned something very special as a curtain-raiser: they would invite back Sir Arthur Conan Doyle who, since his death, had been popping up in India, South Africa, America and beyond. Naturally, the Alliance rather hoped he would prefer to speak to them rather than to anyone else. Though the plans were known to only a small number of people, Price found out about them and aimed to spoil the event. He approached the medium Eileen Garrett to see if she could contact Doyle, who had been a close friend.

The seance took place at the National Laboratory on 7 October. According to Harry, the sitting, asked for by the *Daily Mail*, was just a routine seance, though the newspaper's reporter, Ian D. Coster, later admitted that it was an organised stunt for Eileen Garrett to see if she could contact Sir Arthur and thus promote sales.[16]

The sitting, with Price, Coster and Ethel Beenham as observers, started at 3 p.m., and it became apparent almost immediately that it would go down as one of the most controversial seances in psychic history. After only five minutes, Eileen Garrett's control, an Arab called Uvani, told the sitters in threadbare English that a spirit was coming into the room. It turned out that it was not Doyle but Flight Lieutenant Irwin, captain of the ill-fated airship R101, a huge luxury airborne hotel built under the supervision of Britain's Air Ministry. In October 1929 the hydrogen-filled ship, at 777ft long and with a steady cruising speed of 35mph (and top speed of 77mph), was the largest man-made object ever to fly. But seven hours into its maiden flight from Cardington, in Bedfordshire, to Karachi in India on Saturday 4 October 1930, the airship began to list badly owing to a major escape of gas from its forward gasbags, which subsequently led to the crew momentarily losing control of the ship. The ship crashed and exploded near the treacherous Beauvais Ridge, killing forty-eight of the fifty-four passengers and crew onboard. The dead included the Air Chief Marshal of the RAF, Sir William Sefton-Branckner, and the Air Minister, the Rt Hon. Lord Thompson.

In a long series of spasmodic sentences, 'Irwin' gave the seance listeners a detailed and apparently highly technical account of how the airship had crashed and what its deficiencies were. The communication was so rapid and fluent that Ethel Beenham had some difficulty in taking it down.

During the seance two of Irwin's observations were said to be truly remarkable. One was that the airship had scraped the roofs of the small town of Achy, which no one had heard of and which Price took some time to find on a map. The other was that a new fuel was being secretly prepared for airships and was not yet public knowledge.[17]

At the conclusion of the disjointed but intriguing seance Price decided that the shorthand notes should be handed over to various people conducting the public inquiry into the disaster at the Air Ministry.

At his request, Mollie Goldney interviewed an air officer based at Cardington, named only as Mr X, who knew the R101 airship and crew well and believed that much of the protocol recorded from the seance was accurate and tallied in almost every detail with what was afterwards found in the course of the official inquiry. E.F. Spanner, the well-known naval architect and marine engineer, came to exactly the same conclusions in his book *The Tragedy of the R101*.[18]

If the transcript of the seance is accurate and contemporaneous, we have no explanation as to how Eileen Garrett could have cheated. The official inquiry found that undue pressure from Lord Thompson, which affected the overall design of the airship, was to blame for the crash. No mention was made of the seance.

When, seven months after the sitting, Harry delivered his lecture to a thunderstruck audience at the National Laboratory and for the first time revealed the full story of the seance, it created a sensation. Newspapers and broadcasters from Britain's outposts around the world covered the story. Harry claimed that he had waited until May the following year before disclosing the information because he did not want to hamper the official inquiry. His critics, however, posed searching questions.

By the time of his lecture, they argued, the conclusions of the official inquiry had been published and the full facts of the disaster were in the public domain. Price clung to his earlier statement, suggesting that Irwin's spirit had visited his laboratory on the afternoon of the seance because 'some portion of the mind of a deceased person may linger on for a time of passing'. But it was not just Irwin whom Eileen Garrett traced that day.

Conan Doyle's spirit hoved into the ether too, and back on earth Harry and Sir Arthur 'discussed our old quarrels and I must admit that the verbal mannerisms of the entity . . . were reminiscent of the living Doyle'.[19] By all accounts, it was not a particularly revealing conversation, with the ethereal Scot insisting on discussing the banal rather than saying to Price, 'See, I told you there was an afterlife.'

On 12 November 1930, soon after the momentous seance, Harry addressed a letter (marked 'Private and Confidential') to all members of the SPR proposing an amalgamation similar to that promised to the LSA, the Paris Institut and the British College of Psychic Science. Price buttressed the promise of his library and laboratory with the announcement that his health was getting worse, that he was not tempted to join with a spiritualist society and that he was hesitant to let his belongings fall into foreign hands.

'I should of course expect to take a major part in all investigations brought about through my agency and generally co-operate with the SPR.'[20] In other words, he would carry on much as before but under the aegis of the SPR.

When the offer was flatly rejected, Price travelled to Göttingen as planned, to begin what he hoped would be arrangements to freight the NLPR to Germany. While there, he gave an informal talk to the psychology department and arranged to deliver a lecture to the university's students and the Nobel Prize winner Dr Thomas Mann on 22 January 1931.

But even this newfound friendship was not to last long. Professor Ach was left floundering when he read a copy of 'Conan Doyle's Startling Messages from the Beyond', the article Harry had written on the Doyle seance. Ach could not make sense of a man who had written that 'It is just possible that the views expressed by the entity calling itself Doyle were emanations from the brain of the living Doyle which had been picked up by the medium just as one tunes into a radio set.'[21]

Not surprisingly, Ach passed the article, with Price's mind-boggling conclusion about survival after death, to his colleagues and discussed what they should do. Harry's memory of what happened next, told to Dr Gerda Walther, was that he had prepared his lecture notes and sent them on to the university – and then the fun began. 'Some of the professors were so astonished at my account of what happens through some mediums that they were going to organize an "attack". My friends at the university then advised me to abandon the lecture.'[22] He added that Göttingen cancelled the lecture and scotched any chance of amalgamation with the NLPR.

However, the record of an altogether more likely scenario can be found at Senate House, where a letter from Professor Ach wipes away any lingering hopes of a fresh start for Harry and his laboratory. Hesitantly, Ach told him that he should abandon the arranged lecture because he was certain there would be

a merciless criticism of . . . such a slashing character that I would prefer to spare you the discomfort of it, the more as I would not be myself in a position to offer any effective defence of your argument which, as your article makes clear, would be contrary to my own scientific opinion.[23]

From letters in his archive it seems that Harry had never informed any of his British colleagues, who funded much of the laboratory's research, that he was intending to move to Germany, nor is it clear whether he had told Connie that her future was to lie far away from Pulborough.

Despite this last rebuff, Price continued his hunt for a university to take over the mantle of the laboratory, narrowing his search to those with a history of experimental psychology such as Berlin, Würzburg and Leipzig, where he met the renowned Professor Felix Kreuger, chairman of the German Society of Psychology and director at Leipzig Psychological Institute.

And yet there were encouraging signs that the SPR was about to put the ill feeling between themselves and Price behind them. After his previous offer had been turned down, Harry carried out a private poll of members and found, much to his delight, that two-thirds of the society wanted to ally themselves with the National Laboratory. Harry made the mistake though of relying on Eric Dingwall's support. The SPR's apparent *esprit de corps* did not stretch to Ding, who said the idea could not be achieved: 'it will not get past the present SPR regime . . . nothing could ever succeed with Salter, Wooley and Besterman [respectively the treasurer, chairman and editor of the society's *Journal*]. How could it, I ask you?'[24]

Dingwall had drawn attention to the internecine war raging inside the SPR; indeed many ordinary members had come to the conclusion that, far from fostering and encouraging research, the society was being deliberately obstructive in the search for psychical phenomena. The previous year, influential SPR members, including Dennis Bradley, had charged the society with negligence. Its publications were valueless, he said, its seance room was rarely used, it did not hold sittings, did not conduct investigations, it acted as a brake on progress and was charged with deriding all published accounts of abnormal happenings. With its authority gone the time had arrived for the society to close down.[25]

It is possible that Dingwall's antagonism had been encouraged by his close friend Dr William Franklin Prince, a former Wesleyan with whom he had worked in the early 1920s and who had been elected President of the SPR that year. Certainly Price and Prince had resented each other for a long time. Prince believed Price had been inventing phenomena, while Harry thought the ex-minister hated him 'like poison' and was continually sniping at his work.[26]

In January 1930, some months before his death, Sir Arthur Conan Doyle had resigned his membership, singling out what he saw as the unnecessarily prejudiced views of Theodore Besterman, the society's editor and librarian, whom he regarded as a slovenly critic with very little experience of psychical research. Furthermore, Doyle strongly objected to Besterman's 'insolence and gratuitous offensiveness' towards Gwendolyn Kelley Hack's *Modern Psychic Mysteries*: Besterman had claimed that the book, about an Italian medium, was likely to 'bring our subject into contempt and disrepute'.

Doyle then criticised the society's administrators, accusing them of being a 'small central band of reactionaries'. They were 'anti-spiritualist', and 'everything which tends to prove the truth, no matter how honourable or sane the source may be, is assailed by suppression, mis-representation and every sort of unreasonable and vicious opposition'. He had long waited in hope of some reform of their influence on the society, but had come to the conclusion that the SPR was entirely for evil.[27]

Doyle's resignation had triggered an early mass of others, but the SPR's Council regarded his departure and the fuss it created as a very trivial matter: 'There is nothing but an honest difference of opinion,' they said. 'While Sir Arthur regards Spiritualism as a "cult" the society was founded to carry on critical investigation.'

Price was acutely aware that his chance to sway opinion was rapidly disappearing. As well as being forestalled by Prince and sidelined by Dingwall, there was a growing danger that the SPR could stabilise itself, outflank him and thus deprive him and his allies of the oxygen of crisis, which the NLPR needed in order to succeed.

Price therefore made his amalgamation proposal to the SPR sound apt, fresh and invigorating, demonstrating how it would help the SPR push forward its investigative boundaries. At the Annual General Meeting on 26 February 1931, with Sir Oliver Lodge in the chair, Price's champion Mollie Goldney moved the proposal:

> That this meeting approves of the amalgamation proposed by Mr Harry Price (and supported by an overwhelming majority of SPR voters) of the National Laboratory of Psychical Research with this Society and requests the Council to appoint a committee to discuss the details of the suggested plan with the Administration of the National Laboratory.[28]

In the event, as was universally predicted, the result was a farce. Some members of the council, including Lord Balfour and Stanley de Brath, the noted British psychical researcher, reported there was an impulsive haste about the move and that members had been privately lobbied without knowing the precise terms of the amalgamation. Therefore, the society should stick to its traditional methods.

Balfour accused Price of overestimating his ability, but this hardly seemed to matter, at least in public, since Price had been able to hammer home the differences between the NLPR and the SPR to his largest and most influential audience yet. In private, it was different. No matter how his words were dressed up it was a deeply disappointing episode in his life. In a letter to Dennis Bradley, Price revealed his raging paranoia. Feeling slighted by the society, he sensed 'genuine antagonism' whenever he set foot inside the SPR offices.[29]

In later correspondence with Freddie Bligh-Bond, an influential member of the ASPR and a member of the laboratory, Harry wrote that 'as I anticipated the SPR would not co-operate with us. The move was a political one and I think much good will come of it. The London SPR is getting a nasty jolt over the vote and scores of people are resigning.' He then dangled Bligh-Bond a tempting offer: 'If I really decided that I should take my library and laboratory out of the country I would offer it to the ASPR though the shipping of it would obviously cost a lot of money.'[30]

He had fully expected Bligh-Bond to mention the matter to J.R. Gordon, and was upset to discover in his friend's reply two weeks later that his patron and vice-president had died twelve months previously: no one had told him. In the end, this plea came to nothing. Although he begged the LSA to let him stay at Queensberry Place until he found another address, they refused, eventually forcing the National Laboratory to move to a rented

The epitome of a well-to-do Edwardian couple: Harry and Connie Price pose on their honeymoon in Scarborough, 1908. *(John L. Randall)*

Harry Price's favourite medium Stella Cranshaw. This photograph was taken by Price in 1923 aboard a Channel steamer as they sailed to France to spend a weekend in Paris. (HPC)

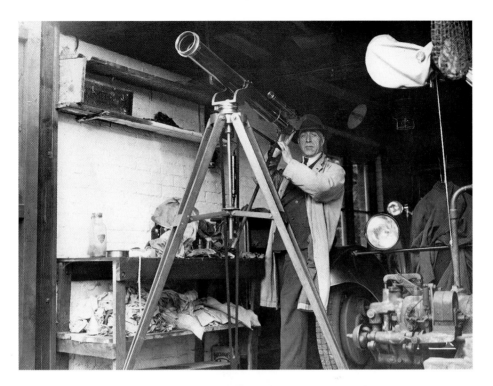

Harry Price in his workshop in Pulborough at a time when he was still keen to contact the planet Mars, *c.* 1930. *(Daily Sketch/Associated Press)*

A stylish Lucy Kay outside 16 Queensberry Place, London, *c.* 1926. Price employed the former model as his personal assistant. The couple later became lovers. *(HPC/DM)*

Harry Price and Lucy Kay with *Daily Mail* reporter Charles Sutton (in front of Price) setting out from the NLPR to visit Borley Rectory, 1929. *(HPC/DM)*

An athletic Harry diving a 'pike' while on holiday in Vienna in 1929, at about the time of his supposed heart attack. *(HPC/DM)*

Close companions:
Harry Price and
Lucy Kay in
Vienna, *c.* 1930.
(HPC/DM)

Harry Price and the Austrian medium Rudi Schneider in the seance room at the NLPR, 1930. *(HPC/DM)*

Price and members of his investigating council, including a youthful Kathleen 'Mollie' Goldney (far left, with cigarette in hand). Mercy Phillimore is standing next to her. *(HPC/DM)*

Publicity photograph of 'Poltergeist Girl' Eleanore Zugun, Harry Price's first notable investigation. *(HPC)*

Lees Farm, aka Parton Magna, at Walcot, Shropshire. It was owned by Harry Price's grandfather and uncle, and was where Price said he first encountered the supernatural. *(John L. Randall)*

The grave of Harry and Connie Price at St Mary's, Pulborough. The grave has been badly vandalised since the photograph was taken in 2001. *(John L. Randall)*

Georgian ground-floor apartment at 13d Roland Gardens, a short walk from Queensberry Place.

In his autobiography Price tried to push the story that the laboratory only moved because its lease had run out. It was such a successful operation, he asserted, that it needed bigger and better accommodation. 'Although I felt I needed a rest, I decided to take larger premises . . . and decided upon a bold policy. I did away with all subscriptions, thus making the members honorary ones. The abolishing of the monetary consideration freed our hands.'

In the public eye, Price was bucking the Depression; and this was the signal for Lucy Kay to ask Harry to back her plan of an early buy-to-let scheme. Despite having dated various men and having worked as a senior secretary for a film company (A. Fried Film Sales), Lucy had never really left Harry's side. She cared for him deeply, while continuing to regard him as an open wallet. Now things were so bad for him financially that for the first time he turned down her request for money. 'I am so sorry but I cannot do what you ask. During the last years, the depression has hit me very considerably and I am more or less living from hand to mouth. I cannot enter into any further responsibilities.'[31]

It was a decision that left Lucy in an appalling mood, though she responded with an abject apology. 'I am sorry I made myself so obnoxious over money matters with you. Your friendship really meant a lot more to me than that and I do so miss seeing you. Please will you forgive me?'[32]

In truth, the NLPR's immediate future was uncertain. It was struggling to find investors, and only twenty former SPR members had switched their loyalty to the laboratory, together with a hundred carried over from the days when Harry was an LSA tenant.

Price sensibly told the press nothing of this slide, proudly stating that NLPR membership stood at over 500 and he had to move to Roland Gardens because, he told the *Scotsman*, 'the museum has grown to such large proportions that larger premises have just been taken to house the exhibits and to provide for the requirements of a rapidly increasing membership'.

The first seance at Roland Gardens took place on 11 March 1931 with the medium and freelance journalist Guy L'Estrange. L'Estrange, a man in his mid-30s, was famous in certain circles for the entertaining saucy materialisations said to occur in his dark seances. One of these included an erotic female ghost known as the French Dancer. One of Price's friends, Alex Dribbell, claimed to have witnessed this phenomenon more than once in his own house in Surrey, and declared that as an added bonus the topless dancer's entire leg from the thigh to the toes could be seen by means of luminous plaques (hand-mirrors covered with luminous paint) as she sashayed naked round the room.[33]

L'Estrange also claimed to have an Islamic spirit guide called Abou ben Mohammed, who was said to appear with the amusing Scot, Hamish Hardy, and a friend, James. This impressive line-up concluded with a springer spaniel called Lady, who often licked people's faces. But just as Harry and his all-male sitters were ready to begin restraining L'Estrange to a chair behind a curtain, Dennis Bradley and a friend showed up a little the worse for wear after enjoying several cocktails in his office and an earlier lunch at the Embassy Club in Bond Street. 'He annoyed the medium and he annoyed us. Nothing happened. I was glad when the seance terminated, as I was sorry for L'Estrange,' Price sourly recalled in his memoirs.

The opening seance aside, the new, fresher, reorganised NLPR tried to recruit everybody and anybody interested in psychical research. Harry's idea, which he sketched out in a letter to Henry Duncan, the husband and business manager of the clairvoyant Helen Duncan, was to include a 'big International Research Council . . . we contemplate having 5,000 members'.[34]

Right from the start Price was very keen to sign up the bovine-faced Helen Duncan, who was nearing the end of an eighteen-month arduous testing period at the LPL, now headed by Robert Fielding-Ould and Sir Ernest Bennett MP. Helen's first seances were reported as violent, nasty affairs, but these halted when the LPL began testing her on fees of £10 a week. At first, they firmly believed she had the power to make the dead walk and jive. *Light* magazine reported short and tall human figures appearing under voluminous linen sheets, almost certainly made from the milky ectoplasm which freely oozed out of Mrs Duncan's every orifice in vast quantities. She herself described the material as 'a liquid spurting from the nipples of my breasts'. The willing onlookers also saw objects, a good few feet away from Mrs Duncan, recoil from her grasp, and felt ghostly fingers stroking their faces.

Under strict instructions not to allow any competing laboratory into the Duncan experiments, Harry persuaded the sculptor James Stevenson, a spiritualist and absolute advocate of 'Mrs D', to collect a small portion of the medium's mysterious spongy and slimy ectoplasm from 'between her chest and tights' during a seance. Fired by his spectacular good fortune, Price supposedly sent the sample to a distinguished London consulting and analytical chemist, whom he would name only as Dr X because 'it would probably harm him professionally if he were to sign his name to an analysis of it. If it ever becomes vital that his name be revealed, doubtless Dr X will give me the necessary permission.'[35] In truth, Price most likely slipped on his white lab coat and analysed it himself.

He spent several weeks and 'dark oppressing weekends' poring over Dr X's chemical analysis and conclusions of the teleplasm, which included the baffling statement that 'in a branch of the arts, plastic masses are made from blood'. Night after night, in a room smelling of wet ink, pipe smoke and hot collars, Price wrote a seventeen-page report, believing he was on the way to discovering a separate branch of science altogether, and in doing so thinking he might become the man of his age.

His analysis of Mrs Duncan's protoplasm – as he now called it in letters to 'Brother Stevenson' – was the 'commencement of a study which one day will occupy the minds of our most brilliant biologists and chemists . . . this is a matter for experimentation which some day will supply us with the facts we so badly need'. He was so confident of his discovery that Helen Duncan was able to give birth to the dead that he invited a reporter from the Press Association to hear his news. The PA, delighted by Price's crazy story, wired it across the world:[36]

MEDIUM IN STRANGE EXPERIMENT –
TELEPLASM UNDER THE MICROSCOPE

The mysterious 'something,' which exudes from tranced mediums, and moves chairs and tables has been captured and examined under the microscope.

Mr Harry Price, hon. director of the National Laboratory for Psychical Research, told a Press Association reporter today that a piece of teleplasm was taken from a medium by permission of the 'dual personality' or 'control'.

He explained teleplasm was exuded during a trance and then returned to the medium's body. The specimen, which had been examined, was left on the medium's chest and legs; although she was examined immediately by doctors, it was impossible to find any change in the physical condition of the woman.

Previous attempts to obtain teleplasm without permission or 'control' said Mr Price had endangered the life of the medium and caused serious illness. It is the first time, he added, that it had been possible in the history of psychical research to chemically analyze the substance.

Whipped up by the fervour around him, Price sent a confidential letter to the spiritualist Freddie Bligh-Bond in his position as editor of the ASPR's *Journal*. With triumphant naivety, he told him that

> some months or so ago I secured a piece of teleplasm from a certain quarter and have no doubt at all that it is the real stuff . . . On account of considerable jealousy by interested parties, I am not able, at the moment, to publish the name of the medium from whom it exuded – but I may do so later.
>
> But I have been to very considerable trouble, and have expended about £20 on it, in analyzing and having analyzed the small portion, which I received. As this is the first serious attempt at analyzing this substance, you will realise that the paper I enclose for publication is of a very considerable importance. I hope you will give it due prominence.[37]

Harry's prospective article for the ASPR, 'An Attempt at the Microscopic Anatomy of Alleged Teleplasm', begins with the news that 'for those impatient folk who are continually making the untrue statement that psychical research is "not progressing", I have a surprise. I have secured, from unimpeachable sources, a specimen of a substance alleged to be Teleplasm and am now engaged upon its histology.'

The article pointed out that although there been previous attempts at analysing the substance – 'Schrenk-Notzing had secured a specimen of it from the French medium Eva C a few years before but I do not think he did much with it' – this was the first time someone who knew its significance had the sense to send it to a chemist.

Price told Bligh-Bond that his shy and retiring friend Dr X was guarded because he was 'dealing with something the very existence of which is denied' and that he was about to exhibit the teleplasm between glass slides at the laboratory's psychic museum.

Bligh-Bond's editorial committee was intrigued by Harry's claims and wrote back asking for the medium's identity to be revealed and more information about the teleplasm sample he had analysed. Harry replied that the medium was of course

> Mrs Duncan who is now at the LSA. When I had spent a great deal of time and money on the analysis, the LSA with that miserable jealousy which is the curse of psychism today, informed the person who gave it to me that no names were to be mentioned. So it is for their sake I withhold the name of the medium . . . If there is the slightest query in the minds of your committee about its authenticity it is much better not to publish.[38]

Slightly nervous about Price's claims, Bligh-Bond decided to spike the article, and in doing so unknowingly rescued Harry's career from the brink of death in America. But Price, ever impatient, had forwarded his paper on protoplasm to Eugène Osty at the Institut Metapsychique and to scientists in Italy and Germany. Osty's reaction to the sample stopped short of incredulity and urged caution:

> I have read your article on the chemical and microscopic examination of the alleged teleplasm. Do you not think that it would be of vital importance to be quite certain, absolutely certain, that you are dealing with actual teleplasm? The publication of such an article would meet with tough opposition.

Price replied that he was personally convinced of its authenticity:

> Several portions were taken and other persons including Sir Oliver Lodge have received specimens. Owing to jealousy by another Society, I am unable to give full particulars as to how I got it and where it came from but someone will eventually write a paper on it and I want to be the first. A piece of my portion was handed to the most eminent analyst in London and his report concludes with my deductions.

Price told Stevenson that 'It looks as if ghosts are made of protoplasm – which is something for the scientists to think about.'[39]

Although Dr Emilio Servadio, editor of *Luce e Ombra*, was unconvinced that the teleplasm was anything but a mash of surgical gauze and albumen soaked in oil of wintergreen (which acted as an emetic), the magazine took

Harry at his word when it insisted that 'the discovery will cause a great sensation, as the most amazing case in the annals of psychic research'.[40]

So excited was Price about testing Helen Duncan that he attempted to poach the impenetrable stronghold of the spiritualist movement from under the LPL's noses by offering the Duncans the almost unheard of sum of £100 in cash (about £4,200 in today's value) in advance, plus £10 a week, matching her wage paid by the LPL, and proposed to them a further £100 when Helen had completed her term of contract with the National Laboratory. Price concluded: 'As you must realise, my Council is making this offer . . . solely in the interest of science. I would also undertake to publish in full the results of our investigation in England, America, Germany and Holland.'[41] Not surprisingly, within a couple of days the Duncans had hotfooted it from their experiments at the LPL to the NLPR, leaving Sir Ernest Bennett and others hopping mad with rage.

Or so it seemed. By this time in early May the LPL was suspicious of the Duncan mediumship. Bennett, speaking with the confidence of an educated man, wrote an unpublished memo to himself which read:

I would like to place on record in connection with the LSA seances held with Mrs Duncan in London 1931, that I never observed in this woman any indications of abnormal gifts or powers and that I am convinced, as a result of my sittings with her that Mrs Duncan indulged in deliberate fraud from start to finish.[42]

Thanks to the LSA's sterling practice of keeping quiet, Harry was none the wiser and accepted Mrs Duncan with open arms. She was closely scrutinised 'by a team of doctors who brought with them a bag of tools and set to work, exploring every orifice and crack where an instrument or hand would go; but at each fresh place they drew a blank.'[43]

Helen Duncan's spirit guide, a Scotsman called Albert, was a rather bumptious man with a measure of contempt for the audience, and spoke in a comically hoarse drawl midway between upper class and cockney. In photographs he resembled a bandaged leg. Helen had a second mouthpiece, Peggy, a mischievous child spirit who wore lipstick, could conjure up a parrot and looked as if she were made out of a flannelette nightdress.

It is no wonder, then, that after four seances as impressive as those at the LSA, where figures were seen dancing in the dark, teleplasm was expelled out of Helen's nose and her ears and objects backed away from her. Again she underwent a thorough gynaecological examination, which still failed to reveal any hiding place for any material she may have used for her materialisations. Price and his council were deeply divided as to whether or not she was genuine. This must have worried him considerably, since he had staked his reputation on telling the world's press that he had discovered the key to human life and that it lay between glass slides in his Kensington laboratory.

At the fourth seance, after various flashlight photographs of materialis-ations had been taken, David Fraser-Harris decided to have the contents of Helen Duncan's stomach examined. He was about to place a stomach pump down her throat when she broke free from his grasp.[44] Price then suggested that she was X-rayed, at which she dashed out into the street, had an attack of hysteria and began to tear her seance garment to pieces. She clutched at some railings and screamed. Her husband tried to pacify her, but it was useless. Price suspected that a wad of tissue had been passed between husband and wife during the mêlée, and when he asked to search Henry, the latter refused, saying he was wearing soiled underwear.

The following day Price sent a letter to the Duncans, who were staying at a house in Beulah Crescent, Surrey, thanking them for the 'strenuous and not very pleasant time which you experienced last night'. He mentioned that he hoped to get some prints of those 'magnificent pictures which we got last night, and I will send you a set. Like ourselves, you will of course keep these prints private – until the great day comes when we can put all our evidence on the table.'[45]

The letter clearly shows that Price still believed that Helen Duncan's protoplasm was capable of summoning the dead and, possibly, life itself. Later, though, his view was to change, partly as a result of Fraser-Harris and William Brown proving that Helen Duncan had produced her seance effects by regurgitating cloth, and partly because her former maid, the feckless Mary McGinlay, contacted Price to persuade him she had first-hand information about Helen's habit of sending her to buy yards of cheesecloth, then asking her to rewash it after the frugal Scot had 'materialised' it.[46]

Knowing the game was up, the slippery Henry Duncan admitted that an hour or two before her sittings his wife would pass into a trance-like state in which she would swallow various articles and bring them back up again in her seances. Theoretically, at least, she was out of his control, and responsible only for herself.

Price shrewdly published his version of events in the NLPR bulletin, in a piece entitled 'The Duncan Mediumship: A Study in Regurgitation', though on legal advice he made edits and renamed it 'Regurgitation and the Duncan Mediumship'. But with insufficient time to publish before the Alliance's own report was in print, he signed a newspaper deal with the *Morning Post* worth 30 guineas for a worldwide exclusive.[47]

Price described Helen Duncan as one of the cleverest frauds in the history of spiritualism, and elsewhere he told the *Post*'s reporter, Dennis Miller, that the NLPR had only paid the Duncans £50 (as opposed to the £270 they really received), that the National Laboratory had led the way in detecting her fraud, and that a well-known spiritualist society was to blame for generating false public interest in her, which caused enormous upset within the LSA.

Although the story that appeared in the *Post* on 14 July helped salvage a little of his standing, Price's reputation in America went into a tailspin when Frederick Bligh-Bond refused to publish a word of criticism against 'the brethren' in the ASPR's *Journal*. Furious, Price wrote to him saying he was

astounded – and a little amazed – at your refusal to print notes regarding the Duncans. As you must realise the LSA has come a frightful cropper over the Duncans and I can visualise them moving Heaven and Earth to suppress our version of the affair.

Mr Letham [editor of *Light*] offered to print the very notes, which you turned down, but arrangements fell through, as we could not agree as to how the press should be informed. Is this upholding the best traditions of both your *Journal* and the ASPR in suppressing remarks you assume would not be palatable to the Spiritualists. In other words is *Psychic Research* still an unbiased scientific journal or not?[48]

Bligh-Bond did two things. First, he contacted Robert Fielding-Ould at the LSA to check Price's story and found it to be baseless. Then he discontinued Price's International Notes. On learning of this, Price wrote to Bligh-Bond: 'It comes as no great surprise . . . perhaps you will be kind enough to get your treasurer to settle my outstanding account of $630.'[49] Price then renounced his membership of the ASPR and his cherished post of Foreign Research Officer, viewing the American stance as treasonous – it was taking a stance against scientific discovery, he huffed.

Eugène Osty published a highly sarcastic review of Price's article in the *Revue Metapsychique*, calling the investigation 'a tragic case of ill-advised chemistry' and added that Price 'also wished to anticipate the report . . . in order to shine in the pages of the press'.[50]

Harry's reaction to this was a letter to Osty in which he tried to sound amused. The article had been a hoax, he claimed:

> In the article 'L'ectoplasme de Mrs Duncan' which I find very amusing, it reads as if I believed, or rather accepted, the genuineness of the 'teleplasm'.
>
> As a matter of fact, I reiterated that I was only concerned with the analysis of it. If *Luce e Ombra* and other publications have elected to say more than I did, that is their affair. The reason why I so much desired to publish my article on the teleplasm was to give the Duncans confidence so that they would come to my laboratory.[51]

Forced to lie to cover up his impetuosity – which by now was almost an habitual reaction – Price realised there was little sense in trying to silence Osty's cheeky criticism. It is difficult to see how the Frenchman, or indeed anyone else, could be expected to take him seriously after this. His theme-park science had become a joke.

Helen Duncan meanwhile, an ill and tortured woman, continued to give seances across the UK, though she was fined £10 for conspiracy to defraud the public in Edinburgh the following year (Price was called on as an expert witness), and was back in the dock twelve years later when police raided a flat above a chemist's shop in Portsmouth, in use as the 'Master Temple Psychic Centre'. In 1944, in one of the most startling episodes in wartime Britain, Duncan and three fellow defendants were brought to trial. She was charged with conspiracy to contravene Section 4 of the Witchcraft Act of 1735, an indictment that had never been brought in a modern court of justice.

Duncan's crime, her many sponsors claimed, harked back to 1941, when at an earlier seance in Portsmouth she had welcomed the spirit of a young sailor who had died a few days previously on the battleship HMS *Barham*, which had been blown apart by a German U-boat off Malta. The sailor was alleged to have said 'My ship has sunk', a source of shock to the Admiralty, which had suppressed news of the ship's loss in order not to shake public morale. After this incident the authorities were fearful Mrs Duncan would reveal the beaches chosen for the D-Day landings; and so she was arrested.

There were nineteen witnesses at her court case at the Old Bailey. One of these, Hannen Swaffer, swore that she was a competent clairvoyant and that she was the victim of a dastardly government plot. He asked why, if the authorities thought she was just a fraudster, had the Home Secretary Herbert Morrison used an antiquated law to try to imprison her rather than charging her with obtaining money by false pretences?

The Chief Constable of Hampshire Constabulary produced Price's X-rays of her stomach and described her as a past master in the art of fraud and an 'unmitigated humbug'. After an eight-day trial, which Winston Churchill called 'absolute tomfoolery to the detriment of necessary work in the court', Duncan was found guilty and sentenced to nine months imprisonment, to be served in London's forbidding Holloway Prison.[52] Duncan's solicitors immediately lodged an appeal, but against fearsome protests from some spiritualists, the Lord Chief Justice, Lord Caldecote, sitting at the Court of Criminal Appeal, believed the prosecution had more than proved its case.

Years earlier, in 1931, Price told his friend Guy L'Estrange that the National Laboratory had expended 'a nasty amount of money on her' and was in some danger of breaking up; but he believed it could recover. Trying to distance himself from Dr X he said: 'As for the doctor certifying that the ectoplasm was genuine, of course this is a sheer impossibility as no-one knows what ectoplasm is or how it can be tested.' Despite these later denials, Price's standing never fully recovered from the uncomfortable fact that he had got things so badly wrong.[53]

But if it was any consolation, so had many others, including Will Goldston and several magicians of the Inner Magic Circle. Later that year Goldston, along with a relatively closed and familiar circle of friends, garlanded Harry with the vice-presidency of the Magicians' Club, a post that came with a gold jewel and an elaborate testimonial. Still Price was doggedly pursuing the fantastic, the motley and the foreign.

10

WHY WARS BEGIN

As he wrote in 1931 to congratulate the physicist James Chadwick on his announcement that he had finally found evidence of the neutron, Harry Price might have thought to himself how good was the feeling of elation. In that same year he believed that he was a whisker away from discovering the secrets of life's biggest mystery.

Although his search had led him astray, and if he was slightly hampered by the completion of the final draft of his first mass-market book, *Leaves from a Psychist's Casebook*,[1] an overblown digest of his major investigations, his life was once again crammed with people, places, obligations and surprises.

It was one of these surprises that set him on another journey of self-discovery. And like most journeys of this kind, it had an unexpected start. With his usual mysterious vagueness, Price told his public in *Confessions of a Ghost Hunter*[2] that at lunchtime on Monday 9 November 1931, a person 'whose name is unknown' called at the laboratory's offices in Roland Gardens. Finding all the doors unlocked, the intruder left behind on Price's desk a cramped handwritten manuscript in English called *The Bloksberg Tryst*.

When he returned from stretching his legs Harry at once identified the manuscript as a translated copy of the High German Black Book, a fifteenth-century volume containing a magical rite for changing a virgin male goat into a beautiful youth. Whoever left the manuscript had also scribbled a note saying they would call again, though they apparently failed to come forward even after Price hurriedly placed a notice in *Light* asking them to contact him at the laboratory.

The problem is that although the mysterious visit apparently made perfect sense to Harry, there is no evidence that the event actually took place. Given what we know of his methodology in the Joanna Southcott affair, papers in the Harry Price Collection suggest that the discovery of the Black Book was the beginning of an explicitly commercial affair, stage-managed with the cooperation of Price's German friend, Dr Erich Bohn.

Bohn was a lawyer, a psychologist-cum-psychic investigator who had first met Price in 1922 when he had visited Munich with Eric Dingwall to take part in the Willi Schneider experiments with Schrenk-Notzing. Since then they had remained good friends, with Bohn arranging for Harry to meet German clairvoyants, including Max Moecke and Erich Jan Hanussen, better known as the mesmeric Prophet of the Third Reich (real name Hermann Steinsschneider), Adolf Hitler's influential Jewish seer. Price in turn had recently elected Erich Bohn as the NLPR's Breslau representative.

By sheer coincidence Bohn was a member of the Johann Wolfgang von Goethe Centenary Committee or Harzer Verkehrsverband, formed to organise celebrations to honour Germany's greatest polymath. Believing that the *Bloksberg Tryst* was Goethe's original source for the Walpurgis night scene in his poetic masterpiece, *Faust*, Price was not going to miss such a spectacular event, especially as people around the Harz Mountain region were keen to host large-scale fire festivities and midnight processions. The heady brew of *Sturm und Drang*, Aryan mystic services and peasant witchcraft offered him the promise of highly charged fun at little expenditure.

Two days after 'finding' the manuscript, Price told the world's press, to great and long peals of hilarity, of his intention to carry out the *Tryst* experiment on top of the Brocken, the highest of the Harz Mountains over-looking the twisty streets and the high-gabled houses of quaint old Weimar. The magic ceremony would see him employing 'a faire ointment' composed of bats' blood, scrapings from a church bell, soot and bees' honey, which in turn he would smear over a he-goat and a thinly clothed actress playing the part of the virgin. 'I am doing this,' he told reporters with a deadpan delivery, 'if only to prove the fallacy of transcendental magic.'

Unsurprisingly, this extreme oddness attracted sledgehammer headlines in newspapers published in Great Britain, Europe and as far as Cuba, India, New Zealand and Canada.

There were headlines such as 'Scientists to Turn He-Goat into Handsome Prince', and 'Innocent Girl and Goat in Magic Ring', which caused both unease and mirth among Price's colleagues, some of whom thought he was rapidly going insane.

A few scientists, such as the Swiss analytical psychologist Carl Jung, the proponent of archetypes, took the event seriously. Missing the point completely, Jung wrote to Price saying: 'For God's sake, tell me that it isn't true! How can a man of science lend himself to superstition!'[3]

In Harry's opinion, he could not lose. Failing to change a goat into a young man was bound to be successful. In the meantime, he continued to build up the momentum of the event by fooling the public and press into believing that the Harzer Verkehrsverband had invited him to stage the event as part of their celebrations. It is a measure of how respected and trusted he was that nobody questioned why the Germans would want to rely on Harry's English version of the *Tryst* when they had their own available to them, in their own language.

Glamour was added to the event by Price choosing the pretty flaxen-haired Urta Bohn-Gordon, the part-Scottish actress and daughter of Erich Bohn, for the part of the unblemished maiden; doubtless he had discussed this with her when she stayed at Arun Bank during a tour of the British Isles the previous year.[4]

Urta, or Gloria Gordon as she was later to call herself when she appeared in comic-book film adventures in Hollywood, told reporters that she had no objection to standing in a silk dress on a mountain as Price smeared her chest with a sticky black substance: 'I guess I am as well qualified as any girl nowadays. I think it will be great fun and if the youth of unsurpassed beauty does appear I shall be terribly thrilled.'[5]

The NLPR published a two-page brochure telling its members that 'elaborate preparations are being made for the experiment and a most enjoyable evening will be the result'.

Addresses on Goethe, Faust, magic witchcraft etc will be given in English and German; Harz Mountain peasant dancers in appropriate costumes will perform the age-old witches' dances on the Hexentanzplatz and it is intended that the evening shall be interesting, enlightening, historical, magical and amusing.

After three postponements, Harry picked 18 June, when the moonlight was at its strongest, to stage the reading. Had the weather been better on 22 March, the day of Goethe's death, he would have performed the experiment in front of seventy-four heads of nations who had earlier paid homage to the poet in the small Thuringian city where he had chosen to live and die. In the end, the weather conditions on the Brocken were too poor to allow the ceremony to go ahead. A little more than two weeks before the experiment Price wrote to Bohn claiming that his doctor had advised him not to go, and asked him to carry out the experiment on his behalf. Slipped in among the prattle of having badly strained his heart, he explained his plan of sending over the fabled bats' blood ointment and incense, just in case Bohn found the latter hard to track down, adding, 'Will you please make sure Urta wears white stockings and shoes; it is an essential part of the manuscript.'[6] An odd requirement of a medieval manuscript.

In view of these claims about his state of health it is odd to find a letter from Price addressed to Cyril Joad asking if he could accompany him and Ethel Beenham to the Brocken because the Canadian physiologist David Fraser-Harris's mother was ill and Fraser Harris was unable to come as planned.[7] After several refusals Joad at last agreed, and before Bohn knew it, Price had shrugged off his 'doctor's advice', packed his bags and with his new trusty companion, travelled to the Harz Mountains to set off on a well-crafted witch-hunt, 'of which there are several in the area'.

But they were to be disappointed. After getting very excited over reports of an old hag who lived in a cave, all they found was a stunted actress in a cottage who had merely played the part of a witch in some long-forgotten and ill-reviewed stage show. Next day their arrival in the area was greeted by a fanfare of massed bands and after an unimpressive ceremony delivered with great courtesy, the pair was given the titular freedom of the town of Halberstadt.

As midnight arrived on 18 June, Price, Joad, Urta Gordon, the goat, forty-two photographers, a party of seventy-three news reporters from across the world, twenty-two radio broadcast units (including one from the BBC) and a MovieTone camera crew made their way up the mountain to be greeted by hundreds of keen spectators, some dressed in period costume.

Standing on a raised dais were several leading members of European nobility, including Her Royal Highness the widowed Grand Duchess Feodora of Saxe-Weimar-Eisenach, the ascetic, pale, thin-lipped and rather nervous Dr Heinrich Bruning, Chancellor of Germany, and representatives of thirty nations. Alongside them stood the dwarfish Wilhelm Frick, Thuringia's Interior and Education Minister and the first Nazi to become a government minister. Standing next to Frick was the author Boris Pasternak, the playwright Gerhardt Hauptmann, the artist Paul Klee, and Ernst Hanfstaengl, one of Hitler's early close collaborators.

As democracy and autocracy looked on to celebrate an ancient rite squired by a genius, everything except the moon's light, which was curtained by a bank of grey cloud, was ready. The sacrificial snowy goat, clothed in a white shroud, trotted into the thickly painted magic pentagram inside a tessellated stone circle, which had been laid down near the natural stone formation called the Granit Altar. Next, in this skeleton plot, was Urta Gordon, who threw water on the crackling fire, lit to encourage the Devil. The thrurible, with streaming wisps of scented incense, was extinguished and then, captured by eerie rays of moonlight, came Price, in full evening dress, top hat and white silk scarf. He began the ceremony by uttering incantations in dog Latin in a weird monotone voice.

Then, in the first moment of action on the stage, and one in which newspaper reports said for an instant the enchantments of the underworld seemed real, Urta poured a flask of red wine over the goat. Harry next anointed the animal and Urta's chest with the so-called 'faire ointment', described by *The Times* as 'looking and smelling exactly like boot polish', and asked Urta to lead the infant ram round the middle circle anti-clockwise three times.

Tossing a white sheet over the startled animal, Harry rather hoarsely counted to ten. To no one's great surprise, and no doubt to Urta Gordon's great disdain, the goat remained a goat. For a moment, everything seemed an anticlimax – until Hanussen dashed forward, recited a spell and, to everyone's bemusement, produced from under a sheet a dwarf clothed in German national dress.

Price boorishly complained that things had not been quite right, so he performed the ceremony again the next day, when the press and spectators had gone home. Still the goat remained unchanged – white with patches of phoney faire ointment sticking to its hair.

Harry had sold his soul to commercialism as surely as Goethe's Dr Faustus had sold his to Mephistopheles; though his price had been not youth but reputation.

The gloriously weird ceremony and Price's part in it won him badly needed money; but he did not expect the merciless attacks on his status from the press. More than forty million readers across four continents read such stories as 'Goat Spurns Maiden to Become Her Young Man'. George Bernard Shaw told the *Morning Post* that the experiment was a 'rather unusual means of amusement'. Journalists such as Charles Sutton from the *Daily Mail*, by then a lobby correspondent and still a friend of sorts, enclosed a note together with the £4 he had borrowed from Harry to help him out of his temporary financial difficulty, saying 'I think you've done yourself a great deal of harm with the Brocken episode. You looked a fool.'[8]

The *Brocken Tryst* had left Price in such a state of high alert that he became irritable at the mere mention of it and panicked about how people began to regard him, aware that the whole saga had flattened his already dented prestige. *Punch*, that once supreme mirror of taste and opinion, reprinted a cartoon drawn by Emilio Coia, published by the French newspaper *Le Monde*, which poked fun at the 'wittily bumptious, goat bearded Joad', showing him and Harry as 'Capricornian fools'.

Once Price reached home he told Joad he found a 'pathetic letter' waiting for him from 'that old haybag' who had given them the freedom of Halberstadt. 'She said she hoped we had not thought her an inquisitive old woman and she was afraid that we despised the Schwab family because they were Jews. In reply I had remarked that I had met several good ones.'[9]

The months that followed Price's return from Germany were inevitably turbulent as the press tried to fathom out what was happening to the promise of the new science. Harry told Hannen Swaffer, then freelancing for the *Daily Sketch*, that the 'experiment was a bit of harmless, knockabout fun. I never intended it to be a serious ceremony. It was a mysterious thing to happen at a mysterious time.'

That September he, Joad and Dennis Dunn of the *Daily Express* made an expedition to West London in another attempt to find psychic wonder by sleeping in a reputedly haunted Louis XV bed at 'a private museum in Chiswick', which, on inspection of a letter Price sent to 'my dear Cyril', turns out to be nothing of the sort.[10]

There was certainly a bed in a room heaving with macabre portents of death (Charles I's death warrant was on a wall, a coffin was next to the bed) but it was above an antique shop at 56 Dalling Road, in Ravenscourt Park in London. Having brought along wine, sandwiches and plenty of smokes, Price set up his electrical flashlight camera to catch the actions of the poltergeist supposed to rock the bed back and forth and throw the wooden coffin over its unfortunate occupants. But they were to be disappointed again. There was no sign of any phenomena, and they failed to find the secret catch on the bed that had reputedly bounced a sleeper to the floor. They left the antique shop before the milkman arrived.

In the first feverish weeks of planning the *Brocken* episode, Harry received a letter from a Miss Florence Milburn, who lived at Peel on the Isle of Man. It told of an animal that looked 'something like a weasel', which had attached itself to the family of a farmer named James Irving who lived at Doarlish Cashen or Cashen's Gap, a run-down and remote farmhouse in the middle of bog-land at the top of the island's Dalby Mountain.

This strange animal, said Miss Milburn, could talk in several languages, was telepathic, could hear whispers from several yards away, sing the Manx National Anthem and liked to catch the bus for a tour round the island to do its shopping and bring back gossip.

At first Harry gave the discovery of the hairy creature a wide berth, instead dispatching a friend, Captain M.H. MacDonald, a keen motorcycle enthusiast who had taken part in the Isle of Man TT Race, to make tentative enquiries. MacDonald brought back a strange tale. The Irvings had settled on Dalby in 1916 to escape the war in Europe. James was well travelled, had been a piano salesman in Canada and then become involved in a failed engineering business in England.

In early 1930 the family had been caught slap bang in the centre of the economic nightmare of the Wall Street crash, and business had begun to slide. They kept themselves to themselves and generally lived a very lonely existence on very little money. Their 14-year-old daughter, Voirrey, the only child then living at home, became the main intermediary, introducing 'Gef' as an 'extra clever mongoose', born in Delhi, India, in 1852. Though he had a history of violent behaviour (he had threatened to kill the Irvings), Gef liked the family enough to spare them. They in turn provided him with his own den at the top of a cupboard and, as a way of thanks, the mongoose kept down the large number of rats in the house, and also brought the Irvings rabbits he had killed.

Captain MacDonald spent a night and two days with the family, and while he heard Gef several times talking in a shrill, feminine voice, telling him how he fancied himself as a singer, he never saw him. Intrepid investigator that he was, MacDonald asked Gef for a few hairs from his tail to take back to London for analysis. Price duly submitted the hairs to the zoologist Martin Duncan, who told him they had come from a dog.

Busy with the preparations in Germany, a supposed haunting of a manor house in Whittlebury Forest in Northamptonshire,[11] a night in with Aleister Crowley[12] and the successful launch of *Leaves from a Psychist's Casebook*, (described by *The Times* as 'a weirdly attractive tome'), Price sensed that his public was not quite ready for Gef and dropped the matter for three years.

Yet, despite all these optimistic pointers (interest and membership in the NLPR was at last on the up in late 1931), Price was discouraged and showing signs of strain. Central to this were events at Borley Rectory and the possibility of a third series of experiments with Rudi Schneider.

Price had been persuaded to revisit Borley by the persistent Ethel Bull, who had called at Roland Gardens with her sister on 29 September.[13] She told him that a new vicar, her cousin Lionel Foyster, was in office at Borley and that the Smiths, having made a successful drama out of their experiences, had moved to Sheringham in Norfolk. An astonishing array of phenomena was now happening at the rectory on an almost daily basis. These included apparitions, bell ringing and the throwing and dropping of bottles, stones and other missiles. There had been outbreaks of small fires. Furniture was knocked over. Doors were locked and unlocked. Voices and footsteps were heard and there was also a curious heady smell of lavender and cooking.

If Harry had an inkling of doubt, he said nothing. The Bull sisters returned to their home near Sudbury in Suffolk and awaited Price's assessment. When he visited the rectory on 13 October he brought with him the loyal Mollie Goldney, Clarice Richards, Ethel Beenham and May Walker.

Since the Foysters were expecting a polite social call, Harry's arrival mob-handed and the announcement that he intended to carry out a full examination of the house caught them off-guard and made them prickly. He did not make a good impression on Lionel's attractive wife Marianne: 'When I was introduced to him in Borley Rectory, he gave me the creeps. He had pointed ears, a balding head with high forehead, and eyes that were startling. They were not polite eyes.'[14] The group talked about Lionel's diary of events, including Marianne's suffering a black eye from the forever irritable poltergeist,[15] and the curious lavender scent, which was stronger than ever.[16] Price, it seems, showed a great deal of interest in examining the messages written on the walls and pieces of paper addressed to Marianne Foyster asking for help, prayers and mass.

He stunned the Foysters by expressing the view that what he had seen on his previous visits to Borley Rectory had been falsified by Mary Pearson, the Smiths' maid. Marianne was also shocked, on a more personal level, to find Price 'slobbering all over' Mollie Goldney.[17]

She was smiling up to Mr Price all the time, very obviously, and he was kind of goofy towards her. They were, I think, in the throes of having a mild romance – I guess that's how you would put it.

They had made several trips and he would go out first and she would follow, and then on another occasion, she went out and he would follow. I wondered what it was all about and I went out as softly as I could – there was a coconut matting in the passage – and then I went and opened the door rather sharply. They were behind the butler's pantry door, he had his arms around her, her dress was all hiked up, and she had pink pants on – the kind that we used to call 'bird cages'. I was very much amused, and sniggered, and I think that that was the reason why she disliked me so intensely.

Price wasted no time in declaring the wall writings, the smashing of crockery and the overturning of furniture to have been faked, perhaps subconsciously, by Marianne. He wrote to David Fraser-Harris:

Well, we went to Borley as arranged on Tuesday last, and have had two nights on the premises. It is the most amazing case, but amazing only in so far that we were convinced that the many phenomena that we saw were fraudulent because we took steps to control various persons and rooms, [and] the manifestations ceased. We think that the rector's wife is respons- ible for the trouble, though it is possible that her actions may be the result of hysteria. Of course we did not wire you because although, psychologically, the case is of great value, psychically speaking there is nothing in it.[18]

While investigating the preternatural rumblings at Borley, Price had learned that experiments with Rudi Schneider at the Paris Institut had proved wildly successful. Under intense scrutiny from an infrared strobe, Rudi had produced what Osty believed was an 'emanation', an invisible force field appearing from his body.

The situation for Price was made more intense by the fact that the seances he had attended that July with Mollie Goldney at Rudi's home in the town of Braunau – also famous as the birthplace of Adolf Hitler – were so impressive that he became paranoid that Osty would storm in and poach Schneider just at the moment the Austrian's supernatural powers were at their height. On his return to London, Harry at once approached Lord Charles Hope and others to secure funding. This achieved, the Austrian and his fiancée Mitzi Mangl were invited back to London for sittings in September.

A few weeks before Rudi was due to arrive in London, however, Price went back on his invitation to Mitzi (who Price found 'very attractive, not bad'[19]) with the result that Rudi refused to come to Kensington, which stuck in the throat of a man not known for his patience and who had brought the medium to London in 1929 after others had all but discarded him.

In the interim the young Austrian was encouraged to return to Paris by Eugène Osty. Rudi had a choice: he could negotiate a better deal with the National Laboratory, or accept the offer from France. Price, on his part, doubtless seeing Schneider's financial detour as a potential threat to his now waning importance, fired off a letter to Gerda Walther, who was still acting as Rudi's manager:

> Rudi gave me his solemn promise both in Paris and three weeks ago . . . We have been put to endless trouble and expense and then Rudi plays me a filthy trick like that. If a son of mine did such a thing, I would thrash him within an inch of his life. I do not know what the Austrian's idea of honour is, but if that is a sample of it, no wonder the Austrians are where they are today . . . If it had not been for me and the Laboratory; Rudi would be earning about £1 a week as a mechanic in Braunau.[20]

This intense enmity calmed down sufficiently for Rudi to come to London together with Mitzi on 29 February 1932, for what would be his most controversial set of seances.

By the end of March it was obvious that whatever powers Rudi possessed were fading, with the result that hints of fraud began to circulate. Eric Dingwall had accused the National Laboratory of cheating in the earlier seances. He wondered who had keys to the door where the experiments were held: was it possible for someone to shift around inside the room and create phenomena?[21]

On several occasions, the keys to the room were handed to different witnesses, but the theory of trickery was dismissed in the minds of the observers. Mollie Goldney sat in Rudi's cabinet and tried to reproduce seance effects to no avail. Whether her opinion of Price was clouded by her intimate relationship with him is a point we shall never know. But the rumours of fraud continued to increase, especially when Price, out of hand, snubbed researchers Dr Guy Brown and Theodore Besterman from the SPR as well as refusing to let the investigator William Marriott in on the sittings, a person who had immensely helped his early career in psychical research, had given him books and made a present of his research notes on various mediums, including William Hope.

Later that March Richard L. Gregory and SPR Research Officer C.V.C. Herbert (later Lord Powis) unveiled infrared equipment comparable to that used in Paris by Eugène Osty. It would take the place of the fiddly electrical shoe and glove arrangement put together by Price. Now the medium would be controlled by two people sitting either side of him, one holding his hands, the other gripping his legs.

Price described the infrared system as a light-tight box that sat inside a gauze cage 4ft 4in long, 1ft 9in high and 1ft 7in wide. A filter was placed in front of the box, which would allow only infrared rays to pass through it. The beam traversed the length of the box, striking a selenium cell or 'bridge' at the other end. By means of a suitable amplifier and relay a bell could be made to ring if the bean were interrupted. If a foreign body (such as the hand) were placed in the cage as if to intercept the beam, the bell would ring.[22]

The handkerchief, which in several seances had proved to be the item 'Olga' reached for first, rested on a counterweighted table-top, so that if anything moved it the other side of the table dropped, completed an electric circuit and fired a magnesium flash. As there were several cameras with uncapped lenses focused on the table, any movement Rudi, the sitters or the entity made would automatically be photographed.

The phenomena seen in the penultimate seance Rudi gave at the National Laboratory on 28 April were weaker but similar to those in the other two series of experiments: objects were moved, the handkerchief was knotted, a wastepaper basket was snatched from a sitter's hands, winds blew through the room and fractional parts of a human trunk and torso were glimpsed. The infrared equipment also recorded a force field emanating from Rudi, similar to that which had been observed in Osty's laboratories in Paris.

It was now that Lord Hope realised that there was something that demanded closer examination, and resolved in his own mind that Rudi's future should not be one dictated by Harry Price, or the National Laboratory, and proposed that an independent investigation under his own and Lord Raleigh's control at the SPR was of paramount importance.

In the end, it looked to Harry as if this was indiscreet fudge. He was angry at having found out about the arrangement only through Mollie Goldney, which naturally put his relationship with Charles Hope under terrific strain. In a huffy letter to him, Price made it clear, seeing that he had brought Rudi to London, that it should be up to him to decide what should happen to the Austrian next. He added:

> I am astonished at the attitude you take in the matter under discussion. The brutal facts of the case are that the very people I am running the Lab for have conspired in a miserable plot against me, and no amount of sophistry will alter them . . . It is like the host at a dinner party having his throat cut by his guests. . . [23]

Developing the classic theme of a man wronged, Price insulted Charles Hope at an emotionally charged meeting of the National Laboratory on 26 April, an event that promptly saw his Lordship resign and created unsettled relationships between all the main parties on the council. More letters flew back and forth now between Arun Bank and London than ever before. In a fit of histrionics, Price called David Fraser-Harris a liar after he had made the point that Hope was only interested in Rudi's future, questioning if he would let Rudi go when his contract with the NLPR expired.

A couple of days later, realising that he had overstepped the mark, Price wrote Fraser-Harris a strange, almost coquettish apology, saying he was sorry he should have been dragged into what amounted to a private argument. He even suggested he was paying for all the laboratory's experiments, which he was not.

> I have had trouble with Lord Charles Hope before. He insists upon 'bossing' things – but he will not 'boss' anything with which I am concerned if I am paying the piper and am doing all the work like I have done for the last ten years. I should never dream of trying to 'boss' another person's show, nor should I dream of doing such a mean, contemptible trick as a certain section of the Council apparently tried to play on me. I am very fond of you and I think your personality is delightful. Let us forget this wretched affair.[24]

The life of a psychic researcher without money or pull was not an easy one, so Fraser-Harris squeezed the issue of letting Rudi do what he wanted to do, slipping in the possibility that if Price held out it might provoke a fresh outbreak of sceptics whispering 'spoof': 'I do not see that you can have any valid objections to my group of genuine investigators, who are prepared to remunerate R, having seances with him. For you to object to this might lead to gravest misconceptions becoming current.'

Immediately afterwards Price was invited to control Rudi in the final seance, an action amply rewarded in the form of Fraser-Harris's letter to *The Times*, saying he wholeheartedly believed that there was something mysterious going on in the sittings:

> I merely wish to say that I, and my wife, have on several occasions, seen phenomena . . . Some of these have been – a four-legged table lifted up and thrown forward so violently that two of its legs were smashed off; a basket tugged out of my hand; a closed cigarette case pulled from the experimenter's hand and later flung open inside a large chest closed with a heavy lid . . .

Fraser-Harris had not been the first to express his feelings to the press. Dr William Brown was also convinced of Rudi's authenticity and wrote to the same newspaper to say so. Price was delighted with these endorsements, jubilant even with the amount of gratifying coverage, immediately writing letters to various scientists exclaiming that the NLPR had ushered in a 'new epoch in psychical research'.[25]

But soon Price was again made to look a fool when Brown was forced to qualify his letter after the Brocken stunt hit the front pages and colleagues questioned how he could believe in the experiments of someone foolhardy enough to try to turn a goat into a handsome prince. 'Intellectual conviction can only come,' predicted Brown in another letter to *The Times* on 14 May, 'if at all, after much stringent scientific investigation carried out in a university laboratory or in the seance room of the SPR with trained scientists and psychical researchers as sitters . . . Further knowledge is required of the exact physiological and psychological nature of Rudi's trance state or so-called trance personality "Olga", whether genuine or spurious.'

From the moment Price had begun testing Rudi in 1929 he had been hungrily eyeing an honorary doctorate and a swift scramble up the academic ladder; now, Brown had seemingly dashed his hopes. 'When I opened *The Times* you can imagine how my appetite vanished! My first reaction was how

Salter, Lord Charles Hope and the rest of the SPR people (mad with jealousy at the success of the Laboratory) will chuckle at your reference to them.'[26] Brown dryly pointed out that when he referred to the 'seance room of the SPR' he was not advocating research under the society.

Soon after Price's tirade, Professor Nils von Hofsten, one of the National Laboratory's flood of honorary foreign correspondents who had been a sitter at two of Rudi's seances in 1929, accused the Austrian of fraud, but offered no evidence for his finger-pointing. Harry righteously attacked von Hofsten for his remarks:

> Do you seriously think that your opinion, voiced after a lapse of two and a half years, will have the slightest weight with scientists anywhere in the world . . . Do you seriously consider that anyone will believe that you had 'proof' of Rudi's fraud and kept silent for two and a half years without saying a word about it . . . and do you not think you should be thoroughly ashamed of yourself? . . . I have much pleasure in removing your name from our list of Foreign Correspondents . . .[27]

Paradoxically, that week Harry had shown Rudi a photograph he had taken at the 28 April seance, suggesting that Schneider had evaded control and cheated. We know that in outline this is accurate, because some years after Price's death Mollie Goldney interviewed Ethel Beenham and took her back to the night on which he had developed the glass plate. A paper in the SPR archive at Cambridge University tells us something of her employer's reaction:

> Mr Price was in the darkroom developing the photograph and called me in. When the negative showing the free arm was before us, we were both [so] astonished that we were speechless. Certainly, Mr Price behaved as if he was amazed and incredulous, as I was. Hardly had we time to discuss the possible implications before Mitzi and Rudi arrived. Mr Price spoke some very halting German, and I had been studying at the Berlitz School of Languages and spoke definitely better than Mr Price but certainly not fluently.
>
>   Between us, we made Rudi understand the photograph; he suggested it must be a spirit arm (it seems he was as surprised and amazed as we had been) but Mr Price or I pointed out it could not be because it was in our

own pajama jacket used in the experiments . . . Rudi was such a nice boy that we all liked, and he left with Mr Price saying we must continue the sittings.

No definite accusation of fraud was made in so many words . . . Mr Price forbade me to say a word about it to anybody until he had thought it over . . . I do know that he intended issuing this accusation in spite against Lord Charles Hope who was having further experiments with Rudi to Mr Price's extreme annoyance. He regarded it as Lord Charles almost 'stealing' the medium he had brought over, paid for etc . . . He was terribly spiteful against Lord Charles and he was waiting for a chance to hit back at him and used this report for that purpose.[28]

Particularly intriguing is Price's next step. Shortly after developing the plate he playfully lured Mollie Goldney to the laboratory, saying he had important news to tell her, but she would have to give her word of honour to keep it secret.[29] Price showed her the photograph with Rudi's hand free and stretched out behind him.

Shocked, Goldney insisted that Price should let other members of the council know immediately, but he refused to do so, saying he intended to publish the photograph if and when it suited him; and was quick to exploit the possibilities.

A few weeks after he had shown the photograph to Goldney Price wrote a veiled menacing letter to Rudi in which he mentioned the 'suspicious looking photograph' in his possession: 'I am just commencing my report on the series of seances we held with you in the spring. I have not yet decided what to do with that photograph we took of you when tying the handkerchief experiment. It is so suspicious looking that there is really only one construction to be put on it. I shall have to consider what to do with it.'[30] It is clear what Price hoped to achieve. If Rudi, courageous enough to go ahead with the Hope–Raleigh experiments at the SPR, ignored him and settled with other investigators, then, out of a fit of pique, he would destroy his reputation. It reaffirmed a threat he had sent in earlier correspondence which stated that if Rudi went into tests with the SPR he would regret it all his life.[31]

Just before the young Austrian's visit to London in 1932, Price, the proud advocate of Schneider's paranormal gifts, wrote to Rudi wishing him a very successful visit, adding that he was 'sorry you are not coming to us but the expenses are so great in connection with your visit that we cannot afford to have you again just yet'. Since the letter was in English, a language Rudi only partially understood, it failed to change his mind. In the autumn of that year he arrived in London to be tested at Tavistock Square.

Almost eighteen months after developing the plate, and in the same week in 1933 that the SPR were due to publish their much vaunted results of the independent seances, with sublime inevitability Price upstaged them by publishing his critical photograph in a pamphlet, alongside an article accusing Rudi of achieving his phenomena through fraud in a fast-moving world exclusive for the brash *Sunday Dispatch*.

Price was desperate to show up Charles Hope and embarrass the SPR. As he wrote to Gerda Walther a week before the exposé, 'It would be a most extraordinary situation if we ended up by the SPR championing Rudi and ourselves throwing doubt on his phenomena.'[32]

Holidaying in France when the news broke, Hope asked Price for an explanation of his almost schizophrenic behaviour:

I shall be interested to hear from you who the 'we' referred to several times in the article as having made this discovery – whether it is meant to refer to your 'Council' or to whom? Also, I would like to know why you did not tell all the Council of your suspicions, especially I should have thought those you asked to subscribe the cost of bringing out the Report . . .[33]

By the end of that long week, eight members of the Council of the National Laboratory, including Dr Gerda Walther, had resigned over Price's article and his increasingly unstable conduct. All except Walther, who sidled back to him shortly afterwards, stayed their distance.

In a letter to Professor Dr Karl Przibram, who was alleged to have detected Rudi's first cheating incarnation in 1924, Price made out that 'we have not made any charges against him. Rudi's friends are still moving Heaven and Earth, but the evidence is too strong for them. I suspect that they might bring legal action.'[34]

Such action may have been considered, but it would never have come to that – a great pity, as Price never allowed anyone to see the negatives of the photograph in his lifetime. Today the photograph forms part of the Harry Price Collection and is freely available for examination. As Anita Gregory found in her tireless investigation into the photograph,[35] there is something suspicious about the photographs Price used to illustrate his Bulletin IV,[36] which were purported to show Rudi breaking from his control. They were of such poor quality that Dr Spencer, then president of the Royal Photographic Society, declared they were out of focus or defective to such an extent as to be almost useless as evidence,[37] scarcely credible for a man with Price's expertise with a camera.

Some of the sitters who took part in Rudi's three series of sittings, notably Mollie Goldney, Clarice Richards, Cyril Joad and Professor David Fraser-Harris, took the wide view that the photograph was an accident and that when Price discovered it he exploited it to the fullest. Then, as now, it would have been seen for what it was, a palpable fake; manufactured by Price to cause the maximum amount of embarrassment to the Society for Psychical Research.

And yet in his reply to Lord Hope's letter Price insincerely said that he failed to understand the problem. 'I do not know why such a fuss is being made over these pictures'.[38] To Joad, by then a close friend, he said that it was quite possible Rudi had been in a state of 'auto-hypnotism or trance, when he twisted round on his chair and picked up the handkerchief from the counterpoise . . . I am convinced he produced much better phenomena, and it was much more spectacular, during the 1929–30 experiments . . . it is curious that these should have been produced under a merciless system of electrical controls when it was impossible for him to cheat in any way. We still hail Rudi as being absolutely genuine.'[39]

Having done the cowardly thing of destroying Schneider's name, psychic research could only come to the conclusion that all analysis of Rudi was unsafe except for Price's own first series. It would have been inexplicable if Harry Price's subsequent split from his colleagues had gone without a hitch, but this was a man with the ability to reject reality, and far from being ruined by the opprobrium heaped on him by almost every psychic researcher in London (the Honourable Everard Fielding and those already mentioned were exceptions) he moved into close friendships with less circumspect psychologists and philosophers. Included among these was the educational psychologist Cyril Burt, who sensed that the University of London might be willing to discuss that familiar subject of housing Price's laboratory and library.[40]

At a lavish dinner held in October at the Hotel Splendide, Piccadilly – then one of the top ten hotels in London – in honour of the innovative and influential French metaphysicist Monsieur René Sudre, a vice-president of the NLPR, Harry gathered together a raft of leading academics and journalists to talk about the importance of psychical research as an academic subject and the idea of beginning an international journal for psychical research.

Richard Lambert, editor of *The Listener*, the mouthpiece of the BBC and then one of the most important literary magazines in the country, Sir Richard Gregory of *Nature* and Peter Quennell, editor of the *New Statesman* (whom Price placed next to the very pretty bookseller Christina Foyle, because he thought it would help the poet and historian's digestion), listened enthusiastically; but with no pot of money it was an impossible pipe dream.[41]

Using two members of the NLPR's reshuffled London Research Board, Professor J.C. Flugel, a former acolyte of Helen Duncan and assistant professor of psychology at University College, and the ubiquitous Cyril Joad, Price picked up Burt's idea of approaching the university's council, the Senate, with a proposal which he wrote with the aid of Joad (who helped to correct Harry's 'grammatification' and who began to pilot the document through a maze of academic bodies and committees).

As well as offering his laboratory and extensive library, which contained extraordinarily scarce first editions such as a 1762 pamphlet of Oliver Goldsmith's account of the Cock Lane Ghost – so rare that a copy in 1930 sold for £900 – he committed himself to setting up an endowment fund necessary to produce a return of £500 a year to continue research work.

During the months he waited for a response Harry turned himself to experimenting with an eccentric device called the psychic telephone, which had been invented by F.R Melton, a Nottinghamshire spiritualist. Simply a wireless set connected to a pair of earphones and a rubber bag, the device was designed to free up time for the busy medium. Melton hoped that eminent scientists who had passed through the 'ether state' would help him invent a loudspeaker, instead of his having to use large trailing earphones that frequently tripped him over as he spoke to the undead.

It was a simple device to use. First, the bag was inflated. Then it was sealed inside a small wooden box for the medium to receive 'spirit' voices over the airwaves; but it was not a success. Price said it was 'not very good. It did nothing but hiss and growl.'

In November the committee of the University of London's Board of Studies finally responded to his offer, deciding that psychical research was indeed 'a fit subject of University study and research'.[42] There were built-in restrictions though. The Academic Council specified that research would only be carried out by 'persons suitably qualified both scientifically and otherwise' and 'with adequate safeguards they feel it would be possible to avoid undesirable forms of publicity'.

It was a poke and a peek at how the majority of academics had come to regard him, his amateur status and his mania for the public exposure. Nevertheless, this offer should have pointed to a bright future, but another letter, this time from Edwin Deller, principal of the University of London and former executive secretary of the Royal Society, led to the university's ultimate rejection of Price's offer, citing lack of space and money – though it is not idle to suppose that influential academics connected to the SPR had a hand in killing off the deal. Deller wrote that it was impossible to make any arrangements for the housing of the laboratory at a school of the university. 'In the circumstances, the University finds itself unable to accept your offer. The decision is reached with regret and I can assure you that your offer and the generous terms with which it was accompanied have been most highly appreciated.'[43]

It seemed that Harry Price was to be permanently disappointed. A while later he mused that:

Academically, Great Britain has shown little interest – officially – in psychical research. Although the Society for Psychical Research has been established for more than fifty years, little had been done in this country to attract organised science until I launched my 'campaign' to interest the University of London.[44]

The implication never far from the surface of Price's writing was that he alone was the pioneer trying to push psychical research into serious study; and it was this conceit that kept respectable scientists from having anything to do with him. There had been a long history of bringing scientific interest to the occult, and throughout their history the SPR had attracted the best scientific brains in Europe to the cause, most of whom were now keeping their distance from Price. As he got used to the idea of being marginalised, Price also had to come to terms with the fact that many of his former council members had in early 1934 fallen in with an initiative of the Survival League, called the International Institute for Psychic Science, cheekily quartered at 16 Queensberry Place. After a slightly bumpy start, the institute, the public was told, 'was not a society for the exposure of mediums but for the finding of genuine phenomena by strictly scientific but very sympathetic and patient inquiry'.[45]

Professor David Fraser-Harris was named research officer, the novelist Shaw Desmond and Professor Julian Huxley were vice-presidents, and among a slew of luminaries sitting on the new body's consultative and executive committees, chaired by Arthur Findlay OBE, were Dr Nandor Fodor, Sir Oliver Lodge, Sir Ernest Bennett MP, Hans Driesch, Dr William Brown and Archibald Montgomery Low. Writing about the institute to Archibald Low, Price said disparagingly: 'I can imagine old ladies going to have their auras tested, with a nice chat and a cup of tea afterwards.'[46]

Forced into dissolving the National Laboratory largely for lack of money, Price considered throwing in his lot, confessing to Joad that he was 'perfectly disgusted with the whole business of psychics' and was content to retire from psychical research. But Cyril and Doreen Joad implored him to reconsider, and, thanks largely to Joad, the University of London Council for Psychical Investigation was formed, which, despite its title, had absolutely no official connection to the University of London. Instead, it had buckets of gravitas, including in its roll-call of distinguished academics the Cambridge philosopher Dr C.A. Mace, the American Freddie A.P. Aveling, the mathematician Dr Samuel Soal and Professor John MacMurray, the Snell Exhibitioner and Fellow of Balliol. It made impressive reading.

At its first meeting on 6 June 1934, chaired by Joad, it was resolved 'That this Committee should carry on the work formerly conducted by the National Laboratory of Psychical Research until such time as it was thought desirable to approach again the University authorities as to the formation of a Department for Psychical Research.' It was an organisation outside academia, which hoped to persuade the University of London that, through proper scientific studies, research into the world of the undead was something of value.

Its headquarters remained at Roland Gardens, though Price was no longer its official head (Joad held that honour): instead he was the body's Honorary Secretary. Reading the minutes of that first meeting it is easy to forget how the council marked a new beginning. Gone were the ill-tempered disputes and the headline-chasing of suspicious finds: the new body represented what Harry called a 'green start where, thanks to the Council, never again would scientists be at risk of being used as cats' paws by spiritualists for propaganda reasons'.[47] The committee believed him when he said his goal was to see psychical research adopted by a British university. Though his quest for proof of survival after death still remained, he began to scout around for remarkable psychological feats of mind over matter rather than anything overtly occult.

In the early summer, he began corresponding with Lieutenant-Colonel Robert Henry Elliot, a distinguished ophthalmologist and head of the Occult Committee of the Magic Circle. Though the principal reason behind his letters was to talk about the fabled Indian Rope Trick, he also mentioned the unfairness of the BBC and Sir Oliver Lodge. That April the Corporation had allowed Gene Dennis, an American clairvoyant who was starring at the London Palladium, to be the first professional medium to broadcast on the *In Town Tonight* programme, but the BBC had refused Price's request for a follow-up discussion on psychical research, a stance supported by Lodge.

An indignant Price, now a member of the clandestine Inner Magic Circle, asked a blustering Elliot, chief constable of the nation's secretive psychical police force, what he intended to do about it.

> I mean to attack the BBC as strongly as I can. I think their present line of action is an abuse of privilege and of opportunity, both of which carry responsibility with them. You have done far more in connection with Spiritualism than I could ever hope to do as I am a very busy man in professional practice and can only give odd spare hours to hobbies like this. It is difficult to understand how Sir Oliver can allow his name to be associated with statements so manifestly incorrect, unless he is getting too old for the work.[48]

His reply so impressed Price that he sent Elliot a silver cigar case by return of post. It is clear that Price was working up to asking if he would kindly allow him on to the panel to discuss the rope trick, which the Occult Committee was strenuously investigating.[49] The favour was granted, and Price appeared on 30 April 1934 at the Oxford House Theatre in

Marylebone, a place notorious for the staging of crude melodramas, to debate whether the rope trick was a supernatural phenomenon or a bit of Indian trickery.

Alongside him were such prickly British imperial favourites as The Lord Ampthill, president of the Magic Circle, former Governor of Madras, assistant Viceroy of India and son of the diplomat Lord Odo Russell, The Lord Meston of Agra and Dunottar and Brigadier-General George Elliott, former adjutant to Queen Victoria.

Opening the case for the prosecution, Lord Ampthill told his sagacious audience that it was in the best traditions of English conjuring to dispel superstitious beliefs. It was stuff and nonsense that Indian magicians could perform certain tricks better than their Western counterparts. The rope trick, he harrumphed, was just a conjuring trick, nothing more.

For his part, Price announced that since there was no mention in his vast library of books on magic and the paranormal to support the theory of the rope trick, it ought to have the funeral it deserved. At the end of the session Elliot summed up the evidence and came to the rapid deduction that the trick was just talk. A rope could not possibly defy gravity and stay rigid enough for someone to climb it and then disappear. If someone could demonstrate that it was in any way supernatural to the satisfaction of his panel, the Magic Circle would pay out 500 guineas.

The outcome of the meeting was a verbal war that rebounded in the letters column of *The Listener* for several months. One letter Richard Lambert received he immediately handed to Price. It was from a reader in Devon claiming to have seen the rope trick performed – and not on the banks of the Ganges, but at the English seaside.

There could be no mistake: enclosed photographs showed the rope, erect and tall, defying gravity. At the bottom sat an Indian fakir named Karachi and there, on the rope, was his son Kyder, biting his lip, looking a trifle worried but unsupported and several feet from the ground. The feat had happened at Pilchard Cove in Plymouth.

The mystic, however, turned out to be a sham fakir whose real name was Arthur Claud Darby, a 45-year-old former soldier from Ramsgate. An erstwhile magician, Darby had adopted the stage name of 'the Phantom', and then thrown in his lot to become the latest in a long line of performers to milk the public's fascination with India. He worked on the sands around Plymouth during the summer months and in winter made the 500-mile round trip to stay with his brother, a silk worker at the Paradise Mill in land-locked Macclesfield.

A Gurkha soldier had taught Darby the rope trick during the First World War, or so he claimed, though even this later turned out to be untrue. There were shouts of 'fake', of course, especially from the Magic Circle, but as one correspondent to *The Listener* asked, 'What is a trick if it is not a fake? Is a trick less of a fake if "genuine" or is a "genuine trick" a trick that is not a trick?'

After several false starts, Karachi met Price, Lambert, an outside broadcast unit of the BBC together with a 'talkie' set-up from Gaumont British Films and several others in a field at Wheathampstead in Hertfordshire, in January 1935. Hoping to perform the trick under near-Indian conditions during a raging blizzard in the English winter was always going to be troublesome, and the Gaumont newsreel shows just how poor Karachi's attempt was. His son Kyder managed to climb the rope but it was hardly the stuff of legends.

This did not matter to Price, who was able to thumb his nose at the Occult Committee and bragged he had seen the Indian rope trick: 'at least I have seen a clever illusion which has intrigued newspaper correspondents for so many years', he declared, conveniently forgetting that a month or so earlier he had taken part in a friendly debate with Elliott and his colleagues.

The Occult Committee was unimpressed, and after Harry's report appeared in *The Listener*, Elliott and others admitted they had seen a type of rope trick but not the one they were looking for, and tenaciously clung on to their 500 guineas.

Darby offered Price the secret of the trick for a knockdown £50, but Price refused. Files in the SPR archive at Cambridge University show how wise this was. Not only had Karachi taken two days to 'prepare the site' but he was seen to leave with his loosely coiled rope and an 8ft length of copper pipe.

Just as Harry was getting ready to travel to Bulgaria on the Simplon Orient Express with Eric Dingwall and Lambert to watch a fire-walk of a 'religious and ecstatic nature', he decided to invite a Kashmiri named Kuda Bux, who was appearing at the Little Theatre in the Strand, to Roland Gardens to test his claim of having X-ray eyes. While he and his examining committee were impressed by the Indian's ability to see whatever was placed in front of him, even though his eyes were bandaged and covered with plugs of cotton wool, Harry concluded he was able to glimpse objects through a mask of wadding, dismissing Bux's fancy claim that he was able to see using his nostrils.

Far more important to Price was Bux's boast of being able to walk on hot embers. After many talks, the University Council drew up a contract to secure the Indian's fire-walking services for 9 and 17 September at Alex Dribbel's house, The Halt, at Woodmansterne Road in Carshalton, Surrey.

In the meantime, Price and Richard Lambert prepared to visit the Isle of Man after the indefatigable Captain MacDonald had paid another visit to the Irving family in May 1935 to study Gef the talking mongoose's latest antics. The Irvings had been writing to Harry Price on and off for the last three years, and when the morning's post brought the news that the creature had begun singing 'Home on the Range', had learned sign language, acquired a smattering of German, French, Italian and Afrikaans, and was taking an active interest in current affairs by studying the newspaper, Harry decided to dispatch MacDonald to find out more.

MacDonald collected little evidence that Gef existed, though he claimed to hear him speak. He also learned that Gef hated Harry Price, demanding an assurance from the Irvings, especially their daughter Voirrey, that he would not be allowed to visit. However, to his credit, Price rowed against the creature's antipathy, later writing:

'This was not the first time Gef had shown signs of fear when any reference to me was made. More than once, he exclaimed "Mr Price is a doubter. Mr Price buts the kybosh on the spirits. I don't like Mr Price and so on."'[50]

Regardless of whether Gef hated him or not, Price thought it his duty to visit Cashen's Gap. After crossing with Lambert from Liverpool to Douglas in July, the pair, extravagantly adorned with sprigs of mountain flax in their buttonholes in order to identify themselves, met James Irving at the Waterfall Inn, on the top of Glen Maye. He told them Gef had been missing for nearly five weeks. Such a thing had not happened before and the Irvings were unsure if he was dead or hiding in a hole behind the skirting board.

To test this theory Price, Lambert and James Irving started back to the farmhouse. There Mrs Irving addressed a little speech to Gef:

In a voice that would have melted the heart of a graven image, or brought tears to the eyes of less hardened investigators than ourselves, she asked the mongoose to show himself.

When this failed, Harry implored him to spit – his favourite way of dealing with doubters – but his jacket remained unspattered by Gef's venom.[51]

Back at their hotel, Lambert and Price reviewed the situation. Believing that it was surely beyond anyone to invent and sustain a story year after year unless there was some foundation to it, they returned to Cashen's Gap to see if Gef had reappeared. Since nothing had been seen or heard of him during the night, Harry and Lambert spent their time on a perfect day, warm and sunny, mooching around the farm searching hedgerows of whitehorn, ash, blackthorn, sycamore and the green pathways that linked them. They lifted stones, looked in barns and stared out to the romantic sea where Price found that 'Without moving one's body, from the outside of the farmstead one can see England, Ireland, Scotland and Wales. St Patrick's Channel sparkled in the sun, and the Mountains of Mourne were a conspicuous landmark on the western horizon. The view was inconceivably wild, grand, and beautiful. It was like being on the roof of the world.'[52]

They spent the remainder of the day in the gloomy farmhouse where they found the decor depressing: 'the whole is panelled with match-boarding stained a deep, dark brown – almost black'. At midnight, they decided it was useless to remain any longer, and left the island the next day.

But during their passage home Gef had made his way back to the house as 'mim as a May Pudding. He clapped his hands and laughed like a maniac', having been out round the island picking up scandal and eating cream buns – 'he has some feminine habits', Price observed. The mongoose was not at all contrite, but to make amends he promised that he would stick his paws in some plasticine so that his tracks could be analysed.

Voirrey Irving took photographs of the bad-tempered animal with the camera Lambert and Harry had bought her and posted them off to London. 'They are not convincing,' Price replied tersely. 'One of them looks like a piece of rock, the other like nothing on earth. I can see no resemblance to a living animal in either of the pictures.'

Gef's paw-prints, cratered in plasticine, arrived during the next few days. Asked by Irving how he made them, Gef apparently said: 'I put my foot in it and gave it a twist, but the stuff was as hard as hell!' A package containing tracks and hair was sent to the distinguished zoologist Robert Pocock at the British Museum. As suspected, Pocock's report was not exactly encouraging. One of the impressions did not represent the footprints of any mammal known to him, except possibly a raccoon. The second paw-print had no possible connection with the other two; and no animal existed in which there is such a disparity in the size of the fore and hind foot. The hair had turned out to be from a dog rather like the Irving's sheepdog Mona. As a parting shot, Pocock concluded his report with the stinging: 'I do not believe the photographs represent footmarks at all. Most certainly none of them was made by a mongoose.'

Despite pretending to bleat that he 'was getting fed up with Gef', and that everything was a 'picturesque swindle', it is quite clear Price enjoyed this markedly odd case, coming up with conclusions of his own about the mongoose's identity. Either, he said, some person had foisted upon them 'bits of Mona's hirsute covering as evidence', or Gef had clipped hair from Mona and raffishly passed it off as his own.

It was around this time that Irving wrote to Harry telling him that he wanted to write a book about Gef's experiences. He had scented the mongoose's desire for self-expression and believed a book might sell well enough to help the family out of their dire financial difficulties; but the idea received a wry response. 'You will have to find a publisher willing to take a first-time author at his word. Gef's story does not have a logical ending to it. I really do not think the book would have much of a chance in a crowded market.'

Perhaps a more cautious man would have written the story first, touted it around various publishers then, if perpetually turned down, asked Price if he could offer it to a publisher on his behalf; but Harry had already made a pre-emptive strike. In March 1936, *The Haunting of Cashen's Gap*, a ragbag of other people's materials, and co-written by Lambert, was on the nation's bookshelves and being marketed as one of the best books of the year.[53]

In Price's defence, although there is hardly a line that can be said to be his in the book, no one else would have taken James Irving's tale seriously enough to pursue it over five years. The sale of the farmhouse shortly after the Price/Lambert book was published probably made up the money the Irvings failed to earn by not publishing the animal's yarns.

An American film director eager to make a movie based on the mongoose's life story offered James Irving $50,000 for full rights; but Gef refused to appear for the screen test, apparently because he hated make-up, and the idea was shelved.

There was also an unexpected turn of events when Lambert sued Sir Cecil Levita (a former chairman of London County Council) for alleged malicious slander after calling him 'unstable' and 'hysterical' for beliving in Gef. Lambert later took Levita to court and received £7,500 in damages.[54]

Price's relationship with preserving ephemera grew closer that year when he helped to set up the National Film Library as part of the British Film Institute, donating around 100,000 feet of old and rare films he had accumulated when he became worried that it might spontaneously combust. He stood as chairman of the library for more than five years ('In my opinion it was the best thing the BFI has done'), then resigned his position when the Second World War prevented his travelling to London for meetings. Harry also found time to become honorary treasurer at the British Institute for Adult Education, a post that brought him into contact with a film director who persuaded Harry to make a short film on psychical research for British MovieTone News. Price did not consider the film a success, packed as it was with awkward pauses, pipe sucking and jerky editing.

'It was difficult to get the atmosphere of the seance room into the story,' he groaned in his autobiography, before suggesting that the film had only been a stopgap arrangement:

> . . . more than once I have been invited to go to the United States in order to make films of the technique of psychical research. But I have always refused. If the right atmosphere cannot be captured in London, in my own Laboratory, I am sure it would still evade us in that land of sin, sun and celluloid – Hollywood.[55]

With charitable giving playing a greater role in his life, Price, along with the actor Sir Frank Benson, became a founding member of the Shakespeare Film Society, which provided him with a salary of £300 a year. The noble aim of producing Shakespearean plays for youngsters died an early death, killed off by petty squabbles and the high fees given to the board.

But the world of psychic research had not disappeared from Harry's life. Just when the public thought they had heard the last of the University Council of Psychical Research, it made the news on 10 September 1935 as Kuda Bux took part in the first scientific recorded fire-walk in the world. After seven tons of oak logs, a ton of pine, a load of charcoal, ten gallons of paraffin, and fifty old copies of *The Times* were ignited, the public were allowed in after paying two shillings (which included tea and hot toasted crumpets) to witness Bux walk a burning trench measuring 11ft long, 6ft wide and 9in deep. Despite appearances, probes measured the heat of the surface at 806 degrees Fahrenheit (430 degrees centigrade).

Bux gathered his thoughts and walked over the red hot embers twice in bare feet without scorching his soles, looking comfortable each time. There was nothing new about fire-walking – the English folklorist Andrew Lang had written on it thirty years earlier, believing it dated to early Shamanism – but contemporaries struggled, just as science does today, to explain it. Sir Leonard Hill, Professor of Physiology at the London Hospital, calculated in the *British Medical Journal* that Bux was able in some way to control the sweat glands of his feet; by way of response, the rump of psychologists and physicists who made up Price's Council reasoned that the secret lay in the short contact and low thermal conductivity of the charcoal.

The University Council repeated the fire-walk experiment two years later when another Indian, Ahmed Hussain from Bithur near Cawnpore, walked along a trench similar to that used in the Kuda Bux experiments, but hotter. Two days later, on 20 April 1937, Price's final tests, filmed by the BBC, took place at Alexandra Palace – the first 'actuality' feature televised in Great Britain.

Also in 1937 Price and Lambert made a trip to Northeim, in the Harz Mountains, to stay with Gerda Walther (his 'little friend') and explore Castle Falkenstein, one of the most beautiful and undamaged medieval castles in the world. Price made time to experiment with Maria Silbert, the medium who claimed to walk on water.

In his memoirs, written between 1940 and 1941 when the threat of invasion by Germany was a daily possibility, he wrote of pockets of 'anti-Hitlerism in Germany'. This was no more apparent than at two informal parties hosted by Walther and the mathematician Ernst von Mohr, a lecturer at Göttingen University, at which 'a number of leading residents and the local chief of police' talked over the political situation.

After seeing that the doors of their home were truly closed, and with the tea-cosy enveloping the telephone 'in case of accidents' we had a heart-to-heart about . . . Hitler. It was quite obvious from the conversation that ensued that every one present was definitely unsympathetic with the Nazi regime – but they were afraid to say so openly. I am sure that if Hitler was present at our little Harz parties, someone would have wrung his neck.[56]

This is Price's safe way of circling around the fact that he had rubbed shoulders with sympathisers of the National Socialist Party. Of course, he had many German friends, both Nazis and those such as von Mohr who were firmly opposed to power by force. Yet Harry's involvement with Nazism was much deeper and much less honourable than his official story makes out; and although there is no overwhelming evidence to suggest that his involvement was anything but timely conviction, it is impossible that he was unconscious of the Nazis' lawlessness and brutality in a country where citizens were daily dispossessed of all their worldly belongings, people disappeared suddenly and free speech was outlawed. Indeed, one surviving unpublished letter and a series of photographs intimates that, at some stage, Price had met Hitler and possibly others of high rank in the Nazi government.

WRITING TO HITLER

B etween 28 February 1933 and 30 April 1945 Germany changed forever. Hitler became chancellor on a nod from Wilhelm Frick and the political wing of the Catholic Church. Nazism, largely an occult-based semi-religion, became the country's pedigree, persona and legacy, defining everything that moved within its borders.

From this point on Harry's friendship with German ideologists begins to look questionable. At Northeim in the summer of 1933 he made an important new friend.

Dr Hans Bender was a National Socialist, the sort of progressive Harry believed could offer him all he was looking for and the sort of person he most wanted to be. A friend and colleague of Gerda Walther and Professor Hans Driesch, Bender had studied French literature, philosophy and psychology in Paris, Heidelberg and Bonn before turning to eidetic imagery and writing a paper on clairvoyance. In this he stated his belief that such imagery played a part in how a medium saw and relayed images to the sitter. Together with the head of experimental psychology at Bonn, the philosopher and psychologist Erich Rothacker, Bender began meeting Price in London. They also had meetings with Sir Ernest Bennett MP, the former vice-president of the LSA and a member of fascist political groups including the Nordic League and later the Right Club, an umbrella organisation of far-right groups formed by his friend, the antisemitic Conservative MP Captain Archibald Ramsay.

Bennett and Dr Erich Rothacker had influential friends, such as Alfred Rosenberg, the official ideologue of the Nazi Party who had popularised *The Protocols of the Elders of Zion*, an absurd collection of tracts that describe a master plan for the restructuring of society, the creation of a new oligarchy and the subjugation of millions by the Jews. Each phase of National Socialist training came under Rosenberg's influence, and ideological concepts were inculcated in every echelon of the Party through his influence. The universities were vital to the new order. Hanussen, who had predicted the Führer's elevation as chancellor, was promised by Hitler early in 1933, just before his murder, that his dream of a university of the occult was not far off.[1] When National Socialist leaders recognised that psychology was vital in helping the German people to accept the legitimacy of Nazi rule, and of course helped the Reich to out-think its enemies, Hanussen became a powerful ally for Rothacker and Bennett.

In early 1936, after first failing to sell the idea of republishing the *British Journal of Psychic Science* as part of the Society for the History of Alchemy and Chemistry's *Ambix* magazine,[2] Price approached Hans Bender with the idea of donating his laboratory and important library to Bonn; he had also heard that Hitler was personally interested in psychic research.[3]

I am anxious to transfer the Laboratory to another authority. Certain officials at the University of London were proposing I receive a doctorate in recognition of the fact that I had established the first chair of psychical research in Great Britain.

I see no reason why I should not make a precisely similar offer to the University of Bonn. You have the accommodation and in yourself someone to look after the department.

Price added cannily that the value of the laboratory and library was £25,000 – a value he seems to have plucked out of thin air – and offered, if the university should be interested in the scheme, to make a visit to discuss the details.[4]

What emerges from this letter is just how far Price was willing to go to gain an honorary doctorate, a motive he flatly denied in *Search for Truth*,[5] where he said he made 'no conscious effort or intention' to win any prestige or honour. There is no written reference from the University of London to support the idea of his receiving an honorary degree, so one can only think that his latest offer was a sly dig in galvanising the Germans to supply him with the academic recognition he so desperately craved.

By March Harry had still received no reply from Bender, but carried on probing curious cases of haunting, including an alleged poltergeist at Dean Manor at Meopham, near Gravesend in Kent. Price believed the account of the owner, Mr G. Varley, who claimed that the spirit was probably that of a fifteenth-century servant girl who was found hanged in the granary after her mistress accused her of theft. Varley had heard groans and other strange noises, like the constant flicking of paper, coming from various parts of the farmhouse – which, in Price's account, was described as a mansion. Yet the investigation was fruitless. Nothing was seen and the house remained quiet, though Price made a speck of radio history as the BBC broadcast him spending a night at the manor, 'the first broadcast ever to be made from a haunted house in this or any other country'; *The Times*, more criticallly, described the experiment as a fiasco. But the publicity was useful for the publication of *Confessions of a Ghost Hunter*, a motley collection of essays that included an ill-masked investigation of Borley, disguised as 'K-Manor' because Lionel Foyster had threatened a libel action should Price identify him, his family or the rectory.

Much of what had been written about Borley could be attributed to normal causes, wrote Price – who could not yet bring himself to believe in all the baffling hype he had written about the house in 1929. Similarly, in a letter to Sir Arnold Lunn in which he acknowledged the truth about the Battersea poltergeist, he also admitted that the so-called unearthly activity at the rectory had been Marianne's doing: 'I think she wanted to drive her husband away from the rectory, which is in a very quiet and lonely spot. But I cannot print this explanation; I daren't even hint at it, so that part of the doings of the Most Haunted House must remain.'[6]

A couple of months after this magnanimous confession, Bender visited Price at his laboratory to bring him some exciting news: the German government, he said, had not rejected his idea out of hand and even now Berlin was considering his proposal. As far as we can surmise, Rosenberg, as the party's theoretician and ideologue, would have studied the proposal first, would then have had it analysed by Goebbels and sent to Hitler and Himmler, who was keen that anything which energised minds about occultism or made them receptive should be encouraged.

The process inevitably took longer than Price wanted or expected, so that in August he approached Reginald Rye, Goldsmiths College Librarian, offering to transfer his library 'on permanent loan' (rather than to donate the library to the university, a story that originated with Paul Tabori) to the University of London so that students eager for information on the occult and magic could make use of the books. The only condition was that the collection should be styled 'The Harry Price Library of Magical Literature' and a plaque put up 'in a prominent place' to signify the donation. Both the Senate and the Court of London University fully endorsed the move, insuring the contents at £10,000.

But Price continued to court German interest, writing to Rothacker and Bender on 7 October that although for the time being he must withdraw the proposals he had put forward to Bonn University, there was still hope of a deal. 'The German authorities have been so long in coming to a decision that I cannot wait any longer . . . please continue your negotiations on the basis as to whether your authorities would accept my proposals if they were renewed.'[7] Exactly what he meant is not hard to work out. If successful, he would have simply snatched back his library and transferred it and the laboratory to Germany, a process that would have furrowed a few academic brows.

Against this sense of urgency, it is no wonder, readers might think, that the committee of the University of London Council for Psychical Investigation presented Price with an illuminated address celebrating his achievements in psychic research at a dinner held at the Hotel Splendide in January 1937. Yet there are no signs that anyone on the council other than Harry knew of his negotiations with Germany. The citation of the council's address read 'Presented to Harry Price, Esq., by the University Council of Psychical Investigation, as a mark of its appreciation of his services to Psychical Research, and especially of the work he has done during the last thirteen years at the Laboratory.'[8]

The newfound understanding between Price and the University of London Council for Psychical Research did not extend to Harry's telling his committee or its Chairman Cyril Joad that he was dealing with fascists. He had good reasons for this: Joad was a supporter of the socialist Popular Front in the Spanish Civil War, a war that raged until 1 April 1939 when Franco became Spain's dictator.

Meanwhile, positive news from Hans Bender about the German government's reaction to the Price proposal was trickling in. In February 1937 one of Bender's colleagues, Fräulein Dr J. Wichert, called on Price to tell him that the Third Reich now recognised psychic research as an official branch of science and had given permission for the founding of a Department of Psychical Research at Bonn University. Hitler had taken a particular interest in the idea.[9]

In March, when the lease of Roland Gardens ran out, the University Council for Psychical Investigation decided it was better to seek administrative offices at 19 Berkeley Street in Mayfair rather than continue with renting an apartment. The laboratory, now seldom used, was packed in crates ready for its secret and seemingly imminent airlift to Bonn.

On 20 March Dr Hans Bender officially informed Price that the Nazis had decided, in principle, to accept his original offer.

They authorise the establishment of a Department of Abnormal Psychology and Parapsychology and think of special interest this Department, besides the research work, questions of a social hygiene in occult matters.

As an acknowledgement of your possible gift and considering its importance for public health, the German Government would confer upon you the Rote Kreuz Medaille, 1 Klasse [order of the Red Cross, 1st Class]. This would not exclude the University honouring you in some other way. Our collaborator told us that you are planning to come to the banks of the Rhine in the beginning of April. I am looking forward to a word from you, when exactly we shall have the pleasure of seeing you in Bonn.[10]

On 13 April 1937 Harry visited Bonn as an official guest of the Third Reich, taking along with him his friend Stuart Worsley, then Acting Principal of the University of London, who it seems was as enamoured of the Nazis as Price was. Now the focus shifted to negotiating the terms of Price's contract with Bonn.

At lunch an inner coterie of trusted academics including Rothacker, Professor Siegfried Behn, Hans Bender, Dr Wichert and others (possibly Nazi officials) entertained Price and Worsley, and while the country as a whole was short of foodstuffs, 'there was no apparent lack of good things at this particular meal. And the Rhine wine was superb.'[11] After the meal, a large car took them for a long ride round the neighbouring countryside, with a visit to Byron's favourite castle of Drachenfels at Königswinter. They made a short ferry ride across the Rhine to Bad Godesberg, and found the town 'be-flagged with swastikas, and learnt that the Fuhrer was staying at the very hotel at which tea had been arranged for us. This was the Rhein-Hotel Dreesen. We stayed there for a couple of hours, listening to the concert, and then left for Bonn and Cologne. We did not see Hitler. He was out motoring.'[12]

Price's account of his trip to Bonn is a diplomatic fib, a happy journey full of bonhomie. The Britain of 1942 did not want to read that he had flashed a salute, as he almost certainly did that summer afternoon, to the man who was bombing the heart out of London.

The trip from Bonn to Bad Godesberg, where Hitler was parading, is little more than 6 miles, so it seems incredible for specially invited guests of the Third Reich to travel to the area and not meet its leader, someone who, according to Price, had taken a great interest in the Bonn project. Although it is true to say there are no surviving letters from Hitler to Price or vice versa, there is a letter in the Price archive that holds a tantalising clue to their relationship. In a hopelessly adolescent letter to Eric Dingwall, Harry wrote on 28 July 1939:

I do not think things are so bad in Germany as they were. I know many people, who have just returned from holidays in Germany, and everything appears normal and they have been kindly treated.

As a matter of fact, it front of me is a letter I have drafted to Hitler asking him if he will give me facilities for attending – in comfort – the Nuremburg Rally in August. I should very much like to see this spectacle.'13

This letter suggests Price was on good enough terms with Hitler to ask him for such privileged access to his set-piece speech. As if that were not strange in itself, there are fifty-three significant photographs dating from 1938 in the Price Collection. It was the year Britain came so close to war with Hitler, the year of Chamberlain's appeasement with the Führer over the Sudeten crisis. The photographs are of important National Socialist architecture, symbols of power such as the Kongresshalle in the Luitpoldhain in Nuremberg, part of the planned neoclassical compound; buildings in Cologne, Berlin and, more importantly, of the very heart of Nazi Germany including the Köningsplatz and the Brown House, the National Socialist Party's headquarters building in Munich.

This is hardly a collection of tourist photographs, or as Price apologists might have it, pictures by someone who was only interested in looking at the occultist symbols used by the German government. On the contrary, they reveal that he was happy about doing business with the Third Reich even after Kristallnacht, when, between 9 and 10 November 1938, the persecution of Jews began in earnest: over 7,500 Jewish shops were destroyed, 400 synagogues razed, 91 Jews murdered and an estimated

20,000 sent to assorted concentration camps to be starved or shot and killed.

Price's motivation was that Nazi interest in his ideas on psychical research was a quick, easy and convenient way of getting his library and laboratory out of Britain. The uncomfortable fact is that Price was a Nazi sympathiser of sorts – he had to be, if he was to accept Hitler's friendship and his offer of supporting the initiative to set up the university of the occult he had once promised Hanussen.

Price may well have been planning to emigrate to Nazi Germany himself, only to see his plan stymied by war. A letter, discovered while researching this book, from Price to Gerda Walther bears this out. It reads like an enforced goodbye to a lover, someone whom he might have been happy to set up home with; and one can imagine tender tears splashing the paper as he typed:

> I have to write you a very sad letter. If hostilities between our two respective countries begin this coming weekend, it will of course be impossible to communicate with you. Please God, that, even at this eleventh hour, someone will find some means of adjusting the differences between our two countries.
>
> But if, in spite of all endeavours, we go to war, I trust that you will not suffer and that your friends and dear ones will be spared. It is obvious that we must face hardships, with I hope, patience and fortitude. Be of good heart and hope for the best.
>
> I will think of you sometimes of our pleasant meetings in Germany. May the time soon come when these meetings can be resumed. We will hope that hostilities will not be prolonged and that both countries will emerge from the conflict with peace and honour.
>
> Remember me sometimes, and pray that our respective countries can soon be friends again.
>
> God bless you![14]

It is important to remember that when Price came to write his autobiography and mentioned 'that there can be little doubt that Hitler's psychical research is due to the fact that he was born in Braunau-am-Inn, the birthplace of the famous Schneider boys', he was speaking from personal knowledge. It gave him no excuse, however, to say that his [Hitler's] mother resided there until her death, and during my many visits to this delightful little town on the Inn (the frontier between Austria and Bavaria) I have more than once seen the placid old lady doing her shopping in the Hoheweg.

No one would dream that she had such a son! Hitler made occasional visits to Braunau, and undoubtedly must have been cognisant of – and interested in – what the Schneider boys were doing, and they had become famous in scientific circles all over the world.

We need look no further for the exciting cause of his interest in psychical research, and why he uttered such an emphatic 'Yes' to the proposal that the Third Reich should give its official blessing to the Bonn project.

Price's claim that he had seen Hitler's mother on several occasions is one of his more far-fetched claims. Klara Hitler (her husband's surname after 1876) was 46 when she died from advanced breast cancer at Linz in Austria on 21 December 1907. It would be seven years before the start of the First World War, in which her son, Adolf, was gassed and five years after that war when he became a National Socialist and began peddling his line about German honour, workers' rights and his dream for a new society.

For Harry Price, civilised society was one that valued the importance of psychical research. He so loved the German way of life that before he died, he declared, 'I want, once more, to have lunch on the terrace of the famous Molkenkur restaurant . . . with the town of Heidelberg and its castle, like a collection of toy houses, hundreds of feet below . . . I want, once more, to watch the peasants making cuckoo clocks at the doors of their Black Forest homes.'

Entranced by German culture, he wrote of his delight in finding out about the 1930s Teutonic nudist cult, the Nachtbadens, 'which was sweeping the Fatherland like a tidal wave, and was somehow mixed up with psychics'.[15] Maintaining that the cult had three million followers, of all ages and both sexes, Harry informed readers that it boasted two hundred clubs and thirty journals, 'much illustrated with pictures of the human form divine in a state of nature'.

Pornographic literature was available in Britain in the 1930s, but it was tame stuff compared to the German variety published under plain wrappers in Berlin, where the very air seemed to transport its citizens to a state of near-irresistible sexual frenzy. Price smuggled the magazines through customs at Harwich, carefully perusing each photograph and text for the psychic content – but he had to admit that he failed.[16]

In the end, Bonn University (later the Reich University) did not become a repository for Price's psychical clutter that so many wealthy patrons had spent money on purchasing. The looming war with Germany thwarted negotiations, and the dialogue petered out to a halt at the end of December 1938. In a letter to Dr Erich Jaensch, the National Socialist spokesman for the Association of German Psychologists, Hans Bender later incautiously accused Price of being a dilettante, a dabbler and of superficial involvement with psychic science. Bender alleged that, like Carl Vett, the former president of the first International Committee for Psychical Research, Price had plenty of money but was unprepared to take the paranormal seriously.[17]

If this is harsh criticism, one should remember that it was Bender and his colleagues who expended considerable funds tempting Price to Germany, and it was he who had to carry the unhappy news to Hitler that his English friend would not be taking up a residency at Bonn.

A month later, on 27 September, Cyril Joad, who still knew nothing of his friend's sinister discussions with Germany, asked Price whether he thought it was worthwhile keeping the University Council for Psychical Investigation in existence. 'It is in no sense at all carrying out the work for which it was intended, and as it does so little, and has become in effect a façade, it might be better to wind it up.'[18] Joad knew that closure would at least stop the bitter recriminations from colleagues, who were increasingly accusing Price of 'arranging things in our name without consultation and the position is getting impossible', a point Dr Guy Brown made to Joad after a news story in *The Times*, endorsing William Trinder's claims of how dowsing with a whalebone and a bobbin could only be done with people who had 'clairvoyant faculties', appeared in the council's name.[19]

Price agreed, and after Cyril Joad had successfully negotiated with the University of London to store much of the old National Laboratory's belongings, the Berkeley Street office was closed straight away, the contents finally packed into eighty-seven tea chests.

The hill-sized X-ray machine was sold to Guy's Hospital, but the rest of the laboratory's scenery, including retorts, bottles of teleplasm, chemicals, the travelling ghost-hunting kit and the psychical museum, ended their days in one of the university's storerooms, which is where they rest today.[20]

Never had it seemed so important to reinvestigate the happenings at Borley Rectory as in the year he began negotiating with Germany. In late spring he heard from Ethel Bull that the new incumbent, Alfred Henning, the thirty-eighth rector of the church, had taken to living in the rectory at nearby Liston – the diocese having combined the two parishes. Price asked the new vicar if he would allow him to rent the now empty rectory for a year so that he could carry out an experiment into the 'the alleged abnormal happenings . . . from a purely scientific point of view; with instruments such as a recording thermograph'.[21] Henning willingly agreed, perhaps believing that since the Church Commissioners had instituted Queen Anne's Bounty – a fund formed by Queen Anne in 1704 to augment poor clergy's income – the diocese would see the vacancy as a chance to sell, or at least for the rectory to earn some money before it was sold.

Instinctively realising that this could be his last hurrah, and not having the time or inclination to sit in a damp, icy, draughty, gloomy, rat-infested house for weeks on end, Harry turned to the most obvious way of keeping an ill legend alive.

He placed an advertisement in the personal column of *The Times* on 25 May asking for 'responsible persons of leisure and intelligence, intrepid, critical and unbiased . . . to join rota of observers in a year's night and day investigation of alleged haunted house in Home Counties. House situated in lonely hamlet so own car is essential.'

From the 200 or so letters Price received he carefully weeded out the critical and the objective, allowing instead only those from the right side of the social spectrum, those observers who had a title or wealth. The Occult Committee of the Magic Circle was banned, as was the SPR, but he allowed in Ellic Howe, a favoured conjurer and author on ritual magic.[22]

To hammer the message home that this was a haunted house, Price dealt out a slender blue booklet to his chosen forty-eight called 'The Alleged Haunting at B—— Rectory – Instructions for Observers'. This was a help manual, a civilised introduction to the rectory, but included among the 'what to do if you see a ghost' chatter was a breakdown of rumoured paranormal activity at the rectory since 1863, the year it was built.

Above all this little booklet helped to sow the psychological message that although there were no corroborated sightings of ghosts, there was substantive gossip about them, so it was impossible even for hard-baked sceptics to interpret each happening as innocuous, whether it be the creaking of a door, the ringing of a bell from rats tripping over bell wires in the attic, odd scents of cooking and perfume, pieces of rotting wood, falling masonry, or tricks played by locals or colleagues.

The more people who heard or saw something semi-ordinary, the more out of proportion the explanatory theories became; the real meaning was lost among a combination of Chinese whispers, fear and a sense of achievement.

In fact nothing happened in the way of phenomena save for some observers believing that Harry Price was behind many of the odd happenings. One of his hand-picked witnesses, Major Henry Douglas-Home, concluded he had furtively drawn pencil marks on walls:

After dark we toured each room, every hour, my friend leading, and Price bringing up the rear. The first few hours we found a number of extraordinary squiggles on walls which we all swore had been unmarked on our previous hour's visit.

We each carried a torch and I was so intent on examining each new mark that I failed, at first, to realise how they were being made. The last man (Price) had a pencil up his sleeve and as he swept his torch over the wall ahead, he made new squiggles in the darkness, which would be found on the next inspection.[23]

Douglas-Home found that by changing places with Price 'no other poltergeist scribbles appeared that night'. The fact that only Ellic Howe and Harry drew attention to abnormal happenings – when they discovered, after their return from dinner in Sudbury, that a few small objects, which they had put on various windowsills upstairs, had been moved – was drowned out by the comfortable way in which they were found.

By now Price had come to the conclusion that he would not buy the rectory (he probably did not have the money to do so and might be moving to Germany in any case) and it was clear that any suggestions it was haunted were baseless. The thermograph failed to show swift changes in barometric pressure, and observers, tripping over themselves with unconvincing sightings, were slated as gossipers.

Henning, for his part, was anxious that he might lose the best chance he had to sell the rectory and face another winter of trying to warm the large vicarage at Liston as well as having to feed and clothe his burgeoning family. He therefore kept up reports of unusual lights, strange noises and mysterious smells to try to counter the overwhelming evidence that the site was quite normal.

Sidney Glanville, a consulting engineer from an ordinary Anglican background, proved the most conscientious of Price's corps of watchmen. It was he who later produced a long and confidential report into the alleged haunting, which Price bound into a book and locked – in the style of Will Goldston – much of which found its way into his first book on Borley.

It was his conscience that made him thoroughly check the various legends of scandal, murder, rape and misinformation, discovering from Essex County Council's archaeological section there had never been a monastery at Borley. He also ascertained that the stage coach manifestation was nothing but country lore, and that the Smiths had been desperate to free themselves from a run-down draughty mansion which was making both of them ill. There was a natural explanation for everything.

In theory, this should have resolved all the outstanding points, but one of Glanville's daughters decided to experiment with a planchette (a device for registering automatic writing) and subsequently came up with the theory that the ghostly nun was a miserable 19-year-old French neophyte called Marie Lairre, who had supposedly come to Borley from a convent at Le Havre and was raped and killed by a member of the Waldegrave family – the local landowners – on 17 May 1667. It was this theory that went some way to convincing Price that should things ever get desperate, a story about this flourishing oral tale, with its mix of love, betrayal and death, would prove explosive.

Just when it appeared that all wonderment had begun to disappear from his life, Harry told his readers in his *Fifty Years of Psychical Research: A Critical Survey* that on 8 December 1937 he received a telephone call at his office from an educated and cultured woman who had heard his talk on haunted houses broadcast by the BBC. She told him that she could guarantee him a ghost, mirroring Price's claim that he could guarantee a ghost at Borley.[24] Not for the first time, Price set aside his quasi-scientific persona and seemed to believe in absolute certainties. The fact that the woman lived in one of the better-class London suburbs somehow gave his investigation an extra dimension, as if cultured people, particularly women, were beyond telling lies. He was rapidly invited to her family's regular Wednesday seance, at which 'a little girl spirit known as Rosalie always materializes'.[25] Of course, certain criteria had to be met before he could take his ringside seat. He could not reveal the woman's identity, so she became another Mrs X; the locality had to remain a secret; there was an embargo on conducting a scientific enquiry; he had to be searched; he could neither talk to nor touch any materialisation. But, if he accepted the invitation, he would be allowed full control of the seance room even to the extent of powdering the room with cornflour (to reveal any footprints). He could rummage around the house from top to bottom, seal all windows, remove furniture, place electrical contacts on each of the proposed sitters and search them immediately before or after the seance.

He asked Mrs X if she minded him bringing along a witness, and suggested Richard Lambert. When she failed to reply he journeyed alone to the mid-Victorian, double-fronted, detached suburban house, 'to the most amazing seance I have ever witnessed'.

Within an hour of arriving on the evening of Wednesday 15th at 7 p.m. he met the socially superior Mr and Mrs X and their 17-year-old daughter. Harry chatted over a light dinner about Rosalie. His anonymous host, 'something in the City', introduced him to the enigmatic-sounding Madame Z, a French spiritualist, who had a tragic life, having married an English officer at the beginning of the First World War and, when he was killed in action in 1916, was left to bring up their daughter Rosalie on her own.

Rosalie, she told him, died of diphtheria in 1921. From the spring of 1925 Madame Z had heard her dead daughter crying 'mother'. This happened so often that she lay awake at night and waited for her daughter to appear, and at one time touched her hand. Through a chance meeting at a church bazaar, she had met the X family, told them of her experiences and from 1928 they began holding regular seances to try to contact her dead daughter.

And so, Harry set about taping windows, dusting starch on the floors, emptying drawers, removing furniture, overturning a sofa and searching all the sitters. The 17-year-old Miss X 'immediately pulled up her skirt and revealed a pair of tight-fitting dark knickers. I was quite convinced she had nothing hidden on her person'; then he frisked the rest of the X family. After turning out the lights, Madame Z laid a series of handmirrors daubed with luminous paint on the carpet. Mr X tuned his portable radio to a foreign station playing classical music, and within five minutes Rosalie was in the room. The level of detail in Price's account made for scintillating copy:

I stretched out my left arm, and, to my amazement, it came into contact, with, apparently, a nude figure of a little girl, aged about six years . . .

I slowly passed my hand across her chest and up to her chin and cheeks. Her flesh felt warm and I could hear her breathing . . . I then placed my hand on her chest and could hear respiratory movements. My hand travelled to her thighs, back and buttocks then traversed her legs and feet. They were the normal limbs of a normal six-year-old.

He described her features as classical, and she looked older than her alleged years.

Price was convinced that if he had witnessed the materialisation of Rosalie in his laboratory he would have proclaimed 'to an incredulous world that survival was proved. But Madame Z is convinced that Rosalie would be frightened away.' He was deeply moved by the experience and friends who saw him the next morning said he looked wan, and appeared perplexed, as if traumatised. He was apparently deeply disturbed, almost distraught, and shaken to the core. He himself stated that:

It was the most remarkable case of materialization, or rather alleged materialization I have ever witnessed . . . as I have had only one sitting and have been unable as yet, to obtain independent corroboration of the extraordinary 'phenomenon' which I witnessed.[26]

Before the account of the seance was published in Price's *Fifty Years of Psychical Research* two years later, he had sent the typescript to Cyril Joad, who found the Rosalie episode unconvincing. It was incredible, he said, that 'little girls' bodies complete with larynxes . . . suddenly materialise out of nowhere . . . it seems to be so totally fantastic that unless I were to see and feel, I do not think anything would persuade me that this had really occurred'.[27]

The single most important piece of evidence about the Rosalie ghost is the absurd picture Price produced to support the fact that she appeared during the sitting. It shows a one-dimensional drawing of a small girl taken through a fish-eye lens, muffled against the cold, which was obviously clipped from a Christmas card or seasonal number of a long-forgotten magazine.

Douglas Craggs, a long-time friend of Price, fellow member of the Inner Magic Circle and a member of the Occult Committee, told newspaper reporters after Harry's death that he had openly criticised him in a newspaper review for publishing the Rosalie story: 'About five months after the publication [*Fifty Years of Psychical Research*] he wrote in a friendly strain saying that he was sure I was right and that he should never have put Rosalie in print.'[28]

By the last quarter of that year, Price had moved away from investigating the undead and found himself interested in miracles such as the liquefaction of the blood of San Gennarro, or St Januarius, Bishop of Benevento and patron saint of Naples, murdered by the Roman Emperor Diocletian during his persecution of Christians in AD 305.

Two phials of St Januarius' solidified blood sit closeted in the tabernacle of the Cappella del Tesoro in the Duomo at Naples. Twice a year, during a special Mass, the blood bubbles and liquefies.

Price, the alchemist, witnessed the spectacle and said he should very much like to study what he believed was a religious phenomenon; others doubted its origins, having made thixotrophic 'blood' of their own which congealed and liquefied, using a mixture of chalk, hydrated iron chloride and salt water.

With spare time on his hands, Harry decided to re-form the Ghost Club he had first joined in 1927. Originally established in 1855 by postgraduates at Trinity College Cambridge, but only formally launched in 1862, the club undertook practical investigations of spiritualist phenomena. Charles Dickens was an early member, as were numerous academics and clergy, but members lost interest and it was dissolved in the 1870s following Dickens's death. It was then re-launched in 1882, at the same time as the Society for Psychical Research, as a very exclusive private members' club with a bias towards spiritualism, populated by people such as Stainton Moses (the founder of the LSA), W.B. Yeats, Sir William Crookes and Conan Doyle. When elected, Harry was the fifty-eighth member on the club's list in its forty-five years of existence.

With attendance falling, Harry, Frederick Bligh Bond (whom Price was now calling 'a fifth rate spiritualist')[29] and a handful of members wound up the club on All Souls' Day, 2 November 1936.

The club was revived the following year, and quickly grew to such a large extent that Price blithely tells us that 139 people crammed into the Royal Societies Club dining room to hear Dr E.H. Hunt's cinematograph talk on the 'Rafai Fakirs of Southern India'. Soon, on account of larger audiences, dinners were held at the Overseas Club in St James's Street.

We decided not to encourage the woolly crank with a bee in his bonnet. The talks we arranged were particularly diverse and interesting. Professor Denis Saurat gave us an account of the 'Seances of Victor Hugo'; Commander Rupert T. Gould gave us a lantern lecture on sea-serpents and the Loch Ness Monster and Captain Trinder gave us a demonstration of his dowsing techniques.[30]

Price gave lectures on Borley Rectory, ectoplasm and snags in extrasensory perception. Members of the Ghost Club included Professor Julian Huxley, Sir Ernest Bennett MP, the novelist Algernon Blackwood, the Romanian Prince and author Matila Ghyka and the influential French philosopher and theosophist Henri Bergson.

While Price now had no laboratory to call his own, he kept himself in the public eye by setting out to deal with the mysteries of the body and its mind, following Hunt's lead on fakirism. In June he experimented, at Joad's suggestion, with an Egyptian called Rahman Bey, who belonged to the Psychic Oriental Union. Like Kuda Bux before him, Bey was appearing at the Little Theatre in John Street, demonstrating the science of fakirism, supported by his cousin Ahmad Mohamed Hassanein, a Royal Chamberlain. He specialised in being imprisoned in a steel casket under water, once remaining submerged in the outdoor pool of Dolphin Court in the City of London for over an hour.

This incredible feat was followed by being buried in a pit in Alex Dribble's garden in Carshalton, although its mysteries had been solved years earlier when Hanussen had described how fakirs survived the ordeal by breathing air through carefully concealed tubes from the surface.

On 15 July 1938 Bey stepped into the prepared pit, measuring 7ft long, 6ft deep and 3ft wide. Wooden posts and support boards shored up the sides to take the weight of the earth, and in the event of an accident would prevent the pit becoming a grave. Price handed the Egyptian a bell push, an emergency button in case he felt ill or wanted help.

In a little over four minutes, and with 2ft of soil on his body, Bey pressed the bell. Diggers worked like fury to release him. Harry, meanwhile, worried about what the legal position was in case of an accident, despite his having secured a document from the Egyptian absolving him from all responsibility in case of any mishap.[31]

He had no need to worry. Rahman Bey emerged unharmed, but suffering from shock. In order to go into a trance, he had pressed the thumbs of both his hands hard against his temples. Just as assistants lowered him into the pit, one of his elbows caught the sides and his concentration was broken.

Harry had filmed the whole incident and proved that Rahman Bey's hand had left his temple; but was adamant that the pit was safe. 'I do not believe he could have suffocated, as the air-space of his "prison" was greater than that allowed for, per person, in air-raid shelters. But he might have died of fright.'[32]

As December 1938 hoved into view, Harry gave thought to the regulation of clairvoyants, which had been niggling since he had formed the National Laboratory. Together with the lawyer Gordon Alchin he drafted what he called the Psychic Practitioners (Regulation) Bill, a strapping great law designed to control mediums. It followed on the heels of Conan Doyle's Spiritualism and Psychical Research (Exemption) Bill, which called for the licensing of mediums in government-approved churches. That bill, which had its first reading in 1930, was blocked by the Home Office after its second reading when it was judged 'ridiculous'.

Price hoped his bill would fare better. He succeeded in attracting the support of John Guy KC, barrister and Conservative MP for Edinburgh Central, who began ushering the prospective law through the Commons before a nervous breakdown ended his political career. Though Price then tried to interest others, such as his friend Clarice Richards and Sir Robert Gower MP, he failed to find any politician willing to pilot the bill's passage through the House. This reluctance allowed him, when he came to write his autobiography, to grumble that it would have been 'presented to Parliament by now had it not been for the present War'.[33]

Besides, Price found his attention was diverted after a tip-off from Mollie Goldney that the SPR were about to hit Cyril Joad a glancing blow: to accuse him of writing bogus material about witnessing psychic phenomena, which he claimed to have first-hand knowledge of.

In the two years since their friendship had suffered a slight eclipse, Joad had been interviewed on numerous occasions about his role of heading the University of London Council for Psychical Investigation; he had also had published various pieces on psychical research, but a long article in the autumn number of *Harper's Magazine* had prompted Eric Dingwall to agitate the SPR into taking action against what he saw as blatant invention.

Faithful readers of the magazine read Joad's article about his experience of what he non-committally called abnormal phenomena. 'This experience has been largely due to the facilities afforded in London by the National Laboratory of Psychical Research,' he claimed, adding that he 'had witnessed at different times a considerable number of varied phenomena', including sittings with Helen Duncan, Rudi Schneider and Eleanore Zugun. Documents published by the National Laboratory, however, showed that he had not.

In January 1939 Mollie Goldney wrote to her former lover to say that Dingwall had enlisted the help of W.H. Salter, who intended to criticise Joad's lack of honesty in a forthcoming issue of the society's *Journal*. Sufficiently concerned about the problems an attack might have on the reputation of his chairman, and wary of anything that might put the brakes on his forthcoming book, Price hurriedly scribbled a letter to Dingwall saying:

> The reason why I am writing to you is about Joad. Mrs Goldney informs me that you have been agitating for the SPR to criticise severely his various published remarks and writing on psychical research. Our council has been in cold storage for some time, and I have, more than once contemplated closing the whole thing down. This action I shall most certainly have to take when the SPR article is published. I shall not be able to help myself. I shall have to see Joad and discuss the position. It is an unfortunate tangle to get into, but of course, it is his own fault. But the Council could not exist for twenty-four hours after such an article, which it is proposed to publish.[34]

Dingwall's response aimed not to reassure Price, who was busy organising a national telepathic test for the readers of *John O'London's Weekly*,[35] but it did helpfully include a copy of Salter's article, which fastened on the suspicion that many of Joad's peerless stories were 'wholly, or partly fictitious'.

Price was relieved that Salter had failed to castigate him, and advised Dingwall that 'Salter will have to be careful. Raise the question of malice and Joad will sue for libel – it looks quite all right. But I am no lawyer.'[36] Pointedly refusing to defend or forewarn his old friend of the SPR's impending attack, Price sat on his hands and let Joad take Salter's battering.

The year 1939 was to be one of gigantic change. On 27 February Borley Rectory was razed to the ground when Captain W.H. Gregson, who had bought it to exploit its ghostly traffic, knocked over a spluttering oil lamp, which set fire to a pile of books; one poltergeist supposedly fled the scene and raced up to nearby Foxearth, where it reportedly settled in at the village's Queen Anne rectory; others gathered their dust and moved into the church at Borley.

At the end of August Hitler invaded Poland. In October the Berkeley Street offices of the University Council for Psychical Investigation were closed and Price's twelfth book, *Fifty Years of Psychical Research: A Critical Survey*, was published to great acclaim.

During the early part of the war, Price carried on much as before. In the late autumn of 1939 he got together with Norman Mansergh-Frost to discuss the latter's *A Bibliography of Automata and Androids*,[37] then gave a talk to the Birmingham Society for Psychical Research, met up with his cousin George and shared family memories with Reverend Ernest Price,[38] a distant cousin who had written to him by chance and whom he had never met. This was the only family on the paternal side he had alive, his sister Annie having died at Weston-super-Mare in 1935.

By the summer of 1940 Price was working flat out. He still travelled to London on business, delivered lectures for the Ghost Club, gave talks at Oxford University and conducted a hefty amount of press interviews for the launch of his first dedicated book on Borley, *The Most Haunted House in England: Ten Years' Investigation of Borley Rectory*.[39]

He also began writing his autobiography, a readable but extremely unreliable life story commissioned by Collins. The book presents tall tales as facts, skids over details, invents and exaggerates anecdotes, omits his unpleasant jousts with the SPR, ignores Connie and their marriage entirely and ends with a hurried look at divinity. In this, he believed in the Christian doctrine of original sin, one Apostolic Church, the forgiveness of sins and the resurrection of the dead.

I have often been asked whether my experiences in the seance room and in haunted houses have made me less inclined to accept the orthodox teachings of the Christian Church. They have not . . . I believe that both this life and the next are centred in God, and I believe in Jesus Christ. I believe in the efficacy of prayer. Many times in my life have I deliberately prayed that a certain thing should happen – or not happen, and often, I am sure my prayers have been deliberately answered. If 'survival', in the Spiritualistic sense, were proven to my satisfaction, I am sure that it would not make me a whit less of an orthodox Christian – as I am pleased to consider myself.[40]

For all his public confidence, he admitted his difficulties in coming to terms with his own mortality. He once asked Mrs Cecil Baines, his chosen successor to the Borley legend, if she believed in resurrection. 'He said to me: "I mean is there an afterlife in which good is rewarded and evil punished?" "I said to him that if you look at Borley from some aspects, it looks like this is the case." Then almost to himself, he said, "If that's the case then we are all in a weak position, now."'[41]

If sections of his autobiography are of doubtful veracity, believers in any of Price's headline investigations, let alone his celebrated portrait of Borley Rectory, must find it difficult not to suspect that many of his accounts rest on his penchant for inventing anecdotes rather than sticking to the banal truth – it was his method of manipulating facts that helped sell copies of his latest books.

The book on Borley was his most valuable asset, a classic of its kind even though his investigation of what he called in a letter to his publisher, Longmans, 'the most important case I have ever handled' would fetch him in a paltry £200 (£5,000 in today's values) by 1945. He was careful to nurture the myth that he did not set out to make money from psychical research, nor wrote his books for profit; nevertheless, he called the first Borley book deal, which he signed in 1938, 'a very bad bargain . . . it has reimbursed me so inadequately for all the time and money I have spent on the investigation. . . . As my private income is derived almost exclusively from the paper trade you can imagine how I have been hit during the war.'

By July 1942 he was indeed seriously short of cash. He refused to hand over to the police two handguns and ammunition he had bought, because his 'income has been seriously affected by the war and I cannot afford to give them away'. He wanted to keep the guns and join the Home Guard, that vast guerrilla army that would mobilise if ever the Nazis invaded; but he was compelled to join the Air Raid Precautions as a warden.

Nowhere, however, is the true nature of Price's war better revealed than in a letter to Mollie Goldney written in mid-1944:

I am working flat out on my Poltergeist over England which is nearly complete. Then I have another Borley book to do, and Mrs Beatrice

Hastings bequeathed to me her 'Diary,' which I am hoping to edit and publish under the title of Diary of a Split Personality.

An amazing case. She died on the day her MS was posted to me! Country Life tell me they could sell 100,000 copies of my Poltergeist book – had they the paper.[42]

Poltergeist over England[43] is a rambling fusion of historic violent spectres and curious U-turns. For example, Price disagreed with his own positive theory regarding apports in *Fifty Years of Psychical Research* a couple of years earlier, by saying 'Very few serious investigators of today accept apports.'[44]

Harry also discussed his own experiences with a destructive, noisy, cruel, erratic, thievish poltergeist, but before we accept his remarkable testimony as evidence of his brush with an actual ghost, it is worth researching its origin. As one author discovered, this experience was no more than a straight steal from two other books. In *Confessions of a Ghost Hunter*, published nine years before *Poltergeist over England*, a remarkably similar story appears.[45] But instead of a poltergeist wailing in his bedroom late at night, it was 'the soft patter of naked feet round my room . . . sometimes the pattering came from under the bed, proving "the intruder" was of very small stature'; then, as if by magic, the 'psychic child' was transformed into the ghost of his favourite dog, 'dear old Nigger', in a book called *The Soul of a Dog*.[46]

But this reckless life was one he was used to, and presumably he saw no reason to change. In the late thirties and early forties he had planned elaborate stories for life after the war. He tried to arrange the hunting of the Loch Ness Monster with two veteran First World War ex-Navy servicemen, the horologist Lieutenant-Commander Rupert T. Gould and Captain D.J. Munro, but this failed to take off because the loch and land beyond was owned by different people, not all of whom granted their permission for the expedition.[47]

Price was always trying to bolster his life with the mysterious. He wanted to investigate the unexplained showers of frogs, winkles and snails and the 'cascade of coffins' that occurred occasionally throughout the British Isles,[48] and he had in mind the investigation of another haunting at an old rectory in Salop, 'his native county', but was kept from these tasks by having deadlines to meet.

The second Borley book he mentioned to Mollie Goldney, *The End of Borley Rectory*, published after the Allied victory in 1946,[49] covered Price's wartime investigations in the supposedly haunted village. This exploration followed on from Harry receiving a letter from a Church of England vicar, Canon Phythian-Adams, who had read *The Most Haunted House in England* and advanced a potty theory, based on his own interpretation of one of the cryptic wall writings (which Price accepted was entirely the work of Marianne Foyster) that the bones of Marie Lairre might be found under the ruins of the rectory.

In 1943 Price enlisted help to dig up the floor of one of the cellars and discovered fragments of a skull. It was a surprise to many people, including the gloriously named Flying Officer Creamer, who according to Harry's *The End of Borley Rectory* had discovered them. But Creamer always denied this, later telling an interviewer he was 'wandering vaguely [in the Rectory's grounds] when I heard a commotion and on going over found some excitement over bone fragments. I was not present when the bones were found. I was walking around in a most casual and haphazard way unlike what was said in *The End of Borley Rectory*.'[50]

The frenzied shout of 'bones' and the exuberance of their discovery happened by more than mere chance. The browned fragments identified as 'sow's bones' by locals were switched in an instant by Price-the-magician's sleight of hand with a human jawbone, in the fashion of Charles Dawson. It was done to add credence to the shaky tale of Marie Lairre, a story that even Sidney Glanville, father of its originator, never believed in.

The remains were later buried by the Reverend Alfred Henning in an unmarked grave in Liston churchyard in May 1945, shortly before which a special service was held at the Church of St Philip Neri at Arundel for the dignified repose of the soul of the Borley nun.

The rot had really set in, but *The End of Borley Rectory* had proved such a popular read that its author received plump bags of mail from haggard-faced, enthralled readers that went so far beyond uneducated scrawl that he felt obliged to continue inventing material. People were so influenced by the stories that the simplest things at this small village, such as a tape recorder failing to work properly, the losing of a pen or a cat refusing to enter a building, were greeted as examples of supernatural forces at work.

Belief in what Price had documented was prevalent among the clergy, dons of prominent universities, scientists, and the nobility – even Sir Ernest Jelf, Senior Master of His Majesty's Supreme Court examined Price's evidence and confessed in the *Law Times* that he was 'at a loss to understand what cross-examination could possibly shake it'. From that time on, Borley Rectory's position as the most haunted house in England went virtually unchallenged. Price's readers apparently failed to spot the yawning variance in his telling of the tale. As Mollie Goldney once told the BBC, in the first edition of Harry's *Confessions of a Ghost Hunter* he had written that she, Ethel Beenham, May Walker and Price 'came to the conclusion that the supernormal played no part in the "wonders" we had witnessed. But this sentence was deleted in further editions of the book, in case, wrote Price, the Foysters took objection to it. When he came to write *The Most Haunted House in England*, he asked Lionel Foyster to contribute a section. Foyster wrote back, not unnaturally expressing surprise at the request, since Mr Price had accused his wife of being responsible for the "phenomena"! Price in turn replied to Mr Foyster admitting that this opinion *was* given in 1931, but added that of course no word of this would appear in his book, and he unequivocally supported the evidence.'[51]

By 1948, while writing a foreword for Jean Burton's well-received biography of D.D. Home,[52] Harry determined to repeat the success, drafting a proposal for Longmans Green of a colossal third book on the haunting; it was a period of his life when he took on anything for money.

At Lucy Kay's urging he again took an interest in the St Ignatius medallion, the object supposedly apported from beyond the grave at the rectory in 1929. For all its supreme importance, he had to excavate his mind as to what this precious find looked like. 'I had completely forgotten about the St Ignatius brass . . . will you lend it to me, so I can have it photographed for a Borley Three I am compiling? I have even forgotten what it looks like.'[53] In February Lucy loaned the medal to him, which he took to wearing on his watch-chain, much in the same way Conan Doyle had worn a spade guinea on his. It clearly had great importance for him.

'Do you find any appreciable difference in your mental outlook or your health since having the St Ignatius brass?' Lucy asked him on 11 March.[54] The end in fact happened very quickly.

On Easter Sunday, 28 March 1948, he had just come back to Arun Bank from posting two letters. One had been to Charles Windham, 3rd Lord Leconfield, a member of the Church of England's Synod, whom Price, as churchwarden at St Mary's Pulborough, had asked to intervene in an anti-rector campaign at the church. The other was to the loyal Mollie Goldney about an impending lecture at the Ghost Club. He had sat back in his favourite chair in his study, ready for a cup of tea, and unexpectedly died from a massive heart attack. He was 68.

The Times paid tribute to someone they saw as an authoritative, significant and influential character. His 'clear and transparent sincerity' coupled with a 'singularly honest mind' made his journalism 'always engaging';[55] but then obituaries are about life, rather than death, and *The Times*, like all newspapers, distilled and shaped a life with copy they had to hand, and without the benefit of hindsight.

The SPR tactfully wrote that 'he succeeded in interesting in the particular aspects of psychical research with which he was most conversant, a very large public to whom a more philosophic approach to the central problems of our subject would have made no appeal. His handling of the Borley Rectory affair is a good example both of his qualities and his defects as a freelance investigator.'[56]

The novelist Dennis Wheatley, who met Price to discuss the occult in the 1930s, believed he should have been awarded a knighthood. In the foreword to a reprint of Paul Tabori's biography of Price, Wheatley wrote: 'Had he survived for another quarter of a century, his long years as a pioneer might have been duly honoured; for today a new generation of scientists is far from being sceptically hostile.'[57]

In public there were surprisingly few savage attacks on his character; indeed, there were agreeing voices who liked his brand of grey honesty. Charles Sutton said 'Harry was one the most plausible rascals I ever had the pleasure of meeting,'[58] and Neil Weaver, chairman of the Magic Circle's Occult Committee, in an interview with the *Daily Mirror*, told the public that 'Harry made a joke out of his investigations – he didn't pretend to us. He wasn't unpopular; he was a most likeable man.'[59]

However, the strongest remarks came from Connie Price. Telephoned and asked to comment a day after her husband's death, she told the *Daily Mail*: 'I know that Harry did not agree with Sir Arthur Conan Doyle and Oliver Lodge, but I am sure he believed in what he was doing and he put his heart and soul into it.'[60]

Camouflage for her distress this cold statement may have been, but here was a woman saying a public goodbye to her partner's life and work, as if there was no love lost between them. She must have been aware that when he was engaged in London, working wherever the laboratory moved to, and whatever case he was engaged on, he had an attractive woman on his arm.

For Harry was a serial womaniser, a jack-the-lad – and so Connie's short sentence helpfully exposes the true nature of their relationship.

Price had established his reputation in the early 1920s for being methodical about psychical investigation and tried to make it his life's work, yet he failed on so many occasions because he knew, as he pointed out in a foreword to J.B Sturge-Whiting's *The Mystery of Versailles – A Complete Solution*,[61] that 'so many people prefer the "bunk" to the "debunk"!' It was something he exploited for thirty-four years, with many phenomenal farces ending up as psychical history.

EPILOGUE

S uch was the reverence for Harry Price that very soon after his death his executors, the Midland Bank, decided that a biography of his compelling life story should be written. It would be a fitting tribute, they said, to this busy, engaging man, and it was recognised that the proceeds of such a book would also help his widow financially.

Sidney Glanville, Price's appointed literary heir, refused the chance of writing the biography and handed the job over to Paul Tabori, an up-and-coming psychical journalist and son of a well-known parapsychologist. When Tabori began leafing through Price's vast collection of correspondence he realised why Glanville had run away from writing his late friend's memoirs. He had second thoughts about writing the biography himself and was sufficiently anxious to tell Mollie Goldney about his concerns.[1] It was then he decided that nothing he wrote should be 'too wounding' for Connie Price to read.[2]

In the foreword to his resultant book, *Biography of a Ghost Hunter*, Tabori tried to make allowances for his subject, writing that 'only those wilfully ignorant of the English libel laws' could blame poor old Harry for saying one thing and believing quite another. 'The same limitations', he wrote, 'must apply to this biography.'[3] In other words, there was no way Tabori could tell the truth about Harry Price for fear of upsetting his followers, who believed all of what he told them. He was seen as the rightful defender of the public's credulity and their promoter of wonder.

If the many authors, broadcasters and day trippers to Borley Rectory, in particular, had cared to study the documents and letters Harry Price had bequeathed to the University of London they would have discovered for themselves that the story was decidedly fishy, as were the case of the Battersea Poltergeist, the alleged mediumship of Stella Cranshaw, and hundreds of similar events their champion had investigated and written about. Although to some it was obvious he was living a pantomime, it is hilarious that this man, who did not seem to have a clue about what he was doing, duped the majority of his colleagues, the public, journalists and some of the greatest minds of his day with his po-faced seriousness, his great passion for phenomena and his bogus academic background. It must have been a fantastic piece of acting.

Richard Lambert, the editor of *The Listener*, who had first met Price in 1933, visited him at Arun Bank, where 'the Magician meditated', and saw in him 'something of Beckford, the collector, something of Priestley, the discoverer of oxygen'. Harry, the paper bag expert, knew that if he surrounded himself with the trappings of science and created the aura of a man deep in thought he could get away with almost anything, helped by his undoubted skill as a magician and showman.

He was an extremely likeable and clubbable man, so few bothered to look beyond his affability. All the grandstanding rows and recriminations followed by wide-eyed making up owed a lot to his ability as a salesman. It was something he had learned from his father and added to over his forty years representing a firm that sold greaseproof paper.

He wanted the National Laboratory to succeed, of course, since this would add to his prestige, but his method of trying to establish the model of a universe no one understood only brought him frustration. Out of his depth, he consciously invented mysterious phenomena and an eccentric personality he thought few would question, hoping cash-rich supporters would keep faith with him and his ideas, knowing positive acclamations of progress in psychical science brought in more money to pay for life's luxuries.

He could not have afforded the Rolls-Royce cars, the antiques, the rare and expensive books, to say nothing of keeping a string of mistresses on his rather puny income, if he had not dipped into the generous funds his supporters had given the NLPR towards furthering his investigations into the unknown. Had he or Connie been wealthy, it makes little sense that he continued to work for Edward Saunders & Son until the day he died. He worked not because he needed to offset his income by ploughing hundreds of pounds of his own money into research, nor because he managed the firm his father owned – he worked because he could not afford to retire.

It was only after his death that his mortal enemy, the Society for Psychical Research, decided to look rather more closely into his reputation as a psychical investigator. Mollie Goldney (tipped off by Paul Tabori) and Eric Dingwall, assisted by Trevor Hall, were commissioned by the SPR to carry out a three-year forensic re-evaluation of Price's cash cow, Borley Rectory. What they discovered appeared in *The Haunting of Borley Rectory* in January 1956.[4] The cries of foul play appeared to bury Price's reputation. Mollie Goldney was deeply shocked at what she had found. She told the psychic researcher P.A. Seward shortly before the report was published: 'I myself will be placed in a very invidious position and it was a very unpleasant shock to me, to find myself unable to escape the unpleasant conclusions suggested in our report . . . and possible hurt to his widow.'[5] Others were less circumspect. In the words of a reviewer for *The Economist*, 'the late Harry Price emerges unmistakably as a rogue, a falsifier, and a manufacturer of evidence'.[6]

It was left up to the loyal duo of another former girlfriend, Lucy Kay (who came to loathe Mollie Goldney and had stonewalled the SPR investigation in 1951), and Mrs Cecil Baines to go on protecting his standing as a first-rate psychic scientist.[7] They picked their way through the forest of Price's contradictions and fabrications, and part of their research found its way into an approved second investigation of Borley Rectory nine years later, by the SPR's Research Advisory Committee. It was an enquiry of sorts, led by Robert Hastings. His work, published in 1969, failed to excuse Price's behaviour. Whether Borley was ever haunted was impossible to determine by the time the report came out because there was a taint of corruption in everything Harry Price had touched.

Ironically, the most convincing series of experiments into supernatural forces Price was involved with, that relating to Rudi Schneider, was sabotaged because of his foot-stomping tantrums and jealousy.

So how should we remember Harry Price? He should be thought of as a supreme bluffer, a hedonistic con man, a terrific raconteur, a great conjuror, a gifted writer and a wonderful eccentric. It is with these last four attributes, if one can call them that, that the 'father of modern ghost hunting' should be laid to rest.

NOTES AND SOURCES

INTRODUCTION

1. Paul Tabori, *Harry Price: The Biography of a Ghost Hunter*, London, Athenaeum Press, 1950.
2. Trevor Hall, *Search for Harry Price*, London, Gerald Duckworth, 1978.

CHAPTER 1: THE RED LION AND THE SANCTUARY OF NEW CROSS GATE

1. SFT, p. 284: 'Salop, my native county'.
2. Frederick Copestick of Bath was prosecuted in 1858 for 'predicting the future'. Unlike mesmerism and phrenology, astrology was illegal. Surprisingly, this provision was not repealed until 1989. Edward Ditcher Price's copy of the Almanac is in the Harry Price Collection (HPC), Senate House, University of London.
3. I found extracts in the HPC which point to Annie living here.
4. Based on deductions in early letters to friends.
5. There seems to be some truth in this. Scraps of paper with the Sequah on them are in the HPC. They are dated 1889 in a childish scrawl. The description comes from Price's *Short Titles Catalogue* published by the National Laboratory for Psychical Research in 1929.
6. William Henry Hartley set up the Sequah Medicine Co., 32 Snow Hill, London, in 1887.
7. SFT, p. 11. *Modern Magic* was first published in 1876. Professor Hoffman was the pseudonym of the barrister Angelo John Lewis. Price wrongly stated that he was a mathematician.
8. First published by Sonnenschein, Le Bas & Lowery in 1889.

9.   SFT, p. 13.

10.   *Man and Boy Magazine*, 19 October 1891: author's collection.

11.   Preface to *Heartbreak House*, London, Constable, 1919.

12.   *Confessions of a Ghost Hunter*, 1936.

13.   Death certificate of Mary Hulse.

14.   It is a story no one has mentioned before and which appears to closely mirror 'The Sceptic'.

15.   HPC: 'Tragedy of the Night', p. 3.

16.   SFT, p. 31.

17.   The basis of the play is unknown.

18.   SFT, p. 28.

19.   *Ibid.*

20.   From documents in the HPC which also tell us that Price was in the top class at school.

21.   SFT, p. 16.

22.   WSRO.

23.   SFT, p. 54.

24.   *Ibid.*

25.   SFT, pp. 54, 55.

26.   John Dumayne was killed in the First Battle of the Somme in 1914.

27.   The photographs taken by Price are in the HPC.

28.   All the plays are in the HPC.

29.   There are three boat tickets to Dieppe in one of Price's four scrapbooks in the HPC, all from around this date. Two have 'Paris, D'Epice' written on them, so I have assumed he travelled to Paris to see what he claimed to have seen.

30.   SFT, p. 23.

31.   HPC: extracted from a short story found in one of Harry Price's scrapbooks.

32.   According to Emma's death certificate, which also tells us that Edward Ditcher Price reported her death at 7 a.m. the following day.

33.   SFT, p. 13.

34.   TNA: BT 31/36784/26645.

35.   Pen-name of R.S. Warren-Bell.

36.   The Royal Societies Club had no connection to the Royal Society, but to become a member of any of the Royal Societies one had to pay a subscription.

37.   SFT, p. 49.

38.   SFT, p. 54. Price later owned two Rolls-Royce cars.

39.   I found this description in *The Last Man*, a narrative about the life of Eldred. It was privately published. London, Goway Press, 1917.

40. SFT, p. 38.

41. 'Exposure of Mr Eldred', *JSPR*, 12, 242–52.

42. SFT, p. 38.

43. SFT, p. 302.

44. Annie married Alfred James Adams, who worked as a clerk in 1901 and lived at 187 Waller Road, Hatcham. Their daughter Evelyn Mary was born the same year.

45. CPS: Harry Price to Mollie Goldney, 13 February 1930.

46. HPC: details of Edward Ditcher Price's estate were found in Price's archive.

47. Trevor Hall believed Price rented rooms in Brockley after Edward had died. He was correct but named the wrong person. Mr Hesson was, according to Edward Saunders's records at TNA, a senior manager at the firm and had obviously been a friend of Harry's father.

CHAPTER 2: UNCOVERING LOST WORLDS

1. Formed in 1873 and still going strong.

2. SFT, p. 45. The Cycle-Yacht is not remembered by any of his surviving relatives, so Harry Price may have invented it when writing his autobiography.

3. *Ibid.*

4. Information from the 1881 census of England and Wales.

5. From probate records at the Probate Registry, York.

6. From a taped conversation John L. Randall conducted with the Knight family in 2001.

7. *Ibid.*

8. Fragments of her planned biography are kept by John L. Randall. A devout Catholic, Mrs Cecil Baines at first liked Price, then distrusted him.

9. There has been a lot of controversy in the Knight family regarding Connie's inheritance, but it cannot have been anything like the fortune some believed she received. This has been checked with documents at the Probate Registry, York.

10. From a taped conversation John L. Randall conducted with the Knight family in 2001.

11. *West Sussex Gazette*, 16 July 1908.

12. HPC: Letter from Tabori to Eric Dingwall 1949: 'Tabori proposes, Mrs Price disposes.'

13. Weiss is better known for his landscape paintings than for his attempts to get airborne.

14. CPS: Laura Baggallay (Frederick's daughter-in-law) to Harry Price, 13 August 1927.

15. SFT, pp. 49, 50.

16. *The Askean*, December 1902.

17. Dean, a local bank manager, published just 500 copies of the book, one of which is now in the author's possession.

18. *West Sussex Gazette*, 28 December 1909.

19. SFT, p. 52.

20. Author's conversation with Harry Price's nephew, Nigel Knight, 2005.

21. It is unusual to be cast out from a teaching post. Uppingham's archives apparently do not reveal why Haines suddenly ended his teaching career.

22. The Society of Antiquaries was founded in 1717, and is one of the UK's oldest learned societies. Its aims, then as now, are 'the encouragement, advancement and furtherance of the study and knowledge of the antiquities and history of this and other countries'. Price applied to become a member, but was turned down.

23. 'Some Recent West Sussex Antiquities', *West Sussex Gazette*, 17 June 1909.

24. *West Sussex Gazette*, 17 June 1909.

25. *Ibid.*, 24 June 1909.

26. Silver is extracted from lead, but this appears to be made entirely of lead.

27. *West Sussex Gazette*, 6 January 1910.

28. *Ibid.*, 30 December 1909.

29. Later finds had been unearthed in France. This find was doubly sensational. Piltdown Man was earlier and English.

30. *West Sussex Gazette*, 13 January 1910.

31. *West Sussex Gazette*, 20 January 1910.

32. *Proceedings of the Society of Antiquaries*, 23, 121–9.

33. *West Sussex Gazette*, 12 December 1911.

34. SFT, p. 51.

35. Two invoices in HPC show this transaction.

36. SFT, p. 51.

37. HPC: Harry Price to Ernest Frost (undated, but undoubtedly 1923).

38. SFT, p. 51.

39. A newspaper cutting announcing the theft is in HPC. Quite who the witness was remains a mystery.

40. HPC: coin archive catalogue no. HP1/5.

CHAPTER 3: HARRY PRICE AND THE PRIMROSE PATH

1. An interesting proposal! *The Stage*, 13 February 1913.
2. As evidenced by one his pocket books in the HPC. Astral travel was based on the idea that you could believe you were in a place and in an instant you were there – the art of guiding the mind. It relied upon a series of intricate mind exercises, underwritten by the power of the mind and the prepared imagination.
3. *Ibid.*
4. There are numerous programmes from these days in the HPC, all of which have Harry Price singing 'a humorous song or two'.
5. From material in the HPC.
6. Newspaper cutting found in volume 3 of Price's scrapbooks, HPC. This cutting is dated 21 September 1913.
7. Mention of Connie attending the march and rally is in the same scrapbook and on the same page as the above.
8. The BCPS was formed at an uncertain date, but it was well before 1920, the date given by Fodor in his *Encyclopedia of Psychic Science*, 1933.
9. HPC: Barbara McKenzie to Harry Price, 13 January 1914. This important letter seems to have been missed by Paul Tabori.
10. From material in the HPC.
11. Price seems to have made quite a bit of money out of taking prints of the picture and, when he donated it to the gallery, selling these on.
12. SFT, p. 70.
13. *Ibid.*
14. TNA: MH 106/2387/13964. The document fails to state what Price was suffering from, but men of fighting age were frequently turned down with minor ailments such as weak chests or fallen arches, at least during the first few months of war.
15. SFT, p. 74.
16. *Journal of the American Society for Psychical Research*, 19/8 (August 1925).
17. SFT, p. 75.
18. *Ibid.*
19. *The Allen-West Story*, published in April 1960.
20. On 29 September 1914 London's *Evening News* published a fictional short story by Edward Machen called 'The Bowmen'. Within a short time tales of archers intervening to help British soldiers spread among the ranks and the stories soon became established fact. The Angel of Mons is the better-known legend.
21. *The History of Spiritualism*, vol. 2, London, Cassell, 1926. The original quotation comes from Job 14:14.

22. SFT, p. 262.

23. *Survival of Man*, London, Methuen, 1909.

24. *Raymond or Life and Death*, London, Methuen, 1916.

25. SFT, p. 76.

26. Tabori, *Biography of a Ghost Hunter*, p. 39.

27. HPC: Dennis Brooks (M.D. Saunders) to Harry Price, 11 May 1919.

28. *Magazine of Magic*, March 1921.

29. He was born in Liverpool in 1872. Inspired to become a magician by reading Professor Hoffman's *Modern Magic*, he founded the Magicians Club in 1911, largely as a self-serving society. This passed into oblivion during the Second World War. He was owner-manager of the Aladdin House, London, and died in 1948.

30. London: Goldston, 1921. Good first editions fetch £400.

31. From catalogue material in the HPC.

32. Cushman was a chemist and palaeontologist, supposedly descended from one of the first Pilgrim families to settle in Massachusetts.

33. HPC: Adeline Perryman to David Gow, 2 March 1921.

34. Formed in 1914 by the magician John Nevil Maskelyne.

35. The majority of people believe Hope was a carpenter. He was not, but his father was.

36. The Circle had various members but the principals were William Hope, Mrs Buxton and William Walker – the first man to obtain psychic 'extras' in colour.

37. Marriott was among the first magicians to try to expose Hope and debunk spirit photographers generally, and was largely instrumental in bringing to an end ghostly forms appearing on photographs.

38. HPC: E. Ford to Harry Price, 7 January 1922.

39. HPC: Harry Price to SPR (no name), 22 January 1922.

40. HPC: David Gow to Harry Price, 14 September 1922.

41. Kegan, Paul, Trench & Trubner, 1922.

42. HPC: James McKenzie to Harry Price, 12 October 1922.

43. HPC: James McKenzie, 14 June 1922.

44. HPC: Sir Arthur Conan Doyle to Harry Price (indecipherable date), June 1922.

CHAPTER 4: HARRY AND THE REVELATION

1. Interview with the *Daily Sketch*, 12 February 1947.

2. University of London, Tabori archive: Dingwall to Tabori, 2 August 1949.

3. Quoted by Trevor Hall in SFHP.

4. HPC: Hon. Everard Fielding to Eric Dingwall, 17 May 1922.

5. Launched in 1920 by C.K. Ogden. The bound version of the entire *Psyche* canon was published by Taylor & Francis in 1995, priced at £2,250.

6. HPC: Dingwall to Harry Price, 26 March 1923.

7. HPC: Harry Price to Dingwall, 2 April 1923.

8. SFT, p. 81.

9. From an interview Harry Price gave to the *Sphinx* magazine describing how he made friendships at the SPR.

10. 'Mediums and their Ways – The Wiles of the Wizard', 17 March 1922.

11. SFT, p. 97.

12. CPS: Harry Price to George Wright, 7 September 1922.

13. Actually published by the NLPR out of their publishing fund.

14. And not the editor as some have confused him with.

15. *Scientific American*, Spring 1923.

16. HPC: Stella Cranshaw to Harry Price, 14 October 1923.

17. HPC: Harry Price to Stella Cranshaw, 16 October 1923.

18. HPC: Harry Price to Barbara McKenzie, 22 October 1923.

19. From 1921 to 1926 Bond edited *Psychic Science*, a quarterly publication of the BCPS. During the 1920s Bond sat with Geraldine Cummins, who produced the 'Cleophas' scripts (the supposed supplement to the Acts of the Apostles and the Epistles of St Paul) by automatic writing. As Bond felt he contributed to the scripts by his presence, he sued for a share of the book's revenue, but the court found against him.

20. SFT, p. 84.

21. HPC: ASPR to Harry Price.

22. HPC: Stella Cranshaw to Harry Price, 30 March 1927.

23. CPS: the letter is undated but talks about the auction. Papers attached to the letter show where and when the auction was held.

24. Contained in a memo written by Mercy Phillimore dated 13 May 1929.

25. HPC: Mercy Phillimore to Harry Price, 4 June 1926.

26. *Light*, 1923.

27. HPC: Arthur Conan Doyle to Harry Price, 1923.

28. HPC: Harry Price to Arthur Conan Doyle.

29. HPC: Harry Price to C.E.M. Joad, 21 August 1929.

30. CPS: Harry Price to Mercy Phillimore, 27 February 1924.

31. CPS: Harry Price to Mercy Phillimore, 4 February 1925.

32. CPS: Dawson Rogers to Harry Price, 13 February 1925.

33. CPS: Harry Price to Dawson Rogers, 14 February 1925.

34. *Morning Post*, 2 May 1925.

35. *The Times*, 13 September 1925.

36. CPS: Lord Raleigh to Harry Price, 18 May 1925.

37. *Morning Post*, 31 May 1925.

38. CPS: Harry Price to Herbert Talbot, salesman at Edward Saunders, 26 June 1925.

39. SFT, p. 90.

40. *Ibid.*, p. 91.

41. CPS: Guide catalogue of Exhibition of Objects of Psychic Interest, 20–21 May 1925, Caxton Hall

42. HPC: Robinson practised as a tax specialist from 21 Spital Yard, Bishopsgate, London.

43. HPC: H. Mansfield Robinson to Harry Price, 11 March 1926.

44. HPC: Harry Price to J.A. Stevenson, 28 October 1930. Price claimed in SFT that it was £14,000. This letter shows otherwise.

45. *Light*, February 1927.

CHAPTER 5: THE BLONDE AND THE CAUSE OF BAD BEHAVIOUR

1. From Lucy Kay's tribute to Harry Price in Tabori, *Biography of a Ghost Hunter*.

2. SPR: Lucy Kay to Mollie Goldney, 11 April 1953.

3. Author's interview with David Meeker, June 2005.

4. HPC: Lucy Kay to Harry Price, 14 October 1931.

5. HPC: Lucy Kay to Harry Price, 11 June 1926.

6. Author's collection: Harry Price to H. Dennis Bradley, 11 September 1925.

7. *The Times*, 4 January 1926.

8. Extract from NLPR's Application for Membership 1925.

9. SPR: memo to herself (undated).

10. HPC: Gregory to Harry Price, 11 December 1925.

11. H. Dennis Bradley . . . *And After*, T. Werner Laurie, 1931, pp. 83–4.

12. Account of Eleanore Zugun from 'An Account of Eleanore Zugun' published in 2004 by the German Psychological Board.

13. From an interview Price gave the *Daily Sketch* headlined 'A Theory about the Poltergeist Girl': Harry Price said he believed that Eleanore 'was possessed'.

14. From papers in the HPC.

15. *Leaves from a Psychist's Case Book*, London, Victor Gollancz, 1933, p. 293.

CHAPTER 6: BEHIND THE SCENES AT QUEENSBERRY PLACE

1. Harry Price quoted the story from the *American* magazine, in which Dr Leonard J. Hartman, in whose house the seance had taken place, had confirmed what happened.
2. CPS: letter from E.J. Powell and Dawson to LSA Council and Sir Arthur Conan Doyle, 24 February 1928.
3. CPS: Sir Arthur Conan Doyle to Mercy Phillimore, 5 September 1928.
4. CPS: Harry Price to Arthur Conan Doyle, 14 September 1928.
5. CPS: Dawson Rogers' advice was communicated by Mercy Phillimore to Sir Arthur Conan Doyle in a letter of 27 September 1928.
6. SPR: Ethel Beenham's 1951 statement to Mollie Goldney as part of an investigation into Price's probity as a psychic researcher.
7. London *Evening Standard*, 12 February 1928.
8. Sidgwick & Jackson, 1961.
9. HPC: Harry Price to Sir Arnold Lunn, 1936. Harry Price disguised the Robinsons in Battersea as the 'Smiths from Brixton'. This is one letter all previous writers have missed.

CHAPTER 7: THE GRATIFICATION OF PERSONAL SPITE

1. *BJPR*, January/February 1929.
2. HPC: Lucy Kay to Harry Price, 14 February 1929.
3. SFT, p. 204.
4. *Ibid.*
5. CPS: note from Sir Arthur Conan Doyle to Mercy Phillimore dated 1929.
6. HPC: letter from Driesch to Price.
7. Extracted from reports in various newspapers including *The Times* and the *Daily Mail*.

CHAPTER 8: PRICE AND THE PERAMBULATING NUN

1. 'The Haunted Rectory – An Impartial Investigation by Peter Eton and Alan Burgess', broadcast on 29 June 1947.
2. SPR: Mrs Smith in a statement to Mollie Goldney dated 1951. Goldney was interviewing her as part of a later SPR investigation into the matter.
3. 'Bluish sparks' were a regular occurrence at late Victorian seances. Mediums used pieces of ferro-cerenium to create flashes of blue light.

4. 'Midnight Séance in the Blue Room', in Harry Price, *The Most Haunted House in England – Ten Years' Investigation of Borley Rectory*, London, Longmans, Green, 1940.

5. HPC: 'The Ghost that Kept Harry Price Awake'.

6. Later identified as a St Ignatius of Loyola pilgrim token. Harry Price later made the claim that there were three tokens found that day, but Lucy Kay remembered only one. Writing to Mrs Cecil Baines in 1951, she wrote (HPC): 'It is the only medal or medallion I remember appearing in the early days, and quite undoubtedly, this is the one that "appeared" on the same night as the keys. I picked it up, and said "Isn't that lovely" and, either that evening or a day or two later Harry Price said I could have it.'

7. *Journal of the American Society for Psychical Research*, 23/8 (August 1929), 455–6.

8. SPR: notes made by Lord Hope on 5 July 1929.

9. Sutton was interviewed by the BBC for their broadcast on Borley Rectory called 'The Haunted Rectory'. The programme was cancelled two days before transmission on 10 September 1956 because it was feared Marianne Foyster would sue for libel after suggestions were made that she faked all the phenomena at the rectory when she lived there.

10. SPR: Sutton's signed statement to Mollie Goldney, 1951.

11. There is no date on the typescript. Lucy Kay documents were donated by her son David Meeker to the HPC in 2005.

12. SPR: Lord Hope's statement to Mollie Goldney, May 1951.

13. *Journal of the American Society for Psychical Research*, 23/9 (September 1929). Price claimed that he visited the area the next year to interview Fred Cartwright, a journeyman who had seen the nun four times. Cartwright was never traced by the subsequent investigation into the Borley legend by the SPR. Nor is there any mention of him in Harry Price's entire archive, which leads me to believe that he was a figment of Price's imagination.

14. SFT, p. 272.

15. Peter Underwood, *Borley Postscript*, Surrey, White House Publications, 2001, pp 150–1.

16. Author's conversation with David Meeker in which he claimed he could not trust one word his mother told him.

17. HPC: Harry Price to A.M. Low, 18 February 1929.

18. HPC: Harry Price to Charles Richet, 25 October 1929.

CHAPTER 9: THE LION, THE WITCH AND HER WARDROBE

1. *Time*, February 1931.
2. *Ibid.*, 5 October 1936.
3. CPS: Mercy Phillimore to Harry Price, 11 February 1930.
4. SFT, p. 145.
5. CPS: Harry Price to Laura Baggallay, 29 March 1930.
6. CPS: all quotations from a letter Harry Price wrote to Mercy Phillimore, 30 March 1930.
7. CPS: Harry Price to Mercy Phillimore, 30 March 1930.
8. CPS: letter from Lord Hope to Mercy Phillimore, 10 May 1930. This valuation shows up in a later draft contract dated 22 May 1930.
9. CPS: Mercy Phillimore to Harry Price, 22 May 1930.
10. From *The Times*, 11 January 1930, where Price was quoted as saying Fielding-Ould was one of the men in London he most respected, and saw him as a loyal and dependable friend.
11. CPS: Harry Price to Mercy Phillimore, 23 May 1930 and 30 May 1930.
12. HPC: Harry Price to Narziss Ach, 28 May 1930.
13. HPC: Narziss Ach to Harry Price, September 1930.
14. SFT, p. 263.
15. CPS: Harry Price to Mercy Phillimore, 20 September 1930.
16. SPR: Coster interview with Mollie Goldney, 1951.
17. CPS: Events are taken from a copy of the original transcript dated 7 October 1930.
18. Harry Price, *Leaves from a Psychist's Casebook*, London, Victor Gollancz, 1933.
19. SFT, p. 159.
20. HPC: Harry Price to SPR Council, October 1930.
21. *Nash's Magazine*, 1930.
22. Harry Price to Gerda Walther, December 1930.
23. Narziss Ach to Harry Price, December 1930.
24. Eric Dingwall to Harry Price, 1931.
25. Bradley, . . . *And After*, pp. 198–216.
26. Harry Price to C.E.M. Joad, January 1933, HPC. Price was advising Joad who 'to steer clear of' on a trip to New York.
27. Bradley, . . . *And After*.
28. SPR.
29. Author's collection: Harry Price to H. Dennis Bradley, 15 May 1931.
30. HPC: Harry Price to Freddie Bligh-Bond, 15 April 1931.

31. HPC: Harry Price to Lucy Kay, 17 May 1931.

32. Lucy Kay to Harry Price, letter has no date, but most likely May 1931.

33. SFT, p. 266.

34. CPS: Harry Price to Henry Duncan, 22 April 1932.

35. 'An Attempt at the Microscopic Anatomy of Alleged Teleplasm'.

36. CPS: it is a mystery as to how this press wire ended up at the former LSA, but it may have been passed around the various psychic research societies at lightning speed by a sympathetic, not to say incredulous, journalist.

37. CPS: Harry Price to Freddie Bligh-Bond, 13 March 1931.

38. HPC: Harry Price to Freddie Bligh-Bond, 15 April 1931.

39. HPC: Harry Price to J.A. Stevenson, 26 June 1931.

40. HPC: Harry Price to Emilio Servadio, 8 April 1931.

41. HPC: 22 April 1931. Price wrote to Henry Duncan saying 'So we are prepared to make you the following offer: we will pay you £100 cash in advance as retaining fee; we will pay you £10 a week over and above all your expenses, and we will pay you £100 upon termination of our agreement, subject to the mutual adjustment of detail between ourselves . . . I have this further offer to make you: should the income from our Members and our Council be greater than the actual amount of cash which we shall pay you, we will hand over the difference to you.'

42. CPS: 11 May 1931.

43. Price, *Leaves from a Psychist's Casebook*.

44. HPC: Harry Price to Dr Emilio Servadio, 8 December 1931.

45. CPS: Harry Price to Henry Duncan, 15 May 1931.

46. HPC: Harry Price to Mary McGinlay, 14 February 1931. McGinlay contacted Price after reading an article about her former employer in the *Morning Post*. She offered him information in return for money and tried to persuade him to pay for her wedding. He refused, saying that after paying for her fare to London, buying her new clothes, and giving her money in lieu of a couple of days off work when she stayed at the Harrington Hall Hotel in Kensington, he felt he had paid her enough.

47. Price claimed to various people that the *Morning Post* offered him 90 guineas for worldwide use. One instance is a letter he wrote to Mollie Goldney on 12 August 1931 in the HPC. However, papers in his archive show he only received 30 guineas.

48. HPC: Harry Price to Freddie Bligh-Bond, 14 August 1931.

49. HPC: Harry Price to Freddie Bligh-Bond, 19 August 1931.

50. 'L'estrange conduite de M. Harry Price', *Revue Metapsychique*, April 1933.
51. HPC: Harry Price to Eugène Osty, 2 November 1931.
52. Trial notes from *The Times*, 28–31 March 1931.
53. CPS: Harry Price to Guy L'Estrange, 14 November 1931.

CHAPTER 10: WHY WARS BEGIN

1. Published in 1933 by Victor Gollancz.
2. Published in 1936 by Putnam.
3. HPC: C.G. Jung to Harry Price, May 1932.
4. HPC: her father had thought it was better for Urta to be away from Germany, the violence in the streets and political uncertainty.
5. Urta appeared in several American comic-book films including *Flash Gordon*. This particular quotation comes from an interview she gave to *The Empire News*, 13 May 1932.
6. HPC: Harry Price to Erich Bohn, June (indecipherable date) 1932.
7. HPC: Harry Price to C.E.M. Joad, 2 June 1932.
8. SPR: Charles Sutton to Harry Price, 21 June 1932. It is interesting to note that, despite Price and Sutton falling out over the 'bricks in the pockets' incident at Borley, Harry was still willing to lend Sutton money. He may have done this for fear Sutton would tell the SPR and others about the incident had he refused the reporter's request.
9. HPC: Harry Price to C.E.M. Joad (indecipherable date), July 1932. This letter on its own does not show that Price was anti-Semitic; if anything it highlights his underlying snobbism.
10. HPC: Harry Price to C.E.M. Joad, July 1932.
11. Wakefield Lodge. Price had been alerted to the house by the editor of the *Northampton Independent*.
12. This appears to have been a dinner. Price's letter to Joad suggests he does not wear a dinner jacket 'as Crowley has left his clothes in Berlin'. The only letter to Crowley in the HPC is a response from Price saying he was sorry to hear that Crowley was 'feeling queer. I am afraid I cannot tell you anything you do not know about Black Magic! It is a phase of our subject to which I have never devoted much time, in spite of its fascination for me.'
13. Andrew Clarke, *The Bones of Borley*, Foxearth, Foxearth and District History Society, 2006.
14. *Ibid.*

15. Marianne suffered the black eye through her lover lunging a throw at her rather than anything supernatural hitting her. See Clarke, *Bones of Borley*.

16. A short distance from Borley in the neighbouring village of Liston stood one of the largest natural medicine essence and flavouring works in Great Britain. Hidden among hornbeams the Stafford-Allen factory (now IFF) used huge quantities of lavender heads to make bases for perfumes. The crop was once grown by several farmers in the district. See Andrew Clarke, *Bones of Borley*, for further information.

17. *The Most Haunted Woman in England*, by Vince O'Neill (Marianne's son). Published on the now defunct www.borleyrectory.com website.

18. HPC: Harry Price to David Fraser-Harris, 15 October 1931.

19. HPC: Price to Walther, 12 March 1931.

20. HPC: Price to Walther, 2 September 1931.

21. HPC: Lord Charles Hope to Harry Price, 1 April 1932.

22. 'An Account of Some Further Experiments with Rudi Schneider', NLPR, 1933.

23. HPC: Harry Price to Lord Charles Hope, 16 April 1932.

24. HPC: Harry Price to David Fraser-Harris, 28 April 1932.

25. HPC: Harry Price to Narziss Ach, 10 May 1932.

26. HPC: Harry Price to Dr William Brown, 12 May 1931.

27. HPC: Harry Price to Von Hofsten, 12 May 1932.

28. SPR: Ethel Beenham interview with Mollie Goldney, 1951.

29. Eric Dingwall and Trevor Hall, *Four Modern Ghosts*, London, Duckworth, 1958.

30. HPC: Harry Price to Rudi Schneider, 27 May 1932. The original was written in German by Lucy Kay.

31. HPC: Harry Price to Rudi Schneider, 27 May 1932.

32. HPC: Harry Price to Gerda Walther, 8 March 1933.

33. HPC: Lord Charles Hope to Harry Price, 10 March 1933.

34. HPC: Harry Price to Karl Przibram, 19 June 1933.

35. Anita Gregory, *The Strange Case of Rudi Schneider*, The Scarecrow Press, 1985.

36. HPC: Bulletin IV of the NLPR, 1933.

37. SPR: Walter Becker to Harry Price, 7 January 1938. Becker sent this criticism from Spencer to Price, but he never received a reply.

38. HPC: Harry Price to Lord Charles Hope, 13 March 1933.

39. HPC: Harry Price to C.E.M. Joad, 12 June 1933.

40. Cyril Burt (later Sir Cyril Burt), the fraudulent educational psychologist, invented data to support his theories about the hereditary component in IQ. Only after his death in 1971 were doubts raised.

41. HPC: Harry Price to Peter Quennell, 12 September 1932.

42. HPC: Edwin Deller to Harry Price, 3 January 1934.

43. HPC: Edwin Deller to Harry Price, 12 February 1934.

44. Harry Price, *Fifty Years of Psychical Research: A Critical Survey*, London, Longmans, Green, 1937.

45. HPC: the institute's constitution.

46. HPC: Harry Price to A.M. Low, 15 March 1934.

47. HPC: Harry Price to A.M. Low, 9 June 1934.

48. HPC: Harry Price to Col Elliott, 12 May 1934.

49. HPC: Harry Price to Col Elliott, 11 June 1934.

50. SFT, p. 231.

51. *Ibid.*, p. 238.

52. *Ibid.*, p. 239.

53. *The Times* of 29 March 1936 said the book was 'a fairytale come to life'.

54. R.L. Lambert, *Ariel and All His Quality*, London, Gollancz, 1940, p. 285. During the course of the trial, suggestions were made that the BBC and its officers brought economic and moral pressure on Lambert to withdraw his writ against Sir Cecil Levita. After the trial was over, the prime minister ordered a Special Board of Inquiry into the matter, which recommended a number of reforms to the mutual benefit of the BBC and its staff.

55. SFT, p. 204.

56. *Ibid.*, p. 172.

CHAPTER 11: WRITING TO HITLER

1. This is the story given by Ismet Dzino, Hanussen's right-hand man when Hitler visited the seer for a private clairvoyancy session at the Hotel Kaiserhof on 11 January 1933. See Bella Fromm's memoir, *Blood and Banquets: A Berlin Social Diary*, London, 1943.

2. HPC.

3. SFT, p. 111 and also supported by Bender's various letters to Price (HPC).

4. HPC: Harry Price to Hans Bender, 19 April 1936.

5. SFT, p. 54.

6. Harry Price to Sir Arnold Lunn, 19 October 1935. This letter ties up with Harry Price's comment about the Battersea poltergeist case.

7. HPC: Harry Price to Hans Bender, 7 November 1936. Although Price mentions this letter in SFT (p. 112) he fails to tell the reader that he asked Bender to continue negotiations on his behalf.

8. Now hanging in the Harry Price Library at the University of London.

9. SFT, p. 112.

10. HPC: Hans Bender to Harry Price, 20 March 1937. The letter also confirms the visit of Dr J. Wichert to Price in February.

11. SFT, p. 114.

12. From papers in the HPC.

13. HPC: Harry Price to Eric Dingwall, 28 July 1939.

14. Dated 28 September 1938. Gerda Walther wrote to Price throughout the war.

15. SFT, p. 177.

16. *Ibid.*

17. Hans Bender to Dr Erich Jaensch, 8 December 1938. From archives at the University of Freiburg.

18. HPC: Cyril Joad to Harry Price, 27 September 1938.

19. The Guy Brown comment appeared in an edited form in Joad's letter to Price which he sent him on 27 September. There was now animosity towards Harry Price, who must have been deeply frustrated that high honours in Germany (he so desperately wanted academic recognition for his work in psychic research) had slipped from his grasp.

20. Harry Price said the laboratory was transferred to the University of London in October 1937. Records at the university show that it was transferred from the University of London Council for Psychical Investigation office at Berkeley Street in October 1938 the offices closed at the same time.

21. HPC: Harry Price to Henning.

22. Ellic Howe was the author of *The Magicians of the Golden Dawn: The Documentary History of a Magical Order, 1887–1923*, London, Routledge & Kegan Paul, 1972.

23. From 'The Haunted Rectory', a planned broadcast by the BBC on the tradition of the Harry Price investigation at Borley Rectory dated 4 September 1956. The transmission never went on air, cancelled for fears Marianne Foyster might sue the broadcaster; SPR.

24. *The Listener*, 1931.

25. Harry Price, *Fifty Years of Psychical Research*, p. 131.

26. *Ibid.*, p. 130.

27. HPC: C.E.M. Joad to Harry Price, 10 November 1938.

28. *Daily Mirror*, 3 April 1948.

29. HPC: Harry Price to C.E.M. Joad, 14 March 1938.

30. SFT, p. 135.

31. *Ibid.*, p. 186.

32. *Ibid.*

33. SFT, p. 214, The Fraudulent Mediums Act was passed in 1951. Supported by Walter Monslow MP (later Baron Monslow), it is still on the statute book 'to provide a safeguard to deal with those who exploit the credulity of others'. There have been six prosecutions and five convictions of clairvoyants since 1980.

34. HPC: Harry Price to Eric Dingwall, 27 January 1939.

35. Following J.B Rhine's telepathic test at Duke University, North Carolina. Price later brought out telepathic cards made by Waddingtons.

36. HPC: Harry Price to Eric Dingwall, 2 February 1939.

37. Published privately in 1939.

38. Ernest lived in Lordswood Road, Birmingham and was connected to St Peter's, Harborne, in the city.

39. Published by Longmans Green, 1940.

40. SFT, pp. 302–3.

41. SPR: Mrs C.C. Baines in an interview with Mollie Goldney, October 1950.

42. HPC: letter from Harry Price to Mollie Goldney, 12 January 1944.

43. Country Life Limited, London, 1945.

44. 'Apports and Psychic Lights', in Harry Price, *Fifty Years of Psychical Research*.

45. SFHP, p. 189.

46. Vivian Evans, *The Soul of a Dog*, London: Frederick Sherlock & Sons, 1913.

47. Lieutenant-Commander Rupert Gould RN restored John Harrison's timekeeper, as detailed in Dava Sobel, *Longitude*, London, Fourth Estate, 1996.

48. Originally sent by Price as a letter to *The Times* dated 28 August 1938, Harry Price duplicated the claim in SFT. All observations were made by Charles Fort in *Lo!*, New York: Claude Kendall, 1931, reprinted most recently by John Brown Publishing, 1997, and the posthumously published *Wild Talents*, New York, Claude Kendall, 1932, reprinted most recently by John Brown Publishing, 1998. A tornado was responsible for the 'cascade of coffins'.

49. Published in London by Harrap & Co., 1946.

50. SPR: Flying Officer Creamer interview with Mollie Goldney, 1951.

51. 'The Haunted House', BBC.

52. *Heyday of a Wizard*, London: George Harrap, 1948 and New York: A.A. Knopf, 1943 (the earlier American version is without Harry Price's foreword).

53. HPC: Harry Price to Lucy Kay (now Meeker), 19 January 1948. This letter shows that only one medallion was ever found at Borley. Price later claimed three. He attached so much importance to the proof of apported evidence at Borley that he failed to photograph it and had forgotten what it looked like.

54. HPC: Lucy Meeker to Harry Price, 11 March 1948.

55. *The Times*, 29 March 1948.

56. *JSPR*, 39, 1947–8.

57. Foreword to Paul Tabori, *Biography of a Ghost Hunter*. Reprint of Tabori's 1950 biography and reissued as part of the Dennis Wheatley Library of the Occult series, Sphere Books, London 1974.

58. SPR: Charles Sutton to Mollie Goldney, 11 January 1951.

59. *Daily Mirror*, 30 March 1948.

60. *Daily Mail*, 29 March 1948.

61. London: Rider & Co., 1938. The Versailles story was the most famous ghost story or psychic adventure in Edwardian Britain. In 1904 two women visiting Versailles as tourists imagined that by 'some strange kink in time' they had been transported back to the eve of the French Revolution in 1789. Sturge-Whiting proved that the Versailles story was a hoax.

EPILOGUE

1. A memo written by Mollie Goldney in the SPR archives at Cambridge University shows that Tabori was surprised to find that almost everything Price had flagged up as truth was nonsense.

2. SPR: William Salter to C.K. Ogden (the publisher of *Psyche*), 29 January 1954.

3. Tabori, *Biography of a Ghost Hunter*, p. 10.

4. Also known as the Borley Report. It was first published in the *Proceedings of the Society for Psychical Research*, 51/18, 6 January 1956. It was published simultaneously as a book by Gerald Duckworth, London.

5. SPR: Mollie Goldney to P.S. Seward, 3 March 1954.

6. *The Economist*, 19 January 1956.

7. HPC: Lucy Meeker to Mrs C.C. Baines, 29 June 1951.

BIBLIOGRAPHY

The Alleyn Lane Story, Brighton, Alleyn Lane, 1960

Bradley, Dennis H., . . . *And After*, London, T. Werner Laurie, 1931

Clarke, Andrew, *The Bones of Borley*, Foxearth, Foxearth & District History Society, 2006

Dingwall, Eric, and Harry Price, *Revelations of a Spirit Medium*, Kegan Paul, Trench & Trubner, London, 1922

Dingwall, Eric, and Trevor Hall, *Four Modern Ghosts*, London, Duckworth, 1958

Evans, Vivian, *The Soul of a Dog*, London, Frederick Sherlock & Sons, 1913

Fort, Charles, *Lo!*, New York: Claude Kendall, 1931 (repr. John Brown Publishing, 1997)

——, *Wild Talents*, New York, Claude Kendall, 1932 (repr. John Brown Publishing, 1998)

Gregory, Anita, *The Strange Case of Rudi Schneider*, New Jersey, The Scarecrow Press, 1985

Griffiths, Richard, *Patriotism Perverted*, London, Constable, 1978

Hall, Trevor, *Search for Harry Price*, London, Gerald Duckworth & Co., 1978

Hoare, Philip, *England's Lost Eden*, London, Fourth Estate, 2005

Howe, Ellic, *The Magicians of the Golden Dawn: The Documentary History of a Magical Order, 1887–1923*, London, Routledge & Kegan Paul, 1972

Lambert, R.L., *Ariel and All His Quality*, London, Gollancz, 1940

Lodge, Oliver, *Survival of Man*, London, Methuen, 1909

——, *Raymond or Life and Death*, London, Methuen, 1916

Price, Harry, *Cold Light on Spiritualistic Phenomena: An Experiment with the Crewe Circle*, London, Kegan Paul, Trench, Trubner, 1922

——, *Stella C: An Account of Some Original Experiments in Psychical Research*, London, Hurst & Blackett, 1925

——, *Rudi Schneider: A Scientific Examination of His Mediumship*, London, Methuen, 1930

——, *Leaves from a Psychist's Casebook*, London, Victor Gollancz, 1933

——, *Confessions of a Ghost Hunter*, London, Putnam, 1936

——, *Fifty Years of Psychical Research: A Critical Survey*, London, Longmans, Green, 1937

——, *Poltergeist over England: Three Centuries of Mysterious Ghosts*, London, Country Life, 1937

——, *The Most Haunted House in England – Ten Years' Investigation of Borley Rectory*, London, Longmans, Green, 1940

——, *Search for Truth*, London, Collins, 1942

——, *The End of Borley Rectory*, London, Harrap, 1946

——, 'A Report on the Telekenetic Phenomena Witnessed through Eleanore Zugun', *Proceedings of the NLPR*, 1/1, January 1927

——, 'Short Title Catalogue of Research Library from 1472 to Present Day', *Proceedings of the NLPR*, 1/2, April 1929

——, 'Regurgitation and the Duncan Mediumship', Bulletin 1 of the NLPR, 1931

——, 'An Account of Some Further Experiments with Rudi Schneider, a minute by minute record of 27 séances', Bulletin 4 of the NLPR, 1933

——, and R.S. Lambert, *The Haunting of Cashen's Gap: A Modern 'Miracle' Investigated*, London, Methuen, 1936

Sobel, Dava, *Longitude*, London, Fourth Estate, 1996

Sturge-Whiting, J.R., *The Mystery of Versailles* (foreword by Harry Price), London, Rider, 1937

Turner, James, *Stella C*, London, Souvenir Press, 1973

Tabori, Paul, *Harry Price: The Biography of a Ghost Hunter*, London, Athenaeum Press, 1950

Underwood, Peter, *Borley Postscript*, Surrey, White House Publications, 2005

INDEX